HOW TO STUDY LAW

HOW TO STUDY LAW
6th edition

ANTHONY BRADNEY, LL.B., B.A.
Professor of Law,
University of Keele

FIONA COWNIE, B.A., LL.B., LL.M.
Barrister, Professor of Law,
University of Keele

JUDITH MASSON, M.A., Ph.D.
Professor of Socio-Legal Studies,
University of Bristol

ALAN C. NEAL, LL.B., LL.M., D.G.L.S.
Barrister, Professor of Law,
University of Warwick

DAVID NEWELL, LL.B., M.Phil.
Solicitor,
Director, The Newspaper Society

SWEET & MAXWELL

THOMSON REUTERS

Published in 2010 by Thomson Reuters (Legal) Limited
(Registered in Engalnd & Wales, Company No 1679046.
Registered Office and address for service:
100 Avenue Road, London NW3 3PF)
trading as [Sweet & Maxwell]

Typeset by Servis Filmsetting Ltd, Stockport, Cheshire
Printed in Great Britain by Ashford Colour Printers, Gosport

No natural forests were destroyed to make this product;
only farmed timber was used and re-planted.

A CIP catalogue record for this book is available from the British Library

ISBN 9780414041806

Thomson Reuters and the Thomson Reuters logo are trademarks of Thomson Reuters.
Sweet & Maxwell® is a registered trademark of Thomson Reuters (Legal) Limited.

Crown copyright material is reproduced with the permission of the Controller of HMSO
and the Queenís Printer for Scotland.

Contents

Acknowledgments

The authors and publishers would like to thank those organisations who have allowed their copyrighted materials to be reproduced as examples throughout this book. Grateful acknowledgment is made to the following authors and publishers for permission to quote from their works: F. Cownie et al., "English Legal System in Context", 4th edn (2007), by permission of Oxford University Press and L. Webley & L. Duff, "Women Solicitors as a Barometer for Problems within the Legal Profession—Time to Put Values Before Profits", Journal of Law and Society, (Wiley-Blackwell, 2007), Vol.34, Issue 3, pp.374–402, by permission of Wiley-Blackwell. All efforts were made to contact the copyright holders and grateful acknowledgment is made to I.C.L.R., TSO, BAILII and Westlaw UK, amongst others for their permissions.

All extracted materials are represented in the format and with the correct content at the time of writing the book and are subject to change.

Preface

A new law student is faced with a potentially bewildering variety of sources of law. A recent case mentioned in a lecture might be found in a database of law reports, a printed report, or a website providing access to recent court judgments. There might be journal articles or newspaper reports that discuss the case. The text of an Act can be found in a number of different ways, using both online sources and editions of statutes found in a law library. It can be difficult to know where to start. This book aims to help you make effective use of the law resources to which you have access. Online sources are placed alongside traditional print sources in each of the chapters of the book and their use explained, in order that you can make the best possible use of both.

In a sense, this book is a labour-saving device. Use it as a reference throughout your time as a student, or indeed thereafter, should you decide to go into legal practice. Though some of the more detailed coverage is most likely to be of use if you are embarking on a legal research module (or a post-graduate qualification), it is not intended to be a textbook associated with a particular course. It is a reference aid to be consulted whenever you have a problem. Consequently, you might use the book selectively, referring to those sections which are useful at a particular point in your studies, or when recommended to look up a case, statute or issue by a member of the teaching staff.

The book concentrates on the law in England and Wales. Detailed coverage is also given of European human rights law and the law of the European Union. A brief appendix covers online sources of Scots and Northern Ireland law.

The title page of the book reflects the contribution made by Philip A Thomas, as co-author and sole instigator, not only of the first edition of *Effective Legal Research*, but also of the four editions of *Dane & Thomas: How to Use a Law Library*. The coverage of print resources is based, in large part, on the coverage of print materials in *How to Use a Law Library*. The coverage of online sources was largely re-written for the first edition of *Effective Legal Revision* and extensively revised for this one.

Part 1

Sources of the law

LAW AND LEGAL INSTITUTIONS

The first question to answer is "what is law?" Most laws are not about something dramatic like ▶ 1.1
murder but are, rather, about the everyday details of ordinary life. Every time a purchase is
made, a contract under state law is created. Both parties make promises about what they will
do; one to hand over the goods, one to pay the price. In this and other ways, everybody is
involved in law every day of their lives. In many instances people are free to make their own
choices about the rules that govern their lives. If they want to join a club, a religion or a company
and be bound by its rules that is a matter for them. Some people regard these rules as being
law just like the law that the state creates. This idea is known as *legal pluralism*. However the
kind of law that comes from the state is what we most frequently think about when we think
about law. Most university courses involving law focus on this type of law and that is what this
book is about.

There are a number of generally acknowledged sources of English law. Some are more
obvious than others. Thus, "the Queen in Parliament" (the House of Commons, the House of
Lords and the monarch) is a vital source of modern English law. Here proposals for legislation
(*Bills*) are presented to, debated by, and voted upon by the House of Commons and the House
of Lords, finally receiving the assent of the monarch and thus becoming legislation (*Statutes* or
Acts). It is also indisputable that judges are significant sources of law, since the English legal
system places great emphasis upon judgments in previous legal cases as guidance for future
judicial decision-making. There are, however, less obvious sources of English law. Some are
direct: for example, in some circumstances the European Union may make law for England and
Wales. Others are more indirect: thus the customs of a particular trade may be incorporated
into the law by the judges or Parliament or international law (the law between states) may be
a basis for national law.

All of the above are sources of *legal rules*. What precisely it is that is meant by the term
legal rules is a subject much debated by philosophers of law. Generally speaking, when the
term is used it indicates that a particular course of action should, or should not, be followed.
Legal rules are said to be *binding*. This means if they are not followed some action in the courts
may result.

It will suffice for present purposes if we consider just two of these sources of law:
Parliament and the judiciary. In so doing, we will discover the central positions occupied within
the English legal system by *statute law* and *judge-made law*. There is a further explanation of
international law and the law of the European Union in Chapter 2.

PARLIAMENT

1.2 ▶ Parliament creates law but not all the law that is created through Parliament is of the same kind. We need, in particular, to distinguish between various levels of legislation.

The legislation with which most people are familiar are statutes. Bills proposed in Parliament become Acts. These Acts may either be *General* or *Personal and Local*. Both of these are sometimes known as *primary legislation*. General Acts apply to everybody, everywhere within the legal system. In this context it is important to remember that there are several different legal systems within the United Kingdom; one for England and Wales, one for Scotland and one for Northern Ireland. Some Acts apply to all the legal systems; many apply only to one or two of them.

Personal and local Acts apply either to particular individuals, institutions or, more usually, to particular areas. Thus, before divorce was part of the general law, it was possible to get a divorce by Act of Parliament. The most common example of local legislation is that which applies to individual cities. The law in Leicester is sometimes not the same as the law in London. General legislation is much more common than personal and local legislation.

A legal rule in a statute can only be changed by new legislation. Judges interpret statutes but they do not have the power to change them. Any statute, no matter how important it seems, can be changed in the same way as any other.

Most legislation consists of a direct statement about how people should behave or indicates the consequences of certain behaviour. For example, a statute may define a crime and say what the punishment will be for that crime. Sometimes Parliament cannot decide exactly what the law should be on a particular point. It may not have the necessary expertise or it may be that the area is one where frequent changes are needed. In such cases Parliament may pass an Act giving somebody else the power to make law in the appropriate area. Such power is often given to government ministers or to local authorities. This is the most common example of what is known as *delegated* or *secondary legislation*. A person or body to whom legislative power is delegated cannot, as can Parliament, make law about anything. The Act (sometimes called *the parent Act*) will determine the area in which law can be made. It may say something about the content of the law but the details of that law will be left to the person or body to whom legislative power is delegated. They may also have the power to change that law from time to time. Most delegated legislation is published as a statutory instrument. Although people are frequently unaware of this type of legislation it is very important, affecting most people's lives. For example, much of the social security system is based on delegated legislation.

The final thing that we have to consider is the range of directives, circulars, and guidance notes produced by various State agencies and bodies such as the HM Revenue & Customs. Some of these documents bind the people to whom they are addressed to behave in particular ways. Many, however, are not legally binding. They do not compel people to do things in the way that statutes or statutory instruments do. Even so, such documents are often very influential. In practice officials receiving them may always act in the way they indicate. Thus we might consider them all as equivalent to legislation.

In Chapter 4 you will find an explanation of how to find statutes and statutory instruments. In Chapter 5 there is an explanation of how you read them to find out where the law stands about something. The methods that the judiciary use to decide how a particular legislative provision is to be interpreted are explained in Chapter 7.

JUDGES, COURTS AND TRIBUNALS

Precedents

Not all legal rules are laid down in an Act of Parliament or some other piece of legislation. A ▶ 1.3 number of legal rules are found in the statements of judges made in the course of deciding cases brought before them. Rules that come from judicial decisions, rather than from legislation, make what is called the *common law*. A common law rule has as much force as a rule derived from statute. Many important areas of English law, such as contract, tort, criminal law, land law and constitutional law have their origins in common law. An explanation of the different divisions of law is to be found in Chapter 2. Some of the earliest common law rules still survive, though many have been supplemented or supplanted by statute. Common law rules are still being made today, though, as a source of new legal rules, common law is much less important than statute.

Strictly speaking, the term common law is confined to rules that have been developed entirely by judicial decisions. It excludes new rules made by judges when they interpret statutes. Most decisions made by judges now involve, at least in part, interpreting statutes. The term *case law* covers both kinds of decisions.

The application of case law is easiest to understand when the issue presently before the court has been raised in some previous analogous case. In such a situation the court will look to see if there is a potential applicable rule in the reports of previously decided cases. Then they will decide whether they have to, or should, apply that rule. It is therefore vital that accurate and comprehensive records be kept of past court decisions and judicial pronouncements. Thus the importance of the numerous and varied series of law reports can be appreciated. Anybody entering a law library in England can hardly help being impressed at the volume of materials falling within this category of Law Reports. Row upon row of bound volumes, containing the judgments in thousands of past cases, dominate the holdings of any major English law library. In the modern era cases are not only published in printed form. They are also published electronically, either by the courts themselves or by various commercial publishers.

More information about the various kinds of Law Reports and how to use them can be found in Chapter 4.

Not every judgement in every case or every part of a judgement is of equal importance in terms of the creation of law. The weight that is to be given to a judgement as an indication of what future judicial decisions will be depends upon two things. One is the level of the court in which that case was decided. In English law there is a principle of a *hierarchy of precedents*. Judgments given by superior courts in the hierarchy are binding on inferior courts; these judgements create a precedent. The second is whether the part of the judgement that is under consideration is the *ratio* of the judgement or whether it is *obiter dicta*. An explanation of the hierarchy of precedents and the rules for determining whether something is ratio or obiter in a judgement is to be found in Chapter 6.

SUPREME COURT, formerly the HOUSE OF LORDS (deals only with appeals)

COURT OF APPEAL (deals only with appeals)

HIGH COURT different divisions deals with different kinds of legal dispute (deals with both appeals and new cases)		
FAMILY DIVISION	CHANCERY DIVISION	QUEEN'S BENCH DIVISION

COUNTY COURT (deals with civil law disputes)	CROWN COURT (deals mainly with criminal law disputes)

MAGISTRATES' COURT (main business—criminal, matrimonial and licensing matters)

Courts

1.4 ▶ Cases are decided in courts or tribunals. We look at what tribunals are in the section below. Different kinds of legal disputes are decided in different kinds of courts. Sometimes it is possible to bring a legal dispute before two or more different kinds of court. In some situations, once a court has given judgment, it is possible to appeal against that judgment to another court. Some courts only hear appeals.

The highest court in the English legal system is the Supreme Court, until very recently known as the House of Lords. Cases in the Supreme Court are normally heard by five judges but in very important cases there can be more than this. Because there is more than one judge in a case before the Supreme Court the decision may be a majority one.

The Privy Council has a varied jurisdiction. It includes hearing appeals from courts in some Commonwealth countries. Its decisions are not technically binding on courts within the English legal system but, because the judges in the Privy Council are mainly the same as the judges in the Supreme Court, its decisions are highly influential within the courts in the English legal system.

The court below the Supreme Court is the Court of Appeal. Like the House of Lords the Court of Appeal has jurisdiction over virtually every area of law. Cases in the Court of Appeal are usually heard by three judges.

The court below the Court of Appeal is the High Court. Both the House of Lords and the Court of Appeal are basically appellate courts. They appear appeals about the decisions of other lower courts. However the High Court has both an original jurisdiction, that is to say it is a place where a case is first heard there, and an appellate jurisdiction. The High Court is divided into three different Divisions. In practice these Divisions function as though they were separate courts. The Chancery Division mainly hears cases that are concerned with mortgages, the sale of land, the administration of estates of deceased persons or other probate business. The Family Division hears cases about matrimonial matters, including civil partnerships, and matters relating to children. The Queen's Bench Division is the largest of the three Divisions and has a much wider jurisdiction than the other two Divisions. Its jurisdiction includes, amongst other things, judicial review, broadly cases challenging the decisions of bodies with statutory powers such as government departments, criminal law, the law of tort and the law of contract.

None of the courts below the High Court create precedents; that is to say that none of their decisions create legal rules that are binding on other courts. This is not to say that these courts are unimportant. They hear more cases when they first come to court than does the High Court. For most people if they have case come to court it will be to a court below the High Court. In terms of the operation of the legal system it is the courts below the High Court that matter most. However, because most law courses at university are concerned with the analysis of legal rules. This means that courts below the High Court are rarely mentioned in these courses.

The courts immediately below the High Court are the County Court and the Crown Court. The county court has a civil jurisdiction whilst the Crown Court has a mainly criminal jurisdiction dealing with the more serious criminal offences. In the Crown Court cases are decided by a judge and a lay jury comprised of 12 people randomly selected from the population at large.

The lowest court in the English legal system is the magistrates' courts. Judges who are legally qualified preside in the other courts within the English legal system. However, most magistrates are lay people who receive only a very minimal training in law. Legally qualified clerks advise them. Magistrates' courts are often thought of as courts with a criminal jurisdiction. However, whilst it is true that magistrates' courts do deal with a very large number of minor criminal cases, dealing with approximately 98 per cent of all criminal cases heard each year, they also have a significant civil jurisdiction dealing with, amongst other things, some family law matters and licensing decisions.

Tribunals

Courts are not the only state institutions that hear cases and make decisions. Tribunals have a ▶1.5
very similar role to that of the courts. Their hearings tend to be more informal and their decisions tend to be about less serious matters than cases that are heard in court. Tribunal cases

are usually decided by a panel comprising of a legally qualified chairperson, who is now some-times called a judge, and two other people who have knowledge of the area that the tribunal is concerned with. Thus, for example, in an Employment Tribunal the panel might consist of an Employment Judge, a trade union official and someone who is an employer. Tribunals have their own appellate system. Most decisions of tribunals will not constitute a precedent and they will not be reported in the way that decisions of the higher courts are. There are, however, exceptions to this such as the Employment Appeal Tribunal.

COMMON LAW AND EQUITY

1.6 ▶ In the section above the term *common law* is used as a synonym for rules of law derived from judicial decisions rather than statute. This is a common way in which the phrase is used. However, another equally frequent sense of the word is as an antonym to *equity*. English law has deep historical roots. The opposition of common law and equity refers to the system of rules that originally develop in different courts within the legal system. Common law rules arose first. Later, these rules were seen as being over-formal and concerned too much with the way a case was presented rather than with the justice in the issues at stake. Thus a less strict system of equitable rules was developed. In time, the rules of equity also became formalised. Eventually, the different courts were merged and now all courts can apply both the rules of common law and equity.

▶ 2
Divisions of law

INTRODUCTION

▶ 2.1

Not all legal rules are of the same type. Legal rules can be divided up in many different ways. This chapter introduces some common ways of classifying law. They show differences in purpose, in origin and form, in the consequences when the rules are breached, and in matters of procedure, remedies and enforcement. The divisions described below are of the broadest kind. One kind of division of legal rules has already been introduced, that between statute and case or common law. This division and the others now described overlap. For example, the legal rule defining murder originates in common law, not statute. It is a rule of criminal law rather than civil law; of public law rather than private law and of national law rather than international law.

CRIMINAL AND CIVIL LAW

▶ 2.2

One of the most fundamental divisions in law is the division between criminal and civil law. Newcomers to the study of law tend to assume that criminal law occupies the bulk of a lawyer's caseload and of a law student's studies. This is an interesting by-product of the portrayal of the legal system by the media. Criminal law weighs very lightly in terms of volume when measured against civil law. There are more rules of civil law than there are of criminal law; more court cases involve breach of the civil law than involve breach of the criminal law. Law degree students will find that criminal law is generally only one course out of 12 to 15 subjects in a three-year law degree, although some criminal offences may be referred to in other courses.

Criminal law means the law relating to crime. Civil law can be taken to mean all the other legal rules within the legal system. The distinction relies not so much on the nature of the conduct that is the object of a legal rule but in the nature of the proceedings and the sanctions that may follow. Some kinds of conduct give rise to criminal liability, some to civil liability and some to both civil and criminal liability.

The seriousness of the conduct does not necessarily determine the type of liability to which it gives rise; conduct that is contrary to the criminal law is not always "worse" than conduct that is against the civil law. Few people would consider every criminal offence a moral wrong (except, perhaps, in the sense that every breach of the law might be thought to be a moral wrong). Equally, some actions that are purely breaches of the civil law might be considered breaches of morality. If you breach your contract you break a promise. Nor is harm, in the sense of damage done to individuals, something that is always found to a greater degree in the criminal law as compared with the civil law. The person who "speeds" at 31 miles per hour on an empty road in broad daylight breaches the criminal law. The company that fails to pay for the goods that it has bought, thereby bankrupting another company, commits only a breach of the civil law. Who has done the greater harm? Concepts of morality have had some influence on the development of English law but historical accident, political policy and pragmatic considerations have played just as important a part in developing our law.

Some conduct which might be considered "criminal" by many people gives rise in law only to civil liability or to no liability at all and some conduct which you may consider "harmless" by some may rise to either criminal or civil liability. It will be easier to see that "harm", "morality" and the division between criminal and civil law do not follow any clear pattern if you consider some fictitious examples. In considering them, ask yourself whether or not the conduct described should give rise to any legal liability; if it should, what form should that liability take and what should the legal consequences be which flow from the conduct described? Should any of the people be compensated for the harm done to them and, if so, by whom and for what? Should any of the characters be punished and, if so, for what reason and how? Who should decide whether or not legal proceedings of any variety should be instigated against any of the individuals? The probable legal consequences that follow from each example are found at the end of the chapter. Do not look at these until you have thought about the examples yourself.

Examples

1. *Norman drinks 5 pints of beer as he does each day. His car suffers a puncture and, as a consequence, he drives into a queue at the bus station injuring a young woman and her child.*
2. *Meena, who is an accountant, regularly takes recreational drugs.*
3. *Sue, who is pregnant, lives with Chris. She smokes 50 cigarettes a day. Sue is also carrying on an occasional affair with Richard.*
4. *Robert agrees to pay Usha, a professional decorator, £5000 if she paints his house. She completes the work to a very high standard. Robert, who is a millionaire, refuses to pay her.*

Even when a person's actions clearly infringe either the criminal law or civil law, it does not necessarily mean that any actual legal consequences will follow. In criminal and civil cases persons with the legal right to take any legal action have a discretion as to whether or not they initiate legal proceedings. There is a difference between *liability* and *proceedings*. Conduct gives rise to liability. It is for someone else to decide whether or not to take the matter to court by starting proceedings.

In criminal proceedings a *prosecutor* prosecutes the *defendant*. The case is heard in the magistrates' court or the Crown Court, depending on the seriousness of the offence. The prosecutor will have to prove to the court, *beyond all reasonable doubt*, that the defendant committed the offence charged. The court will have to determine whether or not the defendant is guilty. In the magistrates' court it will be for the magistrates to determine this question, in the

Crown Court it will be for the jury to decide questions of fact and for the judge to decide questions of law. A finding of *not guilty* will lead to the defendant's acquittal. A finding of *guilty* will lead to a conviction and may lead to a sentence of imprisonment or some other form of punishment such as a fine or probation.

One of the major objectives of the criminal law is to punish the wrongdoer for action that is deemed to be contrary to the interests of the state and its citizens. Criminal proceedings do not have as a major objective the provision of compensation or support for the victim of crime. It is significant that the exercise of the discretion to prosecute is seldom carried out by the victim of the crime. Criminal proceedings are normally initiated by the state or its agents and brought in the name of the Queen or the prosecuting official.

In civil proceedings it is generally the *claimant* (the party harmed) (before April 1999 they were known as the *plaintiff*) who sues the *defendant*, although in some areas of the civil law other terms are used. For example, in the case of a divorce the petitioner sues the respondent. The case will usually be heard in either the county court or the High Court, depending on the nature of the case and the size of the loss involved. The plaintiff usually has to prove, on *the balance of probabilities*, that the events took place in the manner claimed. This is a lower standard of proof than in criminal cases. If the plaintiff proves their case, the court will make some kind of order. What this will be will depend upon the kind of case and what the plaintiff has asked for. The basic choice before the court is whether to order the defendant to compensate the plaintiff for their loss by awarding damages or to order the defendant to act, or refrain from acting, in some specific way in the future, or to make both kinds of orders.

Historically the civil law was primarily founded on the law of contract and tort, which are still mainly areas of common law. The law of contract determines which forms of agreement entered into between individuals are legally binding and on whom they will be binding. The law of tort covers categories of civil wrong, other than breach of contract, which may give rise to legal causes of action. It includes the law of negligence, trespass and libel and slander. Just as a set of facts can give rise to conduct that may result in both civil and criminal proceedings, so a set of facts can give rise to both actions in contract and in tort. Most claimants' primary motivation for bringing civil proceedings will be to obtain an effective remedy for the civil wrong which has been perpetrated. The fact that there is liability will not, however, necessarily mean that they will take action. For example, there may be no point in suing a person for damages if you know they have no money.

In the latter part of the twentieth century areas of civil law other than those related to contract and tort came to be of increasing importance. Some took a very different form to contract and tort. Divorce, for example, necessitates an action in court but, unlike actions in contract and tort, such cases are rarely contested, although there may be separate court cases about what happens to either any children the divorcing couples may have or the property and income that they have. One area of law that has been the source of an increasing number of court cases in the higher courts is public law. Public law is the law that governs those that are given powers by statute. These are largely bodies or individuals which form part of either central or local government. There is a more detailed explanation of the nature of public law in the final section of this chapter.

The emphasis of the civil law has changed over the last hundred years with an increase in the role of the state and the importance of legislation as opposed to case law as the major source of law. Civil law does not just regulate relations between individuals covering such matters as their property transactions, but also deals with relations between the state and individuals. It covers unemployment and social benefit entitlement, tax and planning questions, and council tenants' relationships with their local authorities. All of these areas are covered by statute law that has created new rights and obligations. These are often enforced in tribunals as opposed to courts.

Statutory provisions have also been enacted in order to minimise the common law rights that have resulted from the judicial development of contract law and the notion of freedom of contract. For example, employment protection and landlord and tenant legislation give employees and tenants statutory rights that will often modify or override terms in their contracts that give their employers or landlords specific rights to dismiss or evict them.

NATIONAL, INTERNATIONAL AND EUROPEAN UNION LAW

2.3 ▶ The term *national, municipal* or *state law* is used when referring to the internal legal rules of a particular country. In contrast *international law*, usually termed *public international law*, deals with the law that applies to external relationships of a state with other states. In the United Kingdom, national law is normally unaffected by international legal obligations unless these obligations have been transferred into national law by an Act of Parliament. *European Union law*, however, cuts across this conventional notion that national and international law operate at different and distinct levels. It is a form of international law in that it is in part concerned with legal relations between Member States, but European Union law may also directly affect the national law of Member States. It will therefore be considered separately from both national and international law.

NATIONAL LAW

2.4 ▶ The system of national law has already been considered in Chapter 1.

INTERNATIONAL LAW

2.5 ▶ Public international law regulates the external relations of states with one another. (*Private international law* is a type of national law that deals with cases where individuals find themselves in legal disputes that involve a number of different countries; for example when someone from the United Kingdom makes a contract in France). Public international law, but not private international law, is a form of law very different from national law. There is no world government or legislature issuing and enforcing laws to which all nations are subject. The international legal order is essentially decentralised and operates by agreement between states. This means that the creation, interpretation and enforcement of international law lies primarily in the hands of states themselves. Its scope and effectiveness depends on the capacity of states to agree and the sense of mutual benefit and obligation involved in adhering to the rules.

International law is created in two main ways: by treaty and by custom. Treaties are agreements between two or more states, and are binding, in international law, on the states involved if they have given their consent to be so bound. Customary law is established by showing that states have adopted broadly consistent practices towards a particular matter and that they have acted in this way out of a sense of legal obligation. International law is neither comprehensive nor systematic. Few treaties involve the majority of world states. Most are bilateral understandings or involve only a handful of parties to a multilateral agreement.

Disputes about the scope and interpretation of international law are rarely resolved by the use of international courts or binding arbitration procedures of an international organisation. This is because submission to an international court or similar process is entirely voluntary and few states are likely to agree to this if there is a serious risk of losing their case of where important political or national interests are at stake. Negotiation is far more common. International courts are used occasionally, for example where settlement is urgent, or protracted negotiations have failed, where the dispute is minor or is affecting other international relations; in other words, in cases where failure to settle is more damaging than an unfavourable outcome. Where international law has been breached, an injured state must rely primarily on self-help for enforcement. There is no effective international institutional machinery to ensure compliance when the law is challenged. This means that in practice powerful states are better able to protect their rights and assert new claims.

Breaching established rules is one, rather clumsy, way of changing international law. In a decentralised system, change can only be affected by common consent or by the assertion of a new claim being met by inaction or acquiescence by others. The lack of powerful enforcement machinery does not mean that international law is widely disregarded. On the contrary, legal rules are regularly followed, not least because states require security and predictability in the conduct of normal everyday inter-state relations.

International law also plays an important role in the promotion of common interests such as controlling pollution, restricting over fishing, or establishing satellite and telecommunication link-ups.

A large number of global or regional international organisations have been established for the regulation and review of current inter- state activity. The best-known example, though perhaps not the most effective, is the United States, whose primary function is the maintenance of international peace and security.

In the United Kingdom, international law has no direct effect on national law and, on a given matter, national law may in fact be inconsistent with the United Kingdom's international obligations. The Government has authority to enter into treaties which may bind the United Kingdom vis-a-vis other states. However a treaty will not alter the law to be applied within the United Kingdom unless the provisions are adopted by means of an Act of Parliament. Customary international law may have been incorporated into national law but will enjoy no higher status than any other provision of national law and is, therefore, liable to be superseded by a new statute. However, it is a principle of judicial interpretation that, unless there is clear legal authority to the contrary, Parliament does not intend to act in breach of international law. In some other countries, international law is accorded a different status. In the Netherlands and Germany, for example, international law takes effect in municipal law and, where these conflict, international law prevails.

The lack of direct application should not be taken to mean that international law is of no importance in United Kingdom courts or for United Kingdom citizens. National courts regularly decide domestic cases having presumed the existence and application of international law.

For example, under the Vienna Convention of 1961, diplomats enjoy immunity from criminal prosecution. If a defendant claims immunity, a court must decide whether the defendant falls within the terms of the treaty before proceeding further. Secondly, individuals may have rights under international law, enforceable not through national courts but through international institutions. The European Convention on Human Rights gives individuals the right to complain of breaches of the Convention to the European Commission on Human Rights which may then refer the case to the European Court of Human Rights (these institutions should not be confused with European Union institutions: they are quite separate). Although the United Kingdom ratified the Convention in 1951, it was only in 1966 that the United Kingdom agreed to the articles of the treaty that recognised the right of individual petition and the compulsory jurisdiction of the Court. The Human Rights Act 1998 gives an individual the right to enforce certain rights found in the Convention against public authorities.

EUROPEAN UNION LAW

2.6 ▶ In joining the European Communities in 1973, the United Kingdom agreed to apply and be bound by Community law, accepting that Community law would override any conflicting provisions of national law. Unlike other forms of international law, European Community law is capable of passing directly into national law; it is applicable in the United Kingdom without being adopted by an Act of Parliament. These principles were given legal effect by the passage of the European Communities Act 1972. The European Communities are made up of three organisations: the European Economic Community (EEC), the European Coal and Steel Community (ECSC) and the European Community for Atomic Energy (Euratom). Since the United Kingdom's entry the European Communities have been further enlarged. There are now 27 member states. The European Communities are now part of the European Union, following the Treaty on European Union, signed at Maastricht (since added to by the Treaty of Amsterdam, Treaty of Nice and Treaty of Lisbon). This section will concentrate on the implications of membership of the European Union for United Kingdom law.

The European Union is an international organisation established and developed by treaty between Member States. The basic framework is set out in the EEC Treaty of 1957 (the Treaty of Rome), which defines the objectives of the Community, the powers and duties of Community institutions, and the rights and obligations of Member States. This treaty goes much further than just creating law that binds both Member States and Community institutions. It contains many detailed substantive provisions, some of that create rights for individuals that are enforceable directly in national courts. The EEC Treaty, and certain others which have followed it, are thus primary sources of European Union law. The European Union has a number of major institutions: the Council of European Union, the Commission, the Assembly (or European Parliament), the Court of Justice (and the Court of First Instance) and the Court of Auditors. The terms of the various treaties give the European Union a powerful legislative, administrative and judicial machinery. The Treaty provides that further legislation may be made by the Council of Ministers and the Commission. This is called secondary legislation and takes three forms.

Regulations, once made, pass into the law of a Member State automatically. Regulations are *directly applicable*, that means that Member States do not have to take any action (such as passing an Act of Parliament) to implement them or to incorporate them into national law. Regulations are intended to be applied uniformly throughout the Community, and override any conflicting provisions in national law.

Directives are binding on Member States as to the result to be achieved, but leave each Member State with a choice about the method used to achieve that result. Member States are given a transitional period in which to implement the directive. This may involve passing a new law, making new administrative arrangements, or, where national law already conforms with the directive, taking no action. The Commission can initiate proceedings against a Member State if it believes the steps taken do not achieve the desired result. Although directives are addressed to Member States, in some circumstances an individual may be able to rely directly on certain parts, whether or not the Member State has taken implementing action. This is when the relevant part lays down an unconditional obligation and grants enforceable individual rights.

Decisions can be addressed to Member States, individuals or companies. They are binding only on the person to whom they are addressed and take effect on notification.

European Union law is applied in Member States by their individual system of national courts and tribunals. When a point of European Union law is crucial to a court's decision, the court may refer the case to the Court of Justice for a preliminary ruling on the interpretation of the point in question. Courts against whose decision there is no appeal, (e.g. the Supreme Court) must make a reference to the Court of Justice when the case hinges on European Union law unless the Court has already ruled on that particular issue. Once the Court of Justice has given a preliminary ruling, the case is referred back to the national court from which it originated, which must then decide the case. The Court of Justice will only answer questions put to it about the interpretation of European Union law; it will not rule on national law or on conflict between national and European Union law or apply its interpretation to the facts of the case. These are all matters for national courts. The Commission may bring an action in the Court of Justice against a Member State for breach of an obligation, such as the non-implementation of a directive. Proceedings may be taken against the Commission or the Council for failing to act where the EEC Treaty imposes a duty to act. There are also provisions for annulling legislation adopted by the Commission or Council, for example, where the action has exceeded the powers laid down by treaty.

PUBLIC AND PRIVATE LAW

Another distinction that may be drawn between different types of law is the division between *public law* and *private law*. Public law is largely concerned with the distribution and exercise of power by the state and the legal relations between the state and the individual. For example, the rules governing the powers and duties of local authorities, the operation of the National Health Service, the regulations of building standards, the issuing of passports and the compulsory purchase of land to build a motorway all fall within the ambit of public law. In contrast, private law is concerned with the legal relationships between individuals, such as the liability of employers towards their employees for injuries sustained at work, consumers' rights against

▶ 2.7

shopkeepers and manufacturers over faulty goods, or owners' rights to prevent others walking across their land.

The significance of the public/private law distinction operates at two levels. First, it is a very useful general classification through which we can highlight some broad differences, such as those in the purpose of law, in sources and forms of legal rules, and in remedies and enforcement. This is the way the idea of public/private law will be discussed here. However, the distinction is also used in a second, narrower sense; as a way of defining the procedure by which claims can be raised in court.

One way of thinking about a legal rule is to consider its purpose. The primary purpose underlying most private law rules is the protection of individual interests, whereas the aim of most public law provisions is the promotion of social objectives and the protection of collective rather than individual interests. The methods used to achieve these purposes also differ. A characteristic feature of public law is the creation of a public body with special powers of investigation, decision-making and/or enforcement in relation to a particular problem, whereas private law achieves its ends by giving individuals the right to take action in defence of their interests.

Many problems are addressed by both public and private law. Sometimes a single statute may include both private rights and liabilities alongside public law provisions.

Example

Ann lives next door to an industrial workshop run by Brenda. The machinery is very noisy and the process discharges fumes that make Ann feel ill. This sort of problem is tackled by both public and private law in a number of different ways.

(i) *As a neighbour, Ann may bring a private law action in nuisance, which is a claim that Brenda's activities unreasonably interfere with the use of Ann's land. Ann could claim compensation for the hard she has suffered and could seek an injunction to stop the harmful process continuing.*

(ii) *There are also public law rules that may be invoked whether or not an individual has or may be harmed, aimed at preventing the problem arising in the first place or controlling the situation for the public benefit. For example, when Brenda first started her workshop she would have needed to get planning permission from the local authority if her activities constituted a change in the use of the land. Planning legislation thus gives the local authority an opportunity to prevent industrial development in residential areas by refusing planning permission, or control it by laying down conditions. Other legislation gives the local authority powers to monitor and control various kinds of pollution and nuisances in their area, including noise and dangerous fumes. A further complex set of private rights and public regulations govern the working conditions of the workshop employees, who would also be affected by the noise and smells.*

Public and private law also show differences in their origins and form. Some of the most important principles of private law are of ancient origin and were developed through the common law as individuals took their private disputes to court and demanded a remedy. The rules of private rights in contract, over land and inheritance, to compensation for physical injury or damage to property or reputation, were all first fashioned by judges in the course of deciding cases brought before them. In contrast, most public law rules are of comparatively recent origin first originating in stature, not judicial decisions.

An important function of public law has its roots in constitutional theory. The actions of public bodies are only lawful if there is a legal rule granting the body authority to act in a given situation. A private individual needs no legal authority merely to act. It is assumed that a person acts lawfully unless there is a legal rule prohibiting that behaviour. Public law therefore has a facilitative function, for which there is no equivalent in private law, permitting a public body to take action that would otherwise be unlawful.

A feature of much recent public law is a shift towards the grant of broad discretionary powers to public bodies. This means that the same legislative framework can be used more flexibly, accommodating changes in public policy as to the purposes to which the powers should be put or the criteria for the exercise of these powers. This characteristic form of modern public law contrasts quite sharply with the relatively specific rights and duties to be found in private law, and in turn affects the way public and private law can be enforced. All private law is enforced by granting individuals the right to take action in defence of a recognised personal interest. For example, a householder may make a contract with a builder over the repair of a roof, and may sue the builder if the work or materials are of a lower standard than was specified in the contract. Not all public law can be enforced by way of individual action.

The enforcement of public law can be viewed from two perspectives. First, public law can be enforced when an official ensures that individuals or companies comply with standards set in statutes or delegated legislation, e.g. Environmental Health Officers making orders in relation to or prosecuting restaurants. Secondly, the enforcement of public law can also be seen as the matter of ensuring public authorities themselves carry out their duties and do not exceed their legal powers. Here, the form of public law statutes, mentioned above, rarely ties a public body to supplying a particular standard of service, as a contract may tie a builder, but gives a wide choice of lawful behaviour.

Even where legislation lays a duty on a public authority, there may be no corresponding right of individual action. For example, under the Education Act 1996, local education authorities are under a duty to ensure that there are sufficient schools, in numbers, character and equipment, for providing educational opportunities for all pupils in their area. However, nobody can sue the authority if the schools are overcrowded or badly equipped. The only remedy is to complain to the Secretary of State, who can make orders if satisfied that the authority is in default of their duties. The mechanism for controlling standards of public bodies is generally by way of political accountability to the electorate or ministers rather than the legal process.

Some parts of public law do create individual rights and permit individual enforcement. In social security legislation, for example, qualified claimants have a right to certain benefits and may appeal against decisions of benefit to a tribunal. There is a procedure, special to public law, called *judicial review of administrative action* (usually referred to simply as *judicial review*), whereby an individual may go to the High Court alleging unlawful behaviour on the part of a public body. However, in order to go to court, the individual must show *sufficient interest* in the issue in question (this being legally defined) and the court has a discretion whether to hear the case or grant a remedy. This is quite different from proceedings in private law, where a plaintiff does not need the court's permission for the case to be heard but has a right to a hearing if a recognised cause of action is asserted and also a right to a remedy of some kind if successful.

CRIMINAL LAW AND CIVIL LAW ANSWERS

2.8 ▶ Legal consequences in questions 1–4:

1. Norman's actions may give rise to both criminal and civil proceedings. He may be prosecuted for drink driving and related road traffic offences and, if convicted, will have a criminal record. He may also be sued by the woman or child who would wish to recover damages for the personal injuries they have suffered. Such an action would be a civil action. The same set of facts may give rise to both criminal and civil liability.
2. The use of some drugs is prohibited by law. Legislative changes from time to time alter both which drugs are prohibited and the punishment that follows from conviction.
3. Sue has committed no criminal offence. Neither the unborn child nor Richard have any right of civil action for any harm they may consider Sue has done to them.
4. Robert has not committed any criminal offence. He is in no different a position in law to the person who has no money. Usha will be able to commence civil proceedings against him. She will be able to sue him for breach of contract. Robert's wealth makes it more likely that Usha will consider it worth suing him as she is more likely to be able to recover any damages. However she will also have to remember that Robert will, if he wishes be able to hire the best lawyers so as to delay Joan's inevitable court victory.

3
Law and its Social Context

INTRODUCTION

This chapter is about the different kinds of questions that arise when studying law and the different techniques you need when studying them. ▶ 3.1

You might think that studying law is purely a matter of learning a large number of legal rules. If this were the case only one kind of question would ever arise, what is the content of any particular legal rule? However, simply learning a large number of legal rules is not a very useful way of learning about law. Learning the rules is like memorising the answers to a set of sums. It is of no help when the sums change. If all you do is learn a set of legal rules, when the rules change, when the law is altered, you are back where you started. At the very least, to use your legal knowledge, you also need to know how to find legal rules and how to find out if they have been changed. Thus, to the question "what is the content of the legal rule?" are added questions about how to find them. More importantly all legal scholars would agree that legal rules are sometimes not clear. The content of such rules, and some scholars would argue most legal rules are like this, is the subject of debate. If you are studying law you therefore need to know not just what the legal rules are but how you argue about what the content of legal rules might be.

Not everyone interested in law is interested in questions about the content of legal rules. For example, we might ask whether it is ever right to disobey the law. Here we are concerned not simply with what the rule is but what we ought to do because of that rule. This is a question of ethics that might, in part, relate to the content of a legal rule but is much more about the nature of moral judgement. We need to decide what we should do but we also need to learn how to construct arguments that will convince others that we are right about what we do.

Legal rules are intended to change behaviour; they should have an impact on society. However knowing what a legal rule is does not tell us whether the rule is in fact being obeyed. Equally knowing what a legal rule is does not tell us whether the impact that it is having, even if it is being obeyed, is that which was intended. Scholars have long observed that there is a difference between *the law in books*, legal rules, and *the law in action*, what happens in practice once a legal rule has been created. This is so even if we are just concerned with what happens in the courts. The hierarchical nature of the courts means that the lower courts should obey the rulings in the higher courts but research has shown that this is not always the case. Whether we are concerned with looking at what the law is for an individual client or what influence the law has on society knowing what the legal rules are is not enough. We need to know what happens in practice.

The distinction between the law in action and the law in books is both easy to see and useful to use but it also has its limitations. Some questions about law seem to fit into neither category. For example, is our earlier question about disobedience to law a question about the law in action or the law in books? Information about that actually happens in the legal system will only tell us what people do, not whether their action is morally correct. Equally, being told what the legal rule says is of little help in helping us assess whether we are correct to obey it or not. The question does not appear to fall into either category.

The distinction between the law in action and the law in books is broad but crude. More sophisticated categories provide narrower, more precise distinctions. Thus questions about the nature of law that can include whether or not one has a duty to obey it can be grouped together under the title the philosophy of law or *jurisprudence*. Such categories are not firmly fixed and may be defined by different people in different ways. Thus some people would use the term the *sociology of law* to refer to all questions about the operation of the legal system in practice. Others would distinguish between questions about the relationship between law and other social forces and questions about how effective a legal rule is. They would see the first kind of question as falling within the sociology of law and the second as coming under the heading *socio-legal studies*. It is more important to be able to identify the different kinds of questions than give them the labels.

DIFFERENT QUESTIONS MEAN DIFFERENT ANSWERS

3.2 ▶ Knowing that there are different kinds of questions asked when studying law is of intellectual interest but does it have any further significance? What happens if you fail properly to identify the kind of question that you are asking? We can answer these questions by looking at one way in which different kinds of questions are commonly confused.

For many years it was assumed that legal rules that laid down what should happen were an accurate guide to what actually happened. The law in action was thought to be a reflection of the law in books. It was accepted that there were divergences but these were thought to be on a small scale and of no importance. However, academics have now shown that there is often a very great difference between legal rules and the practice in the legal system. One example of this can be seen in the area of criminal justice, when people are arrested and taken to the police station for questioning.

The Police and Criminal Evidence Act 1984 (generally referred to as "PACE") lays down a large number of rules relating to the treatment of suspects who are detained in police stations. The purpose of these rules is to try and provide a balance between providing safeguards for the person who is being questioned and enabling the police to carry out a thorough investigation. One of the rules that PACE contains is that the suspect must be told of his/her right to seek legal advice. However, researchers have found that most people do not receive legal advice at the police station. This can happen because many suspects do not appreciate how important it is to have legal advice at an early stage in criminal investigations. However, another significant reason influencing suspects in their decision not to seek legal advice is that the police may use a number of ploys to discourage suspects from taking advice, including minimising the significance of what is happening by saying the suspect will only be there for a short time, or emphasising what a long time the detainee will have to wait until their legal adviser arrives. Merely looking at the law in the books could only tell us what is supposed to happen; that suspects are entitled to be told about their right to seek legal advice. It is only when we look at the law in action that we can understand how the law really works in practice; in this case, we come to understand that merely giving a right to people does not mean that they will understand how important it is to exercise that right, nor does giving a right ensure that it will necessarily be implemented in the way it was intended.

The difference between the law in action and the law in books in this area is important for several reasons. First, confusing the different kinds of questions resulted in an inaccurate description. People accepted the wrong kind of material as evidence for their answers, and as a result thought that the law worked in practice in much the same way as the legal rules suggested it should. Secondly, because of that mistake, those involved in advising others on the law may have given misleading advice. Finally, those involved in considering whether or not the law and legal system are effective and just looked not at the real legal system but, instead, at a shadowy reflection of it.

WHICH KIND OF QUESTION AM I ASKING?

Somebody has been divorced and you are asked, how their financial affairs will be settled by the courts. Are you being asked what the relevant rules are, or what will actually happen in court, or both? Outside your course of study it may be very difficult to sort out what kind of question you are being asked. For study purposes the task will generally be simpler. The kind of question that you are being asked is likely to be indicated by the nature of your course as a while. The title of your course may give you a clue. A course on "the sociology of law" is unlikely to be much concerned with questions about the content of legal rules. Some kinds of courses are more usually taught with one kind of question in mind than another. For example, courses on "land law" or the "law of contract" are more often concerned with the law in books than the law in action. These kinds of courses are sometimes termed *black-letter law* courses. Courses on Family Law often include a great deal of material that tells us about the law in action. This kind of course is often described as *socio-legal*.

Even when it is clear what kind of question your course is generally concerned with problems may still arise. It is not only important to know the kind of question that you are interested in. You must also be able to identify the kind of question that the author of a book or article that you are using is interested in. Are they trying only to analyse the legal rules, the cases and statutes in a particular area of law, or are they also interested in exploring how the law works in practice? If you know the type of answer they are trying to give you will be in a better position to judge the quality of their argument and, thus the value of their work. Even when you have identified the kind of question an author is most interested in you will also have to be careful to see that other kinds of question are not introduced. For example, it is not uncommon to find a book largely devoted to discussion of the content of legal rules also including a few remarks on the value or justice of those rules. There is nothing wrong with this if the author realises that a different kind of question is being addressed and uses the appropriate material to answer it. Unfortunately this is not always so.

ARE THERE REALLY DIFFERENT QUESTIONS?

There are some people who would argue that it is misleading to distinguish between different questions in the way we have done above. Some would argue that all the distinctions drawn are

▶ 3.3

▶ 3.4

wrong. Others would argue that only some of them are invalid. Are there really different questions? One argument that might be advanced is about the distinction between the law in action and the law in books. The Court of Appeal has laid down strict rules about when people accused of offences can receive a lesser sentence if they plead guilty (a practice known as *plea-bargaining*). Research in this area has suggested that these rules are not followed in practice. If we assume that the practice of all courts is not to follow these rules, and if this practice continued for many years, what would it mean to say that the legal rule was that which had been laid down by the Court of Appeal? People would only be affected by what happened in practice that would always be different from that which the legal rules said should happen. Could we really say that the legal rule had any significance? If the legal rule has no significance, then surely all we ought to study is what happens in practice, ignoring questions about the law in books?

Other more complicated forms of the above argument exist. Some people would argue that when a judge makes a decision that decision is influenced by the judge's social background, political views and education. The result of any case is therefore not solely determined by the neutral application of legal rules but by factors personal to the particular judge in the case. If this is so, then what kinds of questions will discussion about the content of legal rules answer? If we are to advise people how to act so as to win cases in court what we need to discuss is not, or not only, the content of legal rules but, rather, who are the judges and what their background is. If we want to find out what the law is we have to ask a whole series of questions other than those about ratios or statutes.

In a similar fashion not everyone accepts that questions about the morality of law and questions about the content of law are different. For these people, the very idea of an immoral law is a contradiction in terms. They think that all law must have an irreducible minimum positive moral content. Without that content the "law", in their view, is merely a collection of words that make a command which may be backed by the physical power of the state but do not have the authority of law. Such theories are termed *natural law* theories. Others argue that the questions about something is a legal rule or not and questions about the moral content of that rule are quite distinct. This is usually termed a *positivist* approach to law.

The authors of this book would accept that the distinctions drawn in the previous sections are open to question. The relationship between the different questions, if there are different questions, may be more complicated than the simple divisions above. However most books and most courses in law draw the kinds of distinction outlined. At this early stage in your study of law it will be enough if you understand what the distinctions are. Even if later you come to reject some or all of them, you will still find yourself reading material that is based upon them.

ANSWERING QUESTIONS

3.5 ▶ This chapter has drawn a distinction between three types of question; those concerned with the nature of law, those concerned with the content of legal rules and those which address the operation of law and legal system in practice. Each type of question has a technique appropriate for answering it.

Questions about the nature of law are those that are most difficult to answer. The questions are basic ones, appearing to be very simple. For example, how is law different from other types of command? What is the difference between a gunman telling me to do something and the state, through law, telling me to do some thing? Are both simply applications of power or is there something fundamentally different between them? Neither the content of particular legal rules nor the operation of the law in practice provides any answer. Arguments in this area are abstract and philosophical. In advancing and judging such arguments it is necessary to see that all the terms are explained and that the argument is coherent. Arguments used here must also match the world they purport to explain. In practice these simple conditions are very difficult to meet.

The ultimate source for answers to questions about the law in books is the law reports and statutes that have already been discussed in Chapter 1. Only these sources will give you a definitive answer to any question you are asked. You are told how to find these materials in Chapter 4 and how to use them in Chapter 5. In some cases you may not have either the time or the resources to consult original materials. In such instance you can look at some of the various commentaries on the law. These vary in size, depth of coverage and price. Different commentaries serve different purposes. Some are student texts. Others are written for specific professions or occupations. Most cover only a limited area of law. However there are some general guides to the law and some encyclopaedias of law. The best encyclopaedia of general English law is *Halsbury's Laws of England*. This has a section on almost every area of law. Most good reference libraries will have a copy of this, and your library may also contain some of the other commentaries that are available. All commentaries try to explain legal rules. You should select one suitable to your interests. However, always remember that a commentary is one person's opinion about the law. It may be wrong. You can only be sure what the rule is if you consult the original cases and statutes.

Finding out how the law works in practice is frequently much more difficult than deciding what a legal rule means. It is easy to find opinions about how things work. Almost everybody who has contact with the law, even if only through reading about it in the newspapers, has an opinion on such questions. However, such opinions have little value. At best they are the experience of one person. That experience may be unusual or misinterpreted by that person. What we are trying to understand is how the legal system works. Anecdotes do not give us the answers that we seek. Thus, to answer this kind of question, we need to turn to the materials and techniques of the social scientist.

SEEING THE LAW IN ACTION

One starting point for looking at the law in action is looking at statistical information about the legal system. This is one way of moving from the merely anecdotal to the general. Information about the number of cases handled by a court shows in specific terms what the court's workload is. Changes from year to year may indicate some effects of changes in the law and practice. Statistics here can be used descriptively to provide a clearer picture than general phrases such as "some", "many" or "a few". Statistical tests can also establish that there is a relationship, often called a *correlation*, between different things. For example, the length of a sentence for theft may correlate with the value of the items stolen or the experience of the judge who heard the case. This means that the sentence will be longer if, for example, more items are

▶ 3.6

stolen or the judge is more experienced. Statisticians have produced tests to show whether, given the number of examples you have, there is a strong correlation or not. Where this correlation fits with a theory (sometimes termed an *hypothesis*) it provides evidence tending to confirm the theory. Such confirmation is important; without it we have little to establish the effect that the law has, being forced to rely on personal knowledge of individual instances of its application and having to assume that these have general truth. Empirical study of the operation of law may reveal areas for improvement. It can also confirm that, measured by particular standards, the courts are working well.

If we want to use statistics where will we get them from? Government departments collect and publish a large number of statistical reports relating to their operations. Many of these are now available not only in hard-copy form but on-line via the web. Thus, for example, the Office of National Statistics' data can be seen at *http://www.tics.gov.uk/hub/index.html*. The work of all Government departments is relevant when looking at how the legal system works. Some departments are, however, particularly important in this respect. The Ministry of Justice is one of the largest Government departments and is responsible for the court system, prisons and the probation service. Its web-site is *http://www.justice.gov.uk/*. The Home Office is responsible for things such as the police, immigration and anti-terrorism. Its web-site is *http://www.homeoffice.gov.uk/*. The Department for Children, Schools and Families (*http://www.dcsf.gov.uk/*) and the Department for Work and Pensions (*http://www.dwp.gov.uk/*) also provide useful information. A complete list of Government departments together with their web-sites is to be found at *http://www.number10.gov.uk/Page203*.

Most official statistics are collected from returns filed by local offices of the relevant departments. The content of these is determined by what the department needs to know about its activities and also by what Parliament has asked it to report on. Even minor changes in the collection of official statistics means that it is often impossible to make comparisons over a period of years. The information collected in one year is about something slightly different from that in other years. Moreover, because of the way in which information is collected and the purpose of collecting it, these statistics can only answer a few of the questions about the way the law operates. For example, the judicial statistics list the number of cases brought each year in the County Court, broken down according to the type of claim. They provide little or no information about the applicants, the specific point of law relied on or whether the judgment was successfully enforced.

Official statistics, as a source of information, are limited. They provide information about things of importance to those who collected them. These are not necessarily the things that are important to the researcher. Government departments, the research councils and some private bodies sponsor research into specific areas of law. Small-scale research is often undertaken without sponsorship. Although this research may be based upon official statistics it may involve first collecting the necessary statistics and then deciding what they mean. The researchers must collect the data they need for each project. They have to design the study, that is to select the methods they will use and choose the sample to ensure that they have all the information relevant to their chosen topic. There is a more detailed discussion of some of these issues in Chapter 6, "Reading Research Materials".

The collection of statistics is only one way of gathering information about law and the legal system. Statistics are useful for describing things like numbers of events but are poor for describing things like motivations. Collecting them is one form of *quantitative research*. If researchers want to find out more about the reasons why the law affects people in certain ways, or how it affects them, they will have to carry out different types of research. This may involve interviewing people or even directly observing what is happening in the area in which they are interested. This is known as *qualitative research*. When conducting qualitative research researchers must decide how they can carry out their research so as to ensure that the material they collect is represents not just the particular people or bodies they have studied but is also an accurate reflection of the world as a whole.

Socio-legal research has enabled us to understand in a whole range of situations the way in which the law works in practice. It has revealed, for example, how barristers' clerks affect the working lives of barristers, why business-people often prefer to avoid taking their disputes to court, and how the practice of environmental health officers affects the way in which local authorities deal with industrial pollution. Socio-legal research offers us the opportunity to extend our knowledge of the law and the legal system far beyond the boundaries of the law in the books, showing us how legal rules are affected by the political, economic and social contexts in which law operates.

Part 2

▶ 4
Finding cases and statutes

In Chapter 1 the importance of cases and statutes as sources of law was explained. This chapter   ▶ 4.1
explains how you find reports of cases and copies of statutes and how you make sure that they
are up-to-date. As has been explained, these materials are primary sources of law. From them
it is possible to derive the legal rules in which you are interested. Chapters 5, 6 and 7 will
explain in more detail how this is done.

FINDING CASES

In the following, the task of discovering case reports will be considered for three different sets   ▶ 4.2
of circumstances:

(a) Where a well-stocked and supported library is available.
(b) Where some research or library facilities are available, but without access to a fully-
equipped law library.
(c) With the aid of on-line computerised retrieval facilities.

Most readers will have different facilities available at different times. For example, a reader
who has access to a fully-equipped law library can only use it during opening hours. It is important that you are aware of the different ways in which to find cases so that you can decide which
is the best method to use at any particular time.

USING FULL LAW LIBRARY NON-ELECTRONIC RESEARCH FACILITIES

The traditional, and still the most comprehensive, form of research in relation to law reports is   ▶ 4.3
performed in law libraries containing a wide selection of materials and a variety of support
systems, indexes, catalogues, etc. designed to assist the researcher in the task of locating and
using particular items. Such libraries are found in academic institutions, such as universities, as
well as in professional institutions such as the Inns of Court. In many cases, it is possible to use
such libraries even if you are not a member of the institution. What follows in this chapter is an
introduction to the major series of law reports and the basic methods of locating and checking
up-to-date material and of up-dating earlier materials.

Law reports go back over 700 years, although most of the case reports you will find in a normal law library have been decided during the last 150 years. Reports are divided into different series. The way in which these series are complied varies. Sometimes the series are systematic in their coverage, reporting cases in a particular area of law or from a particular court. In other instances coverage is more general and even idiosyncratic. Older cases can be found in series which bear the title of the name (or names) of the law reporter(s). Such a series is the nineteenth century series of Barnewall and Alderson (Bar & Ald) (all law reports have abbreviations that are customarily used when discussing them. Whenever a series is first mentioned here its usual abbreviation will be given, in brackets, as above. Appendix II to this book is a list of useful abbreviations, including those to the main law reports). The only necessary coherence these cases have is that the reporter thought it was worthwhile to print them. The range and variety of these older cases is enormous, although some help has now been provided to modern legal researchers with some of the old series reprinted in a new collection under the title of *The English Reports* (E.R.). In 1865 the Incorporated Council of Law Reporting introduced *The Law Reports*, a series that was divided according to the different courts of the day. The Council has continued these reports though the current divisions of the reports are different. Today one can find the following divisions:

(a) Appeal Cases (A.C.)—reports of cases in the Court of Appeal, the House of Lords, the Supreme Court and the Privy Council.
(b) Chancery Division (Ch.)—report of cases in the Chancery Division of the High Court and cases appealed from there to the Court of Appeal.
(c) Queen's Bench (Q.B.)—reports of cases in the Queen's Bench Division of the High Court and cases appealed from there to the Court of Appeal.
(d) Family Division (Fam.)—reports of cases in the Family Division of the High Court and cases appealed from there to the Court of Appeal (until 1972 the Family Division was the Probate, Divorce and Admiralty Division (P.)).

This series is the closest to an "official" series of law reports. If a case is reported in several different series and there is a discrepancy between the different reports it is *The Law Reports* that should normally be followed. There is, nowadays, a wide range of privately-published law reports. Most of these series concentrate upon a particular area of legal developments, e.g. the law relating to industrial relations, or the law concerning road traffic. However, there are two series that publish cases dealing with decisions affecting a wide range of legal issues. These general series, with which most students of law will quickly become familiar, are the *Weekly Law Reports* (W.L.R.) and the *All England Law Reports* (All E.R.).

Each of the modern series, just discussed, reports fully any case contained in its volumes. Everything that the judge or judges said in judgement is to be found in the report. There are, in addition, some sources that provide a short summary of, or extracts from, judgments given. The most up-to-date of these sources are those newspapers that print law reports. *The Times* has contained such reports for the longest time and is regarded as being the most authoritative source of such reports. Case-note sections published in legal periodicals such as the *New Law Journal* (N.L.J.) or the *Solicitors' Journal* (S.J. or Sol. Jo.), are also a good source of such summaries. Where a full report of a case is available as well as short summaries or extracts it is the full report that should be considered. Extracts or summaries, where full reports are available, are not primary sources of law. They cannot be cited in court. They reflect what the editor of the report thinks is the important parts of a judgement. The judgement is law. The editor's opinion of the law is merely that, opinion. However such summaries or extracts can be used when there is no full judgement reported elsewhere and they are the only source available.

USING LAW REPORTS

Every case which is reported in a series of law reports can be referred to by way of the names of the parties concerned in the action. Thus, where a court action is brought by somebody called Harriman in dispute with somebody called Martin, the case can be referred to as *Harriman v Martin*. However, referring to a case in this way is of limited usefulness. The reference does not tell the reader the date of the case nor does it indicate the series of reports in which it is found. It does not even tell us to which case involving a Harriman and a Martin the reader is being referred. There may be several. Thus, in addition to its name, each reported case possesses a unique reference indicator. This normally includes (although not always in the same order): ▶ 4.4

(1) a reference to the title of the series of law reports in which the report is to be found;
(2) a date (year) reference. Some series have a volume number for each year. Where the date reference tells you the year in which the case was decided the date is normally enclosed in square brackets;
(3) a reference to the volume number (if there is more than one volume of the particular law reports series in the year concerned);
(4) a reference to the page or paragraph number at which the report of the case may be located.

If the case of *Harriman v Martin* is reported in the first volume of the *Weekly Law Reports* for 1962, at page 739, the reference would be [1962] 1 W.L.R. 739. This is sometimes called the citation for the case. If you know this reference or citation, it is possible to go directly to the shelves of the law library which house the volumes containing that reference and to turn directly to the report of the case.

Increasingly people are turning to the web as a source of law reports. This has led to the creation of a system of *neutral citation* for such reports. Under this system, which first began in 2001 courts and tribunals have their own abbreviation and each case is given a unique official number by the courts. Within judgements, each paragraph has its own number.

References for the Supreme Court look like this:
[2009] UKSC 1
References for the House of Lords look like this:
[2006] UKHL 20
References for the Privy Council look like this:
[2006] UKPC 4
References for the Court of Appeal look this:
Court of Appeal (Civil)   [2003] EWCA Civ 1
Court of Appeal (Criminal)   [2003] EWCA Crim 1

The references for the High Court look like this:

Chancery Division	[2003] EWHC 123 (Ch)
Patents Court	[2003] EWHC 124 (Pat)
Queen's Bench	[2003] EWHC 125 (QB)
Administrative Court	[2003] EWHC 126 (Admin)
Commercial Court	[2003] EWHC 127 (Comm)
Admiralty Court	[2003] EWHC 128 (Admlty)
Technology and Construction Court	[2003] EWHC 129 (TCC)
Family Division	[2003] EWHC 130 (Fam)

Where it is necessary to refer to a precise passage in a judgement by using a paragraph number the paragraph number is put in square brackets. Where a neutral citation is available it is put first before the more traditional citation to a printed hardcopy version of the judgement.

Some tribunals such as the Employment Appeal Tribunal, The Immigration Appeal tribunal and the newly created Upper Tribunal also use a system of neutral citation when reporting their cases.

If you know only the names of the parties in the case, you will need first to search for the specific citation, whether it be a neutral citation or a more traditional reference to a printed volume. Although it would be possible to search the indexes for each individual series of law reports for the names of a case, this would be an inefficient and time-consuming approach. Normally, therefore, recourse is had to a general reference manual, which is known as a *case citator*. One example is the case citator published by *Current Law*. Other means are also available for locating the references of specific cases but *Current Law* is that which is most readily available. What follows is a brief description of the *Current Law Case Citator*. The *Current Law* system of citations for cases works through a combination of three separate reference items:

(1) four hard-bound citators covering the periods 1947–1976, 1977–1997, 1998–2001 and 2002–2004;
(2) a laminated volume for each of the years from 2005 until 2008;
(3) "Monthly Parts", which are issued regularly in pamphlet form, for the current year in which this is being written, 2009. These are subsequently replaced by a bound volume for the year.

The importance of using all three items to complement one another will appear when we consider the problem of locating up-to-date references (see below). Entries in the *Current Law Case Citator* are listed by title of case, arranged alphabetically. Thus, to find the law reports reference to the case of *Harriman v Martin* you need to turn to the alphabetical heading under "Harriman".

This reads: *Harriman v Martin* [1962] 1 W.L.R. 739; 106 S.J. 507; [1962] 1 All E.R. 225 C.A. . . . Digested 61/1249: Referred to, 72/2355.

From this information, we discover not only the law report's reference to the first volume of the *Weekly Law Reports* for 1962, at page 739, but also that there are reports of the same case in:

106 S.J. 507, i.e. the 106th volume of the *Solicitors' Journal* at page 507 and: [1962] 1 All E.R. 225, i.e. the first volume of the *All England Reports* for 1962 at page 225.

We are also told that the court that delivered the decision reported at those locations was:

C.A., i.e. the Court of Appeal.

Next, we are told that a "digest" (a brief summary) of the case has been included in a companion volume to the *Current Law Case Citator* at:

62/1249, i.e. in the companion year volume of *Current Law* for 1962 at paragraph 1249.

Finally, we are told that the case was "referred to" (in another case) and that that case is to be found at:

72/2355, i.e. in the companion year volume of *Current Law* for 1972 at paragraph 2355.

It now only remains to locate one of these volumes in the law library, and to turn to the appropriate page for a report on the case of *Harriman v Martin*. The above is not only a method for finding the reference to a case. If you already have a reference to a case, but you find that volume already in use in the library, you can use the method above to find an alternative citation for the case.

UP-DATING CASES

It is not enough to know merely what was said in a particular case in order to know the importance that should be attached to that case. It is also necessary to know whether such an earlier case has been used or referred to subsequently by the judges, or, indeed, whether it has been expressly approved or disapproved of by a later court. If a case is approved by a court that is further up the hierarchy of courts than the court originally giving judgment (and that approval is part of the ratio of that later case) then the case will take on the status of the later decision. Thus a decision of the High Court approved by the Court of Appeal will take on the status of the Court of Appeal. Even if the approval forms part of the obiter within the later judgment this will be significant, indicating the way in which the court is likely to give judgment once the matter becomes central in a decision at that level. Disapproval of a case will be important in a similar fashion. Such information can be discovered by using the *Current Law Case Citator*. We can regard a case as reliable (or, at least, not unreliable) where we are informed that it has been "referred to", "considered", "explained", "followed", "approved" or "applied". On the other hand, considerable care must be taken with a case that has been "distinguished" while cases that have been "disapproved" or "overruled" are unlikely to prove reliable for future purposes.

▶ 4.5

Example

1. **From the *Current Law Case Citator* for 1977–1997**

   Fort Sterling Ltd v South Atlantic Cargo Shipping NVC (The Finrose) [1994] 1 Lloyd's Rep. 559, QBD. . . . . *Digested 95/***4504**

   This tells us the location of the report of the case as explained above. It also that the case was decided in the QBD (i.e. the Queen's Bench Division) and we are told that there is a digest of the case in the Current Law Year Book *for 1995 at para.4504.*

2. **From the *Current Law Case Citator* for 1998–2001**

   Fort Sterling Ltd v South Atlantic Cargo Shipping NVC (The Finrose) *[1994] 1 Lloyd's Rep. 559, QBD* . . . . Digested 95/**4504.** Applied, 00/244; Considered 00/569.

   This gives us both the information that we had before and also tells us that the case has been applied in another case and considered in yet another case. In both instances we are given the reference to the appropriate Current Law Year Book *that will enable us to look these two new cases up. If we look up the 2000 Year Book we find that the case at paragraph 244 is*

   Thyssen Inc v Calypso Shipping Corp SA *[2000] 2 All E.R. (Comm) 97 David Steel J. QBD (Comm Ct).*

   This gives us the name of the case that applied Fort Sterling Ltd v South Atlantic Cargo Shipping NVC (The Finrose), *a reference to the law report where we can find the case reported (note that All E.R. (Comm) mentioned here is a different series of law reports to the more common All E.R. that we have dicussed elsewhere in this book), the name of the judge in the case and the court where it was heard, the Commercial Court in the Queen's Bench Division. The paragraph also gives a short description of the judgement. Looking up paragraph 569 gives up similar information about* Bua International Ltd v Hai Hing Shipping Co Ltd.

   Looking up the Case Citator for 2002 to 2004, *the year volumes for 2005 to 2008 and the cumulative list of cases in the latest Monthly part to be issued in 2009 gives us no further reference to* Fort Sterling Ltd v South Atlantic Cargo Shipping NVC (The Finrose) *so we now have a complete history of the case.*

USING LIMITED LIBRARY FACILITIES

4.6 ▶ The problems of finding and using cases and law reports where limited resources are available are significant. Clearly, it will not be possible to find reports of all the cases that you may need, since the available reports may only be found in series which are not at your disposal. By the same token, you may not have access to sufficiently comprehensive reference manuals, such as a case law citator or similar. You may have access to one of the general series of law reports. This will often be a set of *All England Law Reports*. Many public reference libraries possess a set of these law reports. If this is the case, some searching for cases can be done using the index contained in those volumes, though this will, of course, be time consuming. Alternatively, if you are concerned only with a limited specialist area you may have access to a specialised series of law reports. Whatever your source of available material, however, it is of paramount importance that you familiarise yourself with the specific indexing and cross-referencing system adopted by that source. If you do this, you will be able to use the material at your disposal, limited though it may be by comparison with the resources of a fully-equipped and supported law library, in the most efficient manner. It will also be important to discover whether you can obtain access to some means for updating the material contained in your available sources. The use of a citator, as explained above, is clearly of major benefit, for the consolidation of information within one reference item avoids the necessity of searching through a range of separate volumes and series. Amongst possible sources of updated information might be the general legal periodicals, such as the *New Law Journal* or the *Solicitors' Journal* (both of which have been referred to above). Many public libraries subscribe to one of these, or to other relevant periodicals. Where your needs related to a specific area, the periodicals available in relation to that area may be of assistance in obtaining up-to-date information. Thus, for example, many human resource management journals contain information about cases decided by the courts in relation to employment law. All of these will probably refer you to sources of information that you do not have but they will also enable you to make the most efficient use of those sources that are available. A further common source of information will be text-books on the subject about which you are seeking information. The important rule here is to check that you have access to the latest possible edition of the book, and to bear in mind the possibility that case-law developments may have overtaken the legal position as it was stated at the time of writing of the book. Most books dealing with the law will contain a statement in the "Foreword" stating the date on which the information given in the book is said to be current. In some instances, you may have access to a case-book. This term is something of a misnomer since case-books frequently contain not just cases but also statutes and comments on the law. Such books are generally concerned with a specific topic, for example "contract law", and contain edited material relevant to the area. These books can be a very useful source where you have access only to limited library facilities. However, they suffer from several deficiencies. First, the reader relies on the editor of the volume to select the most appropriate material. There is no way in which the quality of the work can be checked. Secondly, the material presented may only be given in part. Again, the reader must trust that the editor has not given misleading extracts. Finally, the reader has no means of up-dating the material. In some areas of law encyclopaedias are produced. These are similar to case-books, although they are generally more detailed. Publishers of this kind of work often supply an up-dating service. Increasingly, encyclopaedias are produced in a loose-leaf form and the reader will substitute new pages as supplements are issued.

USING ELECTRONIC RETRIEVAL FACILITIES

4.7 ▶ To complete this section on finding and using reports of cases, mention must be made of the important and fast-developing range of computerised information retrieval systems.

"On-line" Services

4.8 ▶ There are two major, commercially marketed, legal data-bases which are widely used in universities and by practitioners, LEXIS and WESTLAW. Both data-bases cover a number of different jurisdictions and contain not just cases but also legislation and law journals. To use either of these systems effectively requires some training in the way that material is organised and the methods used to search them.

In general both LEXIS and WESTLAW contain the full text of judgements though the format is somewhat different to that in traditional printed law reports. As well as providing access to a large collection of published legal material LEXIS and WESTLAW also include unreported cases, i.e. cases that have been decided but which have not yet been published in hard-copy form and in some cases never will be published in that form.

Searching for a case using electronic retrieval systems is generally done using key words. The user asks whether a specific term or set of words is to be found in the data-base. The user is then given a list of the cases that contain the item that is being searched for and can then look at the cases that have been found. The user will find that on the one hand if they use only very general terms for their search they will be given a very large lit of cases to look at, most of which they will find irrelevant to their needs. If on the other hand they use a very precise term the list provided will not contain any case that is relevant but which uses slightly different terminology in its judgement. The skill in using data-bases like LEXIS and WESTLAW lies in steering a course between these two extremes.

Data-bases such as LEXIS and WESTLAW are highly effective ways of finding cases, finding citations for cases and for seeing if a case has been referred to in any other judgement.

Cases on the net

4.9 ▶ There are many internet sites which discuss law or legal issues or provide material about law. A number of these provide free access to legal materials.

A wide range of material relating to law is available on the British and Irish Legal Information Institute's web site:

http://www.bailii.org/
All decisions of the Supreme Court are available at:
http://www.supremecourt.gov.uk/decided-cases/index.html
Decisions of the House of Lords are available at:
http://www.publications.parliament.uk/pa/ld/ldjudgmt.htm
Privy Council decisions are available at:
http://www.privy-council.org.uk/output/Page31.asp

FINDING AND UP-DATING STATUTES

Statutes are published individually but law libraries and some public libraries have bound col-
lections that include all the statutes for a particular year. Statutes passed since 1988 are available on the internet at:

▶ 4.10

http://www.hmso.gov.uk/legislation/about_legislation.htm

With statutes there are three main problems. Is the statute in force? Has the statute been
repealed by Parliament, (i.e. replaced by some other statute)? Has the statute been amended
by Parliament, (i.e. had part of its contents altered by Parliament)? Starting with a provision in
an Act of Parliament it is necessary to use one of the "citatory" systems in order to discover the
most changes (if any) that have affected that provision. The following example shows how to
update a relatively recent statutory provision using the *Current Law Legislation Citator.*

Example

*Let us take the Children Act 1989 s.8(4). In its original form this provision was set out as
follows:*

Residence, contact and other orders with respect to children

8— *(1) . . .*
   (2) . . .
   (3) . . .
   (4) The enactments are—

   (a) Parts I, II and IV of this Act;
   (b) the Matrimonial Causes Act 1973;
   (c) the Domestic Violence and Matrimonial Proceedings Act 1976;
   (d) the Adoption Act 1976;
   (e) the Domestic Proceedings and Magistrates' Court Act 1978;
   (f) sections 1 and 9 of the Matrimonial Homes Act 1983;
   (g) Part III of the Matrimonial and family Proceedings Act 1984.

*If we assume that in January 2004 we want to discover whether there have been changes
to the wording of section 8(4) it is first necessary to turn to the volume of the* Current Law
Legislation Citator *that covers the period following the enactment of the Children Act
1989. This is the volume for 1989–1995.*

The Current Law Legislation Citator *is arranged in chronological order by year and by
Chapter number for each Act. Chapter numbers are fully explained at page 54. For the
Children Act 1989 this is Chapter 41. We now need to look for our provision, section 8(4).
The entry gives us details of many cases but makes no reference to any amendments. Our
search must be continued in later volumes.*

In the Current law Legislation Citator *for 1996 to1999 there are the following entries:*

s.8, amended: 1996 c.27 Sch.8 para.41, Sch.8 para.60, 1998 c.37 s.119. Sch.8 para.68
    s.8, repealed (in part): 1996 c. 27 Sch.10

We now know that the section was amended by Schedule 8 of the statute whose reference is 1996 Chapter 27 and also by the statute whose reference is 1998 chapter 37. It was also repealed in part by Schedule 10 of the statute whose reference is 1996 Chapter 27.
    We now need to continue our search beyond 1999 by checking the more recent volumes of the Current Law Legislation Citator *for 2000 to 2001 and for 2002 to 2004 and then the subsequent year volumes. In the 2002 to 2004 volume there is an entry that reads:*

s.8, amended: 2002 c. 38 Sch.3 para.55, 2004 c. 33 Sch.27 para.129

There are no further references to section 8 in any of the other volumes.
    We can now look up the statutes that we have found and see what changes have been made section 8(4).

HOW TO USE ENCYCLOPAEDIAS

4.11 ▶ Encyclopaedias are not a source of law (although they may contain sources of law). Cases and statutes are sources of law. They are what will be used when judges are deciding what the outcome of a case is to be. However, for some people encyclopaedias will be the only material they have available. Thus it is important to consider how they can be used most effectively. How to use encyclopaedias Different examples of encyclopaedias vary in form and content. They do not all contain the same kind of material nor are they ordered in the same way. Therefore it is not possible to give a series of rules saying how encyclopaedias should be used. What follows are points that a reader should consider when first using any encyclopaedia. The first thing to look at is the kind of material that the encyclopaedia contains. One advantage of an encyclopaedia can be that it brings together a wide variety of material about particular subject matter. Thus, you may find the encyclopaedia which you are reading contains all the statutes in a particular area, all the statutory instruments, government circulars and other non-statutory material, references to relevant cases (with some description of their contents) together with some discussion of the application of legal rules in the area. On the other hand the encyclopaedia may contain only some of the material or may extract some of it. Thus, for example, instead of having all of a statute you may find that you have only parts of it. Even if the encyclopaedia claims to be fully comprehensive, remember that it is no more than a claim. The editors of the encyclopaedia may feel that they have included all relevant statutes; others may disagree with them. It is always as important to be aware of what you do not know as what you do know. Relying on an encyclopaedia means that there may be gaps in your knowledge of the particular area of law. However, you may feel it worth relying on the encyclopaedia because it is the only source available. Equally, you may find it quicker to use an encyclopaedia and consider the advantage of speedy access more important than any element of doubt in your knowledge of the area. Most encyclopaedias extract at least some of the material that they cover. That is to say that they contain extracts of a statute, statutory instrument, or whatever, rather than the whole. Here the problem is that, in extracting their material, the editors of the encyclopaedia limit your knowledge of the law. You rely on them to extract that which is relevant and cannot check the matter for yourself. As a source of law, the less comprehensive an encyclopaedia is the less useful it will be. However, the more comprehensive an encyclopaedia is the slower it may be to use. Before using the encyclopaedia you need to consider the kind of question that you are trying to answer. If the question is a very broad and general one about the framework of some area of law you may find an encyclopaedia with less detail easier to use. However, if you are trying to answer a very detailed point, perhaps applying the law to a very precise factual situation, you need the most comprehensive encyclopaedia that you can find. Most encyclopaedias, and increasingly many other books about law, are now issued in loose-leaf form. This means that the publisher issues supplements to the encyclopaedia on a regular basis. These supplements, which contain descriptions of changes in the law, are then substituted for the pages that discuss the out-of-date law. The advantage of the loose-leaf form over ordinary books is that it means the encyclopaedia is more likely to be accurate. When using loose-leaf encyclopaedias before looking up the point of law that interests you always see when it was last up-dated. You will usually find a page at the front of the first volume of the encyclopaedia that tells you when it was last up-dated. The technique for finding out about points of law in an encyclopaedia will vary depending upon the encyclopaedia being used. Some are organised according to different areas of law within the subject of the encyclopaedia. Others have different volumes for different kinds of material; one volume for statutes, one for discussion of the law and so forth. Most will have both indexes and detailed contents pages. Most encyclopaedias have a discussion of how they should be used at the beginning of their first volume. Always consult this when first using an encyclopaedia.

FINDING AND USING MATERIAL ON THE LAW OF THE EUROPEAN COMMUNITIES, THE EUROPEAN UNION, AND THE EUROPEAN ECONOMIC AREA

All basic material in relation to the European Communities, the European Union, and the European Economic Area is published in English. However, some material is not made available in all of the official languages of the European Communities immediately. What is said here refers specifically to English language versions of such material.   ▶ 4.12

   The Official Journal of the European Communities is the authoritative voice of the European Communities, and is used to publish daily information. The *Official Journal* (the O.J.) is divided into two major parts (the L and C series). There are also separately published notices of recruitment, notices and public contracts and the like, which are published in a Supplement and in Annexes. Twice a year the O.J. issues a Directory of Community legislation in force and other acts of the Community institutions.

LEGISLATION

The L series (Legislation) contains the text of Community legislation. The series is arranged by Volume, starting in 1958, and by issue number sequentially throughout the issue year. Thus,   ▶ 4.13

the text of Council Directive 95/45/EC of September 22,1994 on the establishment of a European Works Council or a procedure in Community-scale undertakings and Community-scale groups of under takings for the purposes of informing and consulting employees is to be found in the *Official Journal* of September 30,1994.

> The Volume number for 1994 is Volume 37
> The issue number of the OJ L series for 30 September 1994 is L 254
> The text of the Directive is set out on page 64 and thus the page reference is p.64
> The official reference for the Directive will be OJ No L 254, 30.9.1994, p.64

INFORMATION AND NOTICES

4.14 ▶ The C series (Information and Notices) contains, amongst a host of other items, key extracts (*the operative part*) from judgments of the Court of Justice of the European Communities (the ECJ, sitting in Luxembourg) and the Court of First Instance (which also sits in Luxembourg). Where the language of the particular court being reported is not English, the C series will include *a provisional translation*: the definitive translation being found in the separately published Reports of Cases before the Court. There is also brief coverage of actions brought before the ECJ by Member States against the Council of the European Communities, as well as questions referred to the ECJ by national courts of Member States. Also, to be found in the C series will be Preparatory Acts in the course of being made into legislation by the European Communities. Thus, for example, the *Official Journal* for February 19,1994 contains the text of an Opinion delivered by the Economic and Social Committee on a proposal for a Council Regulation on substances that deplete the ozone layer.

> The Volume Number for 1994 is Volume 37
> The issue of the OJ C series for 19 February 1994 is C 52
> The text of the proposed Decision is item 3 in issue C 52, and so the reference is 03
> The full reference for the Opinion is OJ 94/C 52/03.

OTHER MATERIALS

4.15 ▶ Whilst the *Official Journal* is the best official source of information about Community law it should be noted that a wide range of documentation does not find its way into the *Official Journal* and other sources may have to be considered for those wanting a comprehensive list of European materials. In particular, mention should be made of so-called COM documents, which often contain important proposals for future legislation. These are issued by the Commission with a "rolling" numerical reference by sequence of publication during a particular year. Consequently, there is no systematic numbering of such COM Docs a matter which frequently gives rise to criticism about the accessibility of important documentation in the legislative field. By way of example, an important recent Communication concerning the application of the Agreement on social policy, presented by the Commission to the Council and to the European Parliament on December 14, 1993, is simply designated:

> COM(93) 600 final

Various other series, apart from the COM series, are also to be found in relation to a range of spheres of activity within the European Union. Judgments of the European Court of Justice are reported in two series of law reports. One series is that formally published by the European Union itself the *European Court Reports* (E.C.R.). The other series is the privately produced *Common Market Law Reports* (C.M.L.R.). Both can be found in the normal manner. In addition to these specialised law reports series, an increasing number of judgments delivered by the European Court of Justice are now reported as a normal part of general law report series.

EUROPEAN UNION MATERIALS ON THE INTERNET

The official internet site of the European Union is found at:

▶ 4.16

http://europa.eu

From here it is possible to access all the institutions of the European Union in any of the official languages of the Union.

▶ 5
Reading cases and statutes

5.1 ▶ This chapter will explain how you should use the primary sources for legal rules, cases and statutes. You will find a specimen case report and a specimen statute in each section. In addition, there are further examples of case reports in the exercise section of this book (Cases I and II). Skill in the use of the techniques described here can only be acquired with practice. For this reason the exercises in the book enable you to build a range of experience in handling the material contained in cases and statutes.

READING A CASE

5.2 ▶ The contents of law reports are explained here so that you can start to read cases, understand the law which they contain, and make useful notes about them. You will find the court structure, and how cases are decided, explained in Chapter 1. You will find a copy of a case, *R. v Jackson*, on pp.43–45. All specific references in this section will be to that case. The copy is taken from the *All England Law Reports*, which are the most commonly available law reports. However, if you have access to other kinds of law reports you will find that they look very much the same as the *All England Law Reports*. By way of example, in the exercises section of this book there are also to be found law reports taken both from the Court Service internet site (in transcript form) and from a law reports series known as the *Industrial Cases Reports*. The techniques discussed here will be just as useful in reading other series of law reports and court transcripts. The different series of law reports and their use has been explained in Chapter 4.

The case is the criminal law case of *R. v Jackson*. Lawyers pronounce this "Regina (or 'The Queen' or 'King', or 'The Crown') against Terry". Most criminal cases are written like this. In civil cases, the names of the parties are usually given, as in *Donoghue v Stevenson*, the case being pronounced "Donoghue and Stevenson".

R v Jackson

a

COURT OF APPEAL CRIMINAL DIVISION
ROSE L.J., BUTTERFIELD AND RICHARDS JJ
28 APRIL, 1998

Criminal law—Appeal—Leave to appeal—Practice—Single judge granting leave on   *b*
some grounds but refusing leave on others—Need for leave of full court to pursue
grounds in respect of which leave refused.

Where, on an application for leave to appeal to the Court of Appeal, Criminal
Division, the single judge grants leave on some grounds but specifically refuses leave
on others, counsel for the appellant must obtain the leave of the full court if he   *c*
wishes to pursue the grounds in respect of which leave has been refused (see
p. 574g. post).

Notes
For appeal against conviction or sentence following trial on indictment, see 11(2)   *d*
Halsbury's Laws (4th edn reissue) paras 1352, 1355.

Cases referred to in judgment
R v Bloomfield [1997] 1 Cr App R 135, CA.
R v Chalkley, R v Jeffries [1998] 2 All ER 155, [1998] QB 848, [19983] WLR 146, CA.

e

Appeal against conviction
Stephen Shaun Jackson appealed with leave of the single judge against his
conviction on 25 July 1995 in the Crown Court at Croydon before Judge Crush
and a jury of theft. The facts are set out in the judgment of the court.

Marc Willers (assigned by the *Registrar of Criminal Appeals*) for the appellant.   *f*
Hugh Davies (instructed by the *Crown Prosecution Service*, Croydon) for the Crown.

ROSE LJ delivered the following judgment of the court. On 25 July 1997 in the
Crown Court at Croydon, this appellant was convicted by the jury of theft, on the
first count in the indictment. He was acquitted of charges of false accounting on
counts 2, 3 and 4. The trial was a retrial, the jury on an earlier occasion having   *g*
acquitted in relation to certain counts on the then indictment, but failed to agree
in relation to the counts upon which the second jury adjudicated. He appeals
against his conviction by leave of the single judge, which was granted in relation
to the first of the two matters which Mr Willers, on behalf of the appellant, seeks
to canvass before this court.   *h*
    For the purposes of this appeal, the facts can be briefly stated. The appellant
was the proprietor of a minicab firm. Insurance brokers, Thompson Heath &
Bond (South East) Ltd (to whom we shall refer as 'THB') devised a scheme to
enable minicab drivers to pay for their motor insurance by instalments. That
scheme was underwritten by others.
    The scheme allowed the premiums to be collected from the minicab drivers on   *j*
a weekly basis, and passed on to THB each month. THB then paid the
underwriters.
    It was the Crown's case against the appellant that, while he acted as agent for
THB, to collect weekly premiums from the drivers, between February 1991 and
March 1994, he failed to declare to THB the full amount that he had collected,

a   and that he kept a sum of money, in the region of £100,000, for himself and spent much of it on luxury items for his own benefit.

While he was acting in this way, the appellant, it was common ground, devised a form called a Bank 1 form, on which to record payments made by him to THB. At the original trial, the judge had ordered disclosure of Bank 1 forms by the prosecution but, save for one example of such a form, which was in the appellant's possession at the time of the first trial, no such disclosure had been

b   made. Between the first trial and the retrial, however, those documents, which had apparently been in the possession not of the prosecuting authorities but of THB, were disclosed to the defence and were available to them at the time of the retrial.

A submission was made to the trial judge, Judge Crush, by Mr Willers then, as now, appearing for the defendant, that the second trial should be stayed as an

c   abuse of the process of the court. The ground of that submission was that it would not be fair to try the appellant a second time, because the Bank 1 forms had not been available during the first trial and, if they had been, the first jury might have acquitted. The learned judge rejected that submission. That rejection forms the ground of appeal in relation to which the single judge gave leave and which Mr

d   Willers has placed in the forefront of his argument in this court.

Mr Willers accepts that, although the judge at the first trial ordered disdosure and no disclosure took place, that was because the documents had simply not at that stage been found, although they were in the possession of THB.

Mr Willers did not, during the course of the first trial, make any further application, non-disclosure not having been made, either for the jury to be

e   discharged, or otherwise.

Mr Willers does not suggest that, at the first trial or subsequently, there was any bad faith on the part of the prosecution in relation to the non-disclosure. He submits that, during the cross-examination of Det Sgt James at the second trial, it emerged that he had left with THB the responsibility for looking through the vast

f   number of documents and passing to the police those which they thought relevant. Although Mr Willers does not suggest that gave rise to bad faith by the officer, he submits that it would have been better had the officer looked through the documents himself.

By the time of the second trial, however, Mr Willers accepts that the defence had all the documentation that they required, including all the Bank 1 forms. But,

g   he submits, if there was a real possibility of acquittal at the first trial had those forms then been available, it was unfair for the second trial to take place, and the judge should have acceded to the defence application to stay the second trial for abuse of process.

Mr Willers accepted that his submission came to this that, despite the fact that

h   all the relevant material was before the second jury who convicted, this court, in ruling upon the safety of that conviction, should speculate that the first jury, faced with all the relevant material, might have acquitted; and therefore it was unfair to proceed with the second trial. Mr Willers referred to the decision of this court in *R v Chalkley, R v Jeffries* [1998] 2 All E.R. 155, [1998] QB 848. In the course of giving the judgment of the court in that case, Auld LJ commented, adversely, on an

j   earlier decision of this court, differently constituted, in *R v Bloomfield* [1997] 1 Cr App R 135, which had attracted some criticism from the editors of the third supplement to *Archbold's Criminal Pleading, Evidence and Practice* (1997 edn) para 7–45. We make that comment because the argument originally advanced in skeleton form on behalf of the appellant relied, in part, on this court's decision in *R v Bloomfield*.

On behalf of the Crown, Mr Davies submits that the safety of the appellant's *a* conviction depends on the evidence at the second trial, which was followed by an admirably succinct summing up by the learned judge, following a trial which, for reasons which are not manifest, had lasted a considerable number of weeks.

Mr Davies draws attention, in relation to the safety of that conviction, to a number of letters written by the appellant after these apparent defalcations came to light, the first of them, it was common ground, on 21 March 1994 to a man *b* called Andrew Orchard. That letter was written on the day that the defendant left this country, for a period of some seven months in the Canary Islands. The appellant also wrote letters to his sister, Jackie, and to his partner, David. Each of those letter, in various ways, comprises a series of admissions of criminal mis-behaviour of present materiality, coupled with expressions of regret. In the course of the thal, the appellant sought to explain those letters away on the basis of a state of *c* confused mind when he had written them.

In our judgment, it is wholly impossible to accept Mr Willers' submission either that the judge was wrong to rule as he did in refusing a stay, or that that refusal gives rise to any lack of safety in this appellant's conviction. It frequently happens that new evidence comes to light between the time of a first trial when a jury *d* disagrees and a second trial. Such evidence may be favourable to the prosecution or to the defence. But the verdict of the second jury does not become unsafe because it was unfair for there to be a second trial. Indeed, pursuing Mr Willers' argument to its logical conclusion, wherever fresh evidence appears between a first and second trial, it would be unfair, at least if the evidence assisted the defence, to have a second trial at all. That is a submission which we roundly reject. *e* The learned judge was, in our view, correct to refuse the stay on the basis of the application made to him. That refusal, in the light of the overwhelming evidence before the second jury, cannot, in any event, be regarded as rendering the verdict of the second jury unsafe.

The second matter which Mr Willers sought to canvass related to a criticism of the *f* learned judge's direction in relation to dishonesty and the character of the defence case. It is said that the judge misdirected the jury and failed to put the defence case adequately in relation to the way in which money was spent on luxuries.

It is fair to say that Mr Willers sought the leave of this court to pursue the interrelated grounds in relation to that aspect of the case, the learned single judge having refused leave to argue those grounds. For the avoidance of doubt, where, *g* in granting leave to appeal on some grounds, the single judge has specifically refused leave to appeal on other grounds, the leave of this court is required before counsel may argue those other grounds. As we have said, Mr Willers sought the leave of this court. We have read the passage in the summing up in the transcript of which he complains. It is to be noted that, in answer to a question from the *h* jury, the judge gave a dear direction as to dishonesty, relevant to this case, in identical terms to that which he had given at the outset of his summing up.

Nothing in the passage of the summing up about which complaint is made, in our view, renders it arguable that there was any misdirection. Accordingly, as to that aspect of the case, we refused leave to pursue an appeal on that basis. *j*

For the reasons given, this appeal is dismissed.

Appeal dismissed.

Carlone Stomberg   Barrister.

Underneath the name of the case at "**a**" you will see three pieces of information. First, you are told the court in which the case was heard. In this case, it was the Court of Appeal, Criminal Division. It is important to know which court heard a case because of the doctrine of precedent (see pages 101–105 for an explanation of the doctrine of precedent).

The report then gives the names of the judges who took part in the case. This information is used to help evaluate the decision. Some judges are known to be very experienced in particular areas of law. Their decisions may be given extra weight. Finally, you are told when the case was heard and when the court gave its decision. In the House of Lords this process is called "delivering opinions", but in other courts it is known as "giving judgment".

The material in italics, at "**b**" on the first page of the report, is written by the editor of the report. It indicates the subject-matter of the case and the issue which it concerned. The subject index at the front of each volume of law reports includes a similar entry under the first words.

The next section, at "**c**", is called the *headnote*. It is not part of the case proper, and is prepared by the law reporter, not by the judges. The headnote should summarise the case accurately giving references to important parts of the court's opinion or judgment and any cases cited. Because it is written when the case is reported, the headnote may stress or omit elements of the case which are later thought to be important. Therefore, care should be taken when using the headnote.

The notes, just below "**d**", direct the reader to appropriate volumes of *Halsbury's Laws of England* and/or *Halsbury's Statutes of England*. *Halsbury's Laws* provides a concise statement of the relevant law, subject by subject, including references to the main cases and statutes. *Halsbury's Statutes* gives the complete text of all statutes together with annotations that explain them. Although law students and others may need to research the law using *Halsbury* it is not necessary to turn to reference works when reading every case. In most instances, the background law will be sufficiently explained by the judge. In our case of *R. v Jackson* the reference is confined to *Halsbury's Laws*.

At "**e**" there is a list of all the cases referred to by the judges. In relation to each case, a list of different places where the case may be found is given. Where counsel have cited additional cases to which the judges did not refer, this will be given in a separate list under the heading "cases also cited".

At "**e**" to "**f**" you will find a full history of the proceedings of the case. This indicates all the courts that have previously considered the case before the present one. The final sentence of this section indicates where a full account of the facts of the case may be found.

Below "**f**" you will find the names of the counsel (usually barristers but sometimes solicitor-advocates) who appeared in the case. In the case of *R. v Jackson* the barristers on both sides were what are known as "junior counsel". Senior counsel are called "Q.C.s" (Queen's Counsel), or "K.C.s" (King's Counsel) when the monarch is a King.

The appellant was Jackson, while the Crown (in other words the state) was the respondent. The names of the solicitors who acted for the two parties and instructed the counsel are to be found below "**f**" in the law report. Academics may use this information to obtain further information about the case. Solicitors may use it in order to find out which are the best counsel to instruct for particular kinds of cases.

Not all series of law reports have marginal letters as this one does. When they do, these letters can be used to give a precise reference to any part of the case. Thus, the beginning of Lord Justice Rose's judgment is [1999] 1 All E.R. 572g.

Whilst the matters above provide an introduction to the case, the substance is to be found in the judgements. Every law case raises a question or series of questions to be answered by the judge(s). In civil cases, some of these will be questions of fact (in criminal cases these will be answered by the jury). For example, it may be necessary to know at what speed a car was travelling when an accident occurred. In practice, the answers to these factual questions are very important. Once they have been settled, the legal issues in the case may be simple. However, when it comes to the study of law, it is only the legal questions that matter.

For the judge(s) in a case, therefore, there are two clearly distinguishable processes which have to be gone through when hearing the matter and reaching a judgment. First, there is the process of making "findings of fact". Then, in the light of those findings of fact, there is the process of making "findings on the law". The key questions that are posed to the judge(s) in this context are referred to as "the issues in the case".

Lawyers and students of law are concerned primarily not with the outcome of a case but with the reasoning that the judge gave for the conclusion. The reasoning is important because within it will be found the *ratio decidendi* (often referred to simply as "the ratio"). The ratio is that part of the legal reasoning which is essential for the decision in the case. It is the ratio which is binding under the doctrine of precedent and which is thus part of the law. The ratio and the reasons for the decision are not necessarily the same thing. Not all of the reasons given for the decision will be essential. In courts where there is more than one judge, each may give a separate judgment (as can be seen from the examples in the exercises section of this book). If they do, each judgment will have its own reasons, and thus its own ratio. The judges must agree a conclusion to the case (although they may do so only by majority). However, they do not have to have the same reasons for their decision. If they have different reasons the judgements have different ratios and, thus, the case itself may have no ratio. Lawyers will rarely agree that a case has no ratio at all.

Finding the ratio in a case is crucial. It is also the most difficult part of reading cases, particularly when the case involves several judgements. The ratio is the essence of the case and, thus, may not be found simply by quoting from a judgment. Discovering the ratio involves skills of interpretation—understanding and explaining what judges meant, how they reached their conclusions—in order to see the common ground. Although the ratio is the law, it cannot be divorced entirely from the facts. Facts that are essential for a decision provide the conditions for the operation of the rules and are, thus, part of the rule itself. Deciding which are essential, as opposed to subsidiary, facts takes skill and practice. Lawyers frequently disagree on exactly what the ratio to a decision is. Some may view it broadly, seeing the decision as having few conditions but laying down a general rule. Others may take a narrower approach, suggesting that only in very limited circumstances would a decision bind a future court. Subsequent cases often help to clarify what the ratio of a previous case is accepted as being. There is a more detailed explanation of the way in which one decides what the ratio of a case is in Chapter 6 below.

The editors of a law report write what they consider the ratio to be in the headnote. They may be wrong. Even if their interpretation is plausible when they write it, a later case may take a different view. For these reasons, statements of law in the headnote cannot be relied on.

If we look at *R. v Jackson* we can see that some of the things that we are told in the judgment are irrelevant for the purposes of constructing the ratio. The case before the Court of Appeal concerns a question relating to "leave to appeal". Thus, for example, the fact that the accused collected money on a weekly basis, rather than monthly, is of no account. Similarly, the fact that he failed to declare to the insurance brokers the full amount that he had collected is not significant for the purposes of the Court of Appeal on the question concerning "leave to appeal". However, we will be aware that, for the original trial judge in the Crown Court, when the charges brought against the accused were of "false accounting", this would have been a very significant matter.

You will see that in the case of *R. v Jackson* Lord Justice Rose (Rose L.J.) delivers a judgment that is the "judgment of the court". This therefore reflects the shared views of himself, Lord Justice Butterfield and Lord Justice Richards. Judgements in courts with multiple judges like the Court of Appeal and the Supreme Court are not always like this. Each judge may give their own judgement. Having set out the history of the case (at page 572g–h), Lord Justice Rose then gives a brief outline of the relevant facts for the purposes of the appeal (at page 572h–573d). This is followed by a summary of the submissions made by the counsel for each party (at page 573d–574c). You will see that counsel are said to have "submitted" certain things and to have "accepted" other matters during the course of their arguments before the Court of Appeal. Having dealt with these matters by way of preliminary presentation, Lord Justice Rose then moves on to the conclusions of the Court of Appeal. It is here that we look for the reasons and the ratio in the case.

The first matter considered (set out at page 574c–e) is the court's view on a proposition put by counsel for the appellant. You will gather that the Court of Appeal has little sympathy for the argument put forward, and in quite strong terms (at page 574e) "roundly rejects" the proposition that "wherever fresh evidence appears between a first and second trial, it would be unfair, at least if the evidence assisted the defence, to have a second trial". This leads the Court of Appeal to the conclusion that (i) the trial judge acted correctly in refusing to "stay" the trial of the accused, and (ii) anyway, given the evidence before the second jury in this case, that the verdict of that second jury could not be regarded as in any way "unsafe" (see page 574e–f). These conclusions are specific to this case, although the first one follows from the view expressed by the court on counsel's (roundly rejected) proposition. The narrow ratio of the case may thus be discovered by looking at that view, which was essential for reaching the eventual decision delivered by the Court of Appeal.

However, it is the "second matter" dealt with by the Court of Appeal that has drawn the attention of the law report editor to this case. At page 574f–g you will see that the court is faced with a question of what permission (or "leave") is required in order for an appeal to be made against particular aspects of a case. The eventual decision of the Court of Appeal (not to allow an appeal to be pursued on the basis of an alleged misdirection in the trial judge's summing up) is set out at page 574j, and the reasons for arriving at this decision are explained at page 574h. In order to reach that decision, the court has had to decide in what circumstances an appeal such as this may or may not be pursued. In this case the Court of Appeal goes further than to pronounce merely in relation to the specific case before it, relating to Jackson, the accused. Here, the court makes a general statement "for the avoidance of doubt", which is intended to clarify the situation for all future cases where this issue arises (set out at page 574g–h). That ratio, indeed, is also the part of the judgment that has been extracted by the editor of the law reports series to form the headnote that we have already looked at (at page 572c).

R. v Jackson contains only a single judgment. That judgment is a short one. If one had a longer judgment (and most judgements are longer) or multiple judgements in the same case, the task of constructing a ratio would be much more difficult. When one has to consider one judgment and its obscurities in the light of other judgements the process of analysing the law becomes even more uncertain. In order to appreciate some of the problems of constructing a ratio in a less straightforward case, therefore, you should apply the techniques discussed here to the law reports contained in the exercises section of this book.

A court must follow the ratio of any relevant case that is binding on it under the doctrine of precedent. Thus, the question arises, when is a case relevant? A case in the same area must be followed unless it can be "distinguished" on the basis of its facts. If the facts of the case cannot be distinguished—if, as it is commonly put, the case is "on all fours"—then it must be followed. The process of distinguishing cases is really just another way of deciding what the ratio of the case is. If the material facts necessary for the operation of the legal rule in the first case are not found in the second, or are different, there is no precedent. Just as lawyers differ about what the ratio to a case is, so they differ about whether a case is binding in a particular situation or not.

That which is not part of the ratio of the case is said to be the *obiter dictum*. This is usually referred to as "the *obiter*". Obiter is said to have "persuasive authority". That which was said obiter in a court such as the House of Lords may be very persuasive indeed for a relatively inferior court such as a County Court. Moreover, remarks made obiter may indicate which way the law is developing, or which kinds of arguments judges find particularly persuasive. Equally, judges are not always very careful about differentiating between ratio and obiter. There is a further explanation of the place of obiter observations in legal reasoning in Chapter 6 below.

The remainder of this section provides some guidance on how to study cases. The first question a student should ask about a case is "Why has this case been set?" The purpose of studying cases is to obtain an understanding of the relevance of the case to the area of law being studied. Some cases will be more important than others. A leading Supreme Court decision will require more time and closer examination than a decision of the High Court that is merely illustrative of a point mentioned in a lecture or included in a problem. Where a case has developed or defined an area of law it is usually helpful to start by reading what the textbook writers say about it. Where more than one case has to be read on the same point of law, they should, if possible, be read in chronological order and each one digested before moving on to the next.

A second question to ask when reading cases is, "How much time is available?" Try to spend more time on important decisions and important judgements, even if you have to rely on a headnote or a textbook when it comes to the others. Do not spend the greater proportion of your time reading cases which have been overruled or which have novel or interesting facts but no new point of law. The headnote is helpful when allocating time. Treat judgements in the same way as you treat cases. Do not waste your time reading judgements that merely repeat something you have already read. Spend more time on the leading judgements than on the others. Again, the headnote will be helpful for this. Some judgements are more clearly written than others. Some judgements are shorter than others. Neither clarity nor brevity necessarily means that the judgment is more important. Choose what you read because it is the best for your purposes, not because it is the easiest!

Notes on any case should start with the case name and any references. They should then include:

(1) a brief statement of the facts of the case;
(2) the history of the case;
(3) the point of law under consideration;
(4) the decision with the reasons for it, together with any names of cases relied upon.

One page should be enough for this basic information.

When reading judgements in order to make notes, look for agreement and disagreement on each of the points relevant to your study. It is often useful to make separate notes on each of the points raised by the case and then see what different judges said about them. In particular, too, do not forget to make it clear in your notes whether a judge was dissenting or not.

HOW TO READ A STATUTE

5.3 ▶ This section will explain how you should read statutes. The way in which statutes are created is explained on pp.4–5. Looking for a particular legal rule in a statute can be confusing. Some statutes are over 100 pages long, although most are shorter. The language they use often appears complicated and obscure. If you understand the structure of a statute and follow a few simple rules in reading them, statutes will become much clearer.

A copy of a statute, the House of Lords Act 1999, is reproduced below. All subsequent references here are to this statute.

You can find statutes in a number of different ways. Not all of the statutes that you find will look the same as the one that we have reproduced for you. One way to find a statute is to buy it from Her Majesty's Stationery Office, the official stockist for Government publications, or one of its agents. These copies look much the same as the one that we have reproduced, but they have, in addition, a contents list at the beginning. This is also the case in relation to statutes which you may find on the internet. Statutes are also printed in a number of different series with different volumes for each year. The copy of the House of Lords Act 1999 which you are referring to is taken from such a series published by the Incorporated Council of Law Reporting. Some series of statutes are printed in an annotated form. This means that the statute is printed with an accompanying explanatory text, telling you what the statute does. If you use an annotated statute, remember that only the words of the statute are definitive. The explanatory text, although often helpful, is only the opinion of the author. Statutes are also available on-line at a number of different websites (see, for example, *http://www.statutelaw. gov.uk/, http://www.opsi.gov.uk/acts* and *http://www.bailii.org/*).

c. 34

ELIZABETH II

House of Lords Act 1999 ①

1999 Chapter 34 ②

An Act to restrict membership of the House of Lords by virtue of a hereditary peerage; to make related provision about disqualifications for voting at elections to, and for membership ③ of, the House of Commons; and for connected purposes.

[11th November 1999] ④

BE IT ENACTED by the Queen's most Excellent Majesty, by and with the advice and consent of the Lords Spiritual and Temporal, and Commons, in this present Parliament assembled, and by the authority of the same, as follows:—

⑤

1. No-one shall be a member of the House of Lords by virtue of a hereditary peerage.

Exclusion of hereditary peers.

⑥

Exception from section 1.

2.—(1) Section 1 shall not apply in relation to anyone excepted from it by or in accordance with Standing Orders of the House.

(2) At any one time 90 people shall be excepted from section 1; but anyone excepted as holder of the office of Earl Marshal, or as performing the office of Lord Great Chamberlain, shall not count towards that limit.

(3) Once excepted from section 1, a person shall continue to be so throughout his life (until an Act of Parliament provides to the contrary).

(4) Standing Orders shall make provision for filling vacancies among the people excepted from section 1; and in any case where—

(a) the vacancy arises on a death occurring after the end of the first Session of the next Parliament after that in which this Act is passed, and
(b) the deceased person was excepted in consequence of an election,

that provision shall require the holding of a by-election.

(5) A person may be excepted from section 1 by or in accordance with Standing Orders made in anticipation of the enactment or commencement of this section.

(6) Any question whether a person is excepted from section 1 shall be decided by the Clerk of the Parliaments, whose certificate shall be conclusive.

Removal of disqualifications in relation to the House of Commons.

3.—(1) The holder of a hereditary peerage shall not be disqualified by virtue of that peerage for—

    (a) voting at elections to the House of Commons, or
    (b) being, or being elected as, a member of that House.

(2) Subsection (1) shall not apply in relation to anyone excepted from section 1 by virtue of section 2.

Amendments and repeals.

4.—(1) The enactments mentioned in Schedule 1 are amended as specified there.

(2) The enactments mentioned in Schedule 2 are repealed to the extent specified there.

Commencement and transitional provision.

5.—(1) Sections 1 to 4 (including Schedules 1 and 2) shall come into force at the end of the Session of Parliament in which this Act is passed.

(2) Accordingly, any writ of summons issued for the present Parliament in right of a hereditary peerage shall not have effect after that Session unless it has been issued to a person who, at the end of the Session, is excepted from section 1 by virtue of section 2.

(3) The Secretary of State may by order make such transitional provision about the entitlement of holders of hereditary peerages to vote at elections to the House of Commons or the European Parliament as he considers appropriate.

(4) An order under this section—

    (a) may modify the effect of any enactment or any provision made under an enactment, and
    (b) shall be made by statutory instrument which shall be subject to annulment in pursuance of a resolution of either House of Parliament.

Interpretation and short title.

6.—(1) In this Act "hereditary peerage" includes the principality of Wales and the earldom of Chester.

(2) This Act may be cited as the House of Lords Act 1999.

SCHEDULES

SCHEDULE 1

AMENDMENTS

Peerage Act 1963 (c.48)

1. In section 1(2) of the Peerage Act 1963 (disclaimer of certain hereditary peerages) for the words from "has" to the end there shall be substituted the words "is excepted from section 1 of the House of Lords Act 1999 by virtue of section 2 of that Act".

Recess Elections Act 1975 (c.66)

2. In section 1 of the Recess Elections Act 1975 (issue of warrants for making out writs to replace members of the House of Commons whose seats have become vacant), in—

(a) subsection (1)(a), and

(b) paragraph (a) of the definition of "certificate of vacancy" in subsection (2),

for the words "become a peer" there shall be substituted the words "become disqualified as a peer for membership of the House of Commons".

SCHEDULE 2

REPEALS

Chapter	Short title	Extent of repeal
1963 c.48.	The Peerage Act 1963.	In section 1(3), paragraph (b) and the word "and" immediately preceding it. Section 2. In section 3, in subsection (1)(b), the words from "(including" to "that House)" and, in subsection (2), the words from "and" to the end of the subsection. Section 5.

THE DIFFERENT PARTS

① This is the *short title* of the Act, together with its year of publication. When you are   ▶ 5.4
writing about a statute, it is normal to use the short title and year of publication to
describe the statute. Sometimes, when a statute is referred to constantly, the short
title is abbreviated. Thus, the Matrimonial Causes Act 1973 is often referred to as
"the M.C.A. 1973". If you work in a particular area of law, you will quickly learn the
standard abbreviations for that area.

② This is the official *citation* for the statute. Each Act passed in any one year is given its own number. This is known as its *chapter number*. Thus you can describe a statute by its chapter number and year. The citation "1999 Chapter 34" could only mean the House of Lords Act 1999. "Chapter" in the official citation may be abbreviated to "c.", as in the top right hand corner of your copy of the statute. This form of official citation began in 1963. Before that, statutes were identified by the "regnal year" in which they occurred, followed by their chapter number. A regnal year is a year of a monarch's reign. Thus, "30 Geo 3 Chapter 3" refers to the Treason Act 1790, which was passed in the 30th year of King George III's reign. It is much easier to remember and use the short title of an Act rather than its official citation.

③ This is the *long title* of the Act. The long title gives some indication of the purpose behind the Act. It may be of some use in deciding what the Act is all about. However, the long title may be misleading. For example, the long title of the Parliament Act 1911 indicates that the Act is part of a process of abolishing the House of Lords— although, nearly 100 years later, that institution is still in existence, even though the House of Lords Act 1999 has introduced restrictions upon membership of the institution by virtue of a hereditary peerage. Long titles are sometimes vague and may conflict with the main body of the Act. In the event of such a conflict, the legal rule is that expressed in the main body of the Act.

④ This indicates when the *royal assent* was given and the House of Lords Bill 1999 became an Act. Statutes become law on the date when they receive the royal assent *unless the Act says otherwise*. The statute itself may say that it becomes law on a fixed date after the royal assent, or it may give a Government Minister the power to decide when it becomes law. When a Minister brings a statute into effect after the date on which it has been passed a "commencement order" must be made. This is a form of delegated legislation. Statutes do not have a retrospective effect unless the Act expressly says so.

⑤ This is known as the *enacting formula*. It is the standard form of words used to indicate that a Bill has been properly passed by all the different parts of the legislature.

⑥ By each section you will find a short explanation of the content of that section. These *marginal notes* may help you to understand the content of the section if it is otherwise unclear.

The main body of the statute that follows is broken up into numbered *sections*. Each section contains a different rule of law. When you refer to a rule of law contained in a statute, you should say where that rule of law is to be found. This enables others to check your source and to see whether or not they agree with your interpretation of the law. Instead of writing "section", it is usual to abbreviate this to "s.". Thus, "section 1" becomes "s.1". Sections are often further subdivided. These sub-division are known as *subsections*. When you wish to refer to a subsection, you should add it in brackets after the main section.

In larger statutes, sections may be grouped together into

Example

Q. *How many people are excepted from s.1 of the House of Lords Act 1999?*
A. *90 people at any one time. See s.2(2) House of Lords Act 1999.*

different *Parts*. Each Part will deal with a separate area of law. Looking for the correct Part will help you to find the particular legal rule that you want.

Some statutes have one or more *Schedules* at the end. The content of these varies. Some contain detailed provisions that are not found in the main body of the act. Others are merely convenient reminders and summaries of legal rules, and changes to legal rules, found elsewhere in the Act.

In the House of Lords Act 1999, for example, there are two Schedules. The first Schedule says which sections of previous statutes have been changed (amended) by the 1999 Act. This Schedule sets out the detailed effect of the amendments, which are given their legal effect by virtue of s.4(1) of the Act. The second Schedule sets out which sections of a previous statute have been repealed by the 1999 Act. Those repeals are given their legal effect by virtue of s.4(2) of the Act.

References to Schedules are often abbreviated as "Sched.". Where a Schedule is divided up, the divisions are known as *paragraphs*, and can be abbreviated as "para.".

USING A STATUTE

Your use of statutory material will vary. Sometimes you will be referred to a particular section or sections of a statute in a case, article, or book that you are reading. In other instances, a new statute will be passed which you need to assess as a whole in order to see how it affects those areas of law in which you are interested. In either case, when first reading statutory material, you may be able to gain some help in deciding what it means from commentaries.

Commentaries are explanations of the law written by legal academics or practitioners. Annotated statutes, which were discussed earlier, are one useful source of such commentaries. You may also find such commentaries in books and articles on the area of law in which the statute falls. Always remember that a commentary represents only one author's opinion of what the statute says. In the case of a very new statute there will probably be no commentary. Therefore, you will need to be able to read a statute yourself, so that you can assess the value of other people's opinions and form your own view when there is no other help available.

When reading a statute, do not begin at the beginning and then work your way through to the end, section by section. Statutes do not necessarily use words to mean the same things that they do in ordinary conversation. Before you can decide what a statute is about you need to know if there are any special meanings attached to words in it. These special meanings can be found in the Act, often in sections called *definition* or *interpretation sections*. These are frequently found towards the end of the Act. For example, in the House of Lords Act 1999, there is a guide in s.6(1) to the interpretation of the expression "hereditary peerage" when used in the context of the Act. An Act may have more than one definition section. Sometimes, Parliament, when laying down a particular meaning for a word, will say that the specified meaning will apply in all statutes in which that word appears. Unless a statute specifically says this, however, you should assume that a definition in a statute applies only the use of the word in that statute.

You are now in a position to decide what new legal rules the statute creates. Some people begin this task by reading the long title of the Act to give themselves some idea of the general

▶ 5.5

aim of the statute. Although this can be helpful, as we saw above in the section on the different parts of the Act, it can also be misleading.

Statutes should be read carefully and slowly. The general rule is that a statute means precisely what it says. Each word is important. Because of this, some words that we use loosely in ordinary conversation take on special significance when found in a statute. For example, it is important to distinguish between words like "may" and "shall", one saying that you *can* do something and the other saying that you *must* do something. Conjunctives, such as "and", joining things together, must be distinguished from disjunctives, such as "or", dividing things apart.

Example

Section 26A(1) of the Race Relations Act 1976 provides that:

"It is unlawful for a barrister or barrister's clerk, in relation to any offer of a pupillage or tenancy, to discriminate against a person—

    (a) in the arrangements which are made for the purpose of determining to whom it should be offered;
    (b) in respect of any terms on which it is offered; or
    (c) by refusing, or deliberately omitting, to offer it to him."

As a result, a barrister or a barrister's clerk will discriminate unlawfully if they do any one of the acts spelled out in (a) or (b) or (c).

This would be a very different provision if it had said that it was necessary for all three of the acts (a) and (b) and (c) to be present before discrimination occurred. As the law stands, any one of the acts listed will make the actor guilty of unlawful discrimination. If a conjunctive were substituted, then it would be necessary to show all three acts in order for unlawful discrimination to be established.

So far, the emphasis has been upon closely reading the particular statute. You should also remember that the statute should be read in the context of the general Acts, rules and principles of statutory interpretation discussed in Chapter 7.

One further thing to remember when reading a statute is that the fact that it has been printed does not mean that it is part of the law of the land. It may have been repealed. It may not yet be in force. Re-read pp.37–38 if you cannot remember how to find out if a statute has been repealed. Go back and read about the royal assent on p.54 if you cannot remember how to find out if a statute is in force.

STATUTORY INSTRUMENTS

What statutory instruments are, the way in which they are created, and the purposes that they   ▶ 5.6
have, are discussed on p.4.

Statutory instruments should be read in the same way as statutes. However, whilst stat-utes make relatively little reference to other sources, statutory instruments, because of their purpose, make very frequent reference either to other statutory instruments or to their parent statute. The legislative power has been given only for a limited purpose, the statutory instru-ment is a small part of a larger whole. For this reason, you will find it much more difficult to understand a statutory instrument if you do not have access to the surrounding legislation. Before reading a statutory instrument, it is vital that you understand the legislative framework into which it fits.

Exercise 1

STATUTES I

5.7 Start by re-reading the appropriate parts of Chapters 5 and 7 and then look at the Fur Farming (Prohibition) Act 2000. Then answer the questions. When answering the questions make sure you include the correct statutory references. Answers to Section A for each exercise can be found in Appendix III.

ELIZABETH II   c. 33

Fur Farming (Prohibition) Act 2000

2000 CHAPTER 33

An Act to prohibit the keeping of animals solely or primarily for slaughter for the value of their fur; to provide for the making of payments in respect of the related closure of certain businesses; and for connected purposes.   [23rd November 2000]

BE IT ENACTED by the Queen's most Excellent Majesty, by and with the advice and consent of the Lords Spiritual and Temporal, and Commons, in this present Parliament assembled, and by the authority of the same, as follows:—

1.—(1) A person is guilty of an offence if he keeps animals solely or primarily—   *Offences relating to fur farming.*

    (a) for slaughter (whether by himself or another) for the value of their fur, or

    (b) for breeding progeny for such slaughter.

(2) A person is guilty of an offence if he knowingly causes or permits another person to keep animals as mentioned in subsection (1).

(3) The references in this section to keeping animals for slaughter or to breeding progeny for slaughter include keeping or (as the case may be) breeding them for sale for slaughter.

(4) A person who is guilty of an offence under subsection (1) or subsection (2) is liable on summary conviction to a fine not exceeding £20,000.

2.—(1) If a person is convicted of an offence under section 1(1) in respect of animals of a particular description, the court may make a forfeiture order in respect of any animals of that description which are kept by that person when the order is made or which come into his keeping during the relevant period.   *Forfeiture orders.*

(2) If a person is convicted of an offence under section 1(2) in respect of animals of a particular description kept by another person, the court may make a forfeiture order in respect of any animals of that description which are kept by that other person when the order is made or which come into his keeping during the relevant period.

(3) For the purposes of this Act, a forfeiture order is an order for the forfeiture and destruction or other disposal of the animals to which the order applies (including any subsequent progeny of those animals).

(4) The court may make a forfeiture order whether or not it also deals with the offender in respect of the offence in any other way.

(5) Where—

(a) the court proposes to make a forfeiture order, and

(b) a person claiming to have an interest in the animals concerned applies to be heard by the court,

the court shall not make the order unless that person has been given an opportunity to show cause why the order should not be made.

(6) In this section "relevant period" means the period beginning with the making of the forfeiture order and ending with the destruction or other disposal of the animals in pursuance of the order.

Effect of forfeiture orders.

3.—(1) A forfeiture order operates in relation to the forfeiture of animals so as to deprive any person of his rights in those animals.

(2) Any person claiming to have an interest in the animals concerned may appeal against a forfeiture order to the Crown Court.

(3) Where the court makes a forfeiture order, it may in particular—

(a) appoint a person to carry out the order,

(b) impose requirements on any person in relation to the keeping of the animals concerned pending their destruction or other disposal,

(c) order the offender to pay such sum as the court may determine in respect of the reasonable expenses of carrying out the order and, where he does not keep the animals himself, of keeping them pending their destruction or other disposal,

(d) make such provision as the court considers appropriate in relation to the operation of the order pending the making or determination of any appeal or application relevant to the order.

(4) Any sum ordered to be paid under subsection (3)(c) shall be treated for the purposes of enforcement as if it were a fine imposed on conviction.

Powers of entry and enforcement.

4.—(1) A person authorised in writing by the appropriate authority (whether generally or in a particular case) may at any reasonable time enter any premises on which he has reasonable grounds for suspecting that an offence under section 1(1) has been or is being committed and may inspect the premises and any animals or things found there.

(2) A person appointed by the court under section 3(3)(a) to carry out a forfeiture order may at any reasonable time enter any premises on which he has reasonable grounds for suspecting that animals to which the order applies are being kept, and carry out the order.

(3) A person seeking to enter any premises in the exercise of his powers under subsection (1) or (2) shall, if required by or on behalf of the owner or occupier or person in charge of the premises, produce evidence of his identity, and of his authority or (as the case may be) appointment, before entering.

(4) A person who has entered any premises in the exercise of his powers under subsection (1) or (2) shall, if required as mentioned in subsection (3), state in writing his reasons for entering.

(5) A person is guilty of an offence if he intentionally obstructs or delays any person in the exercise of his powers under subsection (1) or (2).

(6) A person who is guilty of an offence under subsection (5) is liable on summary conviction to a fine not exceeding level 3 on the standard scale.

(7) In this section—

"premises" includes any place but not any private dwelling, and

"private dwelling" means any premises for the time being used as a private dwelling excluding any garage, outhouse or other structure (whether or not forming part of the same building as the premises) which belongs to or is usually enjoyed with the premises.

5.—(1) The appropriate authority may (and, in the case of the Minister of Agriculture, Fisheries and Food, shall) by order make a scheme for the making of payments by that authority to persons in respect of income and non-income losses incurred by them as a result of ceasing, by reason of the enactment or coming into force of section 1, to carry on their businesses so far as they consist of activities prohibited by that section.

Compensation for existing businesses.

(2) A scheme shall, in particular, specify—

(a) the description or descriptions of income losses and the description or descriptions of non-income losses in respect of which payments are to be made, and

(b) the description or descriptions of businesses in respect of which payments are to be made,

but need not provide for the making of payments in respect of all income losses or all non-income losses or (as the case may be) in respect of all businesses.

(3) A scheme shall also, in particular—

(a) specify the basis or bases of valuation for determining losses,

(b) specify the amounts of the payments to be made or the basis or bases on which such amounts are to be calculated,

(c) provide for the procedure to be followed (including the time within which claims must be made and the provision of information) in respect of claims under the scheme and for the determination of such claims.

(4) Before making a scheme under this section, the appropriate authority shall consult such persons as appear to it to be likely to be entitled to payments under such a scheme and such organisations as appear to it to represent such persons.

(5) Subsection (6) applies to any dispute as to a person's entitlement to payments under a scheme or the amounts of any such payments which—

(a) has not been resolved within nine months of the day on which the original decision as to entitlement or amounts was notified in writing to the person concerned by the appropriate authority, and

(b) has not been referred by agreement to arbitration.

(6) The dispute shall be referred by the appropriate authority to, and determined by, the Lands Tribunal.

(7) An order under this section shall be made by statutory instrument which, except in the case of an instrument made by the National Assembly for Wales, shall be subject to annulment in pursuance of a resolution of either House of Parliament.

(8) In this section—

"income losses" means losses of income, and

"non-income losses" means losses other than income losses.

Interpretation.   **6.**   In this Act "the appropriate authority" means—

(a) in relation to England, the Minister of Agriculture, Fisheries and Food, and

(b) in relation to Wales, the National Assembly for Wales.

Short title, commencement and extent.   **7.**—(1) This Act may be cited as the Fur Farming (Prohibition) Act 2000.

(2) Sections 1 to 4 shall come into force on such day as the Minister of Agriculture, Fisheries and Food may by order made by statutory instrument appoint; but no day before 1st January 2003 shall be appointed.

(3) Section 5 shall come into force at the end of the period of two months beginning with the day on which this Act is passed.

(4) This Act extends to England and Wales only.

Section A

1. What criminal offences does this Act create?
2. To which parts of the United Kingdom does it apply?
3. Is the Act in force?
4. Why do you think the statute was passed?
5. Does the Act provide for compensation for a person who gives up fur farming because of the legislation?

6. a) Mr McGregor runs a business breeding exotic rabbits. He sells their fur for use in the fashion industry. Until a year ago he also sold the carcasses to a pie factory but this no longer makes rabbit pies. Is Mr McGregor committing an offence under the Fur Farming (Prohibition) Act 2000?

b) Mr McGregor rents the land for his business from Potter Land Holdings Plc. Does this company commit any offence by allowing Mr McGregor to breed rabbits on the land?

c)Would your answer in b) be any different if Mr McGregor ran a mink farm?

7. Mr McGregor is prosecuted and convicted but he is not fined. The court makes forfeiture order in respect of 'rabbits kept at Mr McGregor's address.' Mr Fisher goes to the property to carry out the order. As well as destroying the farm rabbits he kills Thumper, Mr McGregor's daughter's pet rabbit.

a) Advise Mr Fisher whether he has acted lawfully.

b) Would your answer be different if Thumper had only been bought after the forfeiture order was made?

Section B

8. What is the short title of this Act?

9. What is the purpose of regulations (orders) made under s.5?

10. a) Before making regulations whom must the Minister consult?

b) How many sets of regulations have been made under s.5?

c) Give the title and statutory instrument number (SI number) of the current regulations

11. Have there been any reported cases on the Act or the regulations?

12. Why was it necessary to replace the regulations made in 2002?

13. Is there similar legislation for Scotland?

Exercise 2

STATUTES II

Hunting Act 2004

2004 CHAPTER 37

An Act to make provision about hunting wild mammals with dogs; to prohibit hare coursing; and for connected purposes. [18th November 2004]

B E IT ENACTED by The Queen's most Excellent Majesty, by and with the advice and consent of the Commons in this present Parliament assembled, in accordance with the provisions of the Parliament Acts 1911 and 1949, and by the authority of the same, as follows: —

PART 1

OFFENCES

1 Hunting wild mammals with dogs

> A person commits an offence if he hunts a wild mammal with a dog, unless his hunting is exempt.

2 Exempt hunting

> (1) Hunting is exempt if it is within a class specified in Schedule 1.
>
> (2) The Secretary of State may by order amend Schedule 1 so as to vary a class of exempt hunting.

3 Hunting: assistance

> (1) A person commits an offence if he knowingly permits land which belongs to him to be entered or used in the course of the commission of an offence under section 1.
>
> (2) A person commits an offence if he knowingly permits a dog which belongs to him to be used in the course of the commission of an offence under section 1.

4   Hunting: defence

It is a defence for a person charged with an offence under section 1 in respect of hunting to show that he reasonably believed that the hunting was exempt.

5   Hare coursing

(1)   A person commits an offence if he—
  (a)   participates in a hare coursing event,
  (b)   attends a hare coursing event,
  (c)   knowingly facilitates a hare coursing event, or
  (d)   permits land which belongs to him to be used for the purposes of a hare coursing event.

(2)   Each of the following persons commits an offence if a dog participates in a hare coursing event—
  (a)   any person who enters the dog for the event,
  (b)   any person who permits the dog to be entered, and
  (c)   any person who controls or handles the dog in the course of or for the purposes of the event.

(3)   A "hare coursing event" is a competition in which dogs are, by the use of live hares, assessed as to skill in hunting hares.

PART 2

ENFORCEMENT

6   Penalty

A person guilty of an offence under this Act shall be liable on summary conviction to a fine not exceeding level 5 on the standard scale.

7   Arrest

A constable without a warrant may arrest a person whom he reasonably suspects—
  (a)   to have committed an offence under section 1 or 5(1)(a), (b) or (2),
  (b)   to be committing an offence under any of those provisions, or
  (c)   to be about to commit an offence under any of those provisions.

8   Search and seizure

(1)   This section applies where a constable reasonably suspects that a person ("the suspect") is committing or has committed an offence under Part 1 of this Act.

(2)   If the constable reasonably believes that evidence of the offence is likely to be found on the suspect, the constable may stop the suspect and search him.

(3)   If the constable reasonably believes that evidence of the offence is likely to be found on or in a vehicle, animal or other thing of which the suspect appears to be in possession or control, the constable may stop and search the vehicle, animal or other thing.

(4) A constable may seize and detain a vehicle, animal or other thing if he reasonably believes that—

    (a) it may be used as evidence in criminal proceedings for an offence under Part 1 of this Act, or

    (b) it may be made the subject of an order under section 9.

(5) For the purposes of exercising a power under this section a constable may enter—

    (a) land;

    (b) premises other than a dwelling;

    (c) a vehicle.

(6) The exercise of a power under this section does not require a warrant.

9   Forfeiture

(1) A court which convicts a person of an offence under Part 1 of this Act may order the forfeiture of any dog or hunting article which—

    (a) was used in the commission of the offence, or

    (b) was in the possession of the person convicted at the time of his arrest.

(2) A court which convicts a person of an offence under Part 1 of this Act may order the forfeiture of any vehicle which was used in the commission of the offence.

(3) In subsection (1) "hunting article" means anything designed or adapted for use in connection with—

    (a) hunting a wild mammal, or

    (b) hare coursing.

(4) A forfeiture order—

    (a) may include such provision about the treatment of the dog, vehicle or article forfeited as the court thinks appropriate, and

    (b) subject to provision made under paragraph (a), shall be treated as requiring any person who is in possession of the dog, vehicle or article to surrender it to a constable as soon as is reasonably practicable.

(5) Where a forfeited dog, vehicle or article is retained by or surrendered to a constable, the police force of which the constable is a member shall ensure that such arrangements are made for its destruction or disposal—

    (a) as are specified in the forfeiture order, or

    (b) where no arrangements are specified in the order, as seem to the police force to be appropriate.

(6) The court which makes a forfeiture order may order the return of the forfeited dog, vehicle or article on an application made—

    (a) by a person who claims to have an interest in the dog, vehicle or article (other than the person on whose conviction the order was made), and

    (b) before the dog, vehicle or article has been destroyed or finally disposed of under subsection (5).

(7) A person commits an offence if he fails to—

    (a) comply with a forfeiture order, or

    (b) co-operate with a step taken for the purpose of giving effect to a forfeiture order.

10 Offence by body corporate

(1) This section applies where an offence under this Act is committed by a body corporate with the consent or connivance of an officer of the body.

(2) The officer, as well as the body, shall be guilty of the offence.

(3) In subsection (1) a reference to an officer of a body corporate includes a reference to—

   (a) a director, manager or secretary,

   (b) a person purporting to act as a director, manager or secretary, and

   (c) if the affairs of the body are managed by its members, a member.

PART 3

GENERAL

11 Interpretation

(1) In this Act "wild mammal" includes, in particular—

   (a) a wild mammal which has been bred or tamed for any purpose,

   (b) a wild mammal which is in captivity or confinement,

   (c) a wild mammal which has escaped or been released from captivity or confinement, and

   (d) any mammal which is living wild.

(2) For the purposes of this Act a reference to a person hunting a wild mammal with a dog includes, in particular, any case where—

   (a) a person engages or participates in the pursuit of a wild mammal, and

   (b) one or more dogs are employed in that pursuit (whether or not by him and whether or not under his control or direction).

(3) For the purposes of this Act land belongs to a person if he—

   (a) owns an interest in it,

   (b) manages or controls it, or

   (c) occupies it.

(4) For the purposes of this Act a dog belongs to a person if he—

   (a) owns it,

   (b) is in charge of it, or

   (c) has control of it.

12 Crown application

This Act—

   (a) binds the Crown, and

   (b) applies to anything done on or in respect of land irrespective of whether it belongs to or is used for the purposes of the Crown or a Duchy.

13 Amendments and repeals

(1) Schedule 2 (consequential amendments) shall have effect.

(2)   The enactments listed in Schedule 3 are hereby repealed to the extent specified.

14   Subordinate legislation

An order of the Secretary of State under this Act—
- (a)   shall be made by statutory instrument,
- (b)   may not be made unless a draft has been laid before and approved by resolution of each House of Parliament,
- (c)   may make provision which applies generally or only in specified circumstances or for specified purposes,
- (d)   may make different provision for different circumstances or purposes, and
- (e)   may make transitional, consequential and incidental provision.

15   Commencement

This Act shall come into force at the end of the period of three months beginning with the date on which it is passed.

16   Short title

This Act may be cited as the Hunting Act 2004.

17   Extent

This Act shall extend only to England and Wales.

SCHEDULES

SCHEDULE 1

Section 2

Exempt Hunting

Stalking and flushing out

1 (1) Stalking a wild mammal, or flushing it out of cover, is exempt hunting if the conditions in this paragraph are satisfied.

 (2) The first condition is that the stalking or flushing out is undertaken for the purpose of —
 (a) preventing or reducing serious damage which the wild mammal would otherwise cause —
 (i) to livestock,
 (ii) to game birds or wild birds (within the meaning of section 27 of the Wildlife and Countryside Act 1981 (c. 69)),
 (iii) to food for livestock,
 (iv) to crops (including vegetables and fruit),
 (v) to growing timber,
 (vi) to fisheries,
 (vii) to other property, or
 (viii) to the biological diversity of an area (within the meaning of the United Nations Environmental Programme Convention on Biological Diversity of 1992),
 (b) obtaining meat to be used for human or animal consumption, or
 (c) participation in a field trial.

 (3) In subparagraph (2)(c) "field trial" means a competition (other than a hare coursing event within the meaning of section 5) in which dogs —
 (a) flush animals out of cover or retrieve animals that have been shot (or both), and
 (b) are assessed as to their likely usefulness in connection with shooting.

 (4) The second condition is that the stalking or flushing out takes place on land —
 (a) which belongs to the person doing the stalking or flushing out, or
 (b) which he has been given permission to use for the purpose by the occupier or, in the case of unoccupied land, by a person to whom it belongs.

 (5) The third condition is that the stalking or flushing out does not involve the use of more than two dogs.

 (6) The fourth condition is that the stalking or flushing out does not involve the use of a dog below ground otherwise than in accordance with paragraph 2 below.

(7) The fifth condition is that—

    (a) reasonable steps are taken for the purpose of ensuring that as soon as possible after being found or flushed out the wild mammal is shot dead by a competent person, and

    (b) in particular, each dog used in the stalking or flushing out is kept under sufficiently close control to ensure that it does not prevent or obstruct achievement of the objective in paragraph (a).

Use of dogs below ground to protect birds for shooting

2   (1) The use of a dog below ground in the course of stalking or flushing out is in accordance with this paragraph if the conditions in this paragraph are satisfied.

    (2) The first condition is that the stalking or flushing out is undertaken for the purpose of preventing or reducing serious damage to game birds or wild birds (within the meaning of section 27 of the Wildlife and Countryside Act 1981 (c. 69)) which a person is keeping or preserving for the purpose of their being shot.

    (3) The second condition is that the person doing the stalking or flushing out—

        (a) has with him written evidence—

            (i) that the land on which the stalking or flushing out takes place belongs to him, or

            (ii) that he has been given permission to use that land for the purpose by the occupier or, in the case of unoccupied land, by a person to whom it belongs, and

        (b) makes the evidence immediately available for inspection by a constable who asks to see it.

    (4) The third condition is that the stalking or flushing out does not involve the use of more than one dog below ground at any one time.

    (5) In so far as stalking or flushing out is undertaken with the use of a dog below ground in accordance with this paragraph, paragraph 1 shall have effect as if for the condition in paragraph 1(7) there were substituted the condition that—

        (a) reasonable steps are taken for the purpose of ensuring that as soon as possible after being found the wild mammal is flushed out from below ground,

        (b) reasonable steps are taken for the purpose of ensuring that as soon as possible after being flushed out from below ground the wild mammal is shot dead by a competent person,

        (c) in particular, the dog is brought under sufficiently close control to ensure that it does not prevent or obstruct achievement of the objective in paragraph (b),

        (d) reasonable steps are taken for the purpose of preventing injury to the dog, and

        (e) the manner in which the dog is used complies with any code of practice which is issued or approved for the purpose of this paragraph by the Secretary of State.

Rats

3   The hunting of rats is exempt if it takes place on land—

    (a)   which belongs to the hunter, or

    (b)   which he has been given permission to use for the purpose by the occupier or, in the case of unoccupied land, by a person to whom it belongs.

Rabbits

4   The hunting of rabbits is exempt if it takes place on land —

    (a)   which belongs to the hunter, or

    (b)   which he has been given permission to use for the purpose by the occupier or, in the case of unoccupied land, by a person to whom it belongs.

Retrieval of hares

5   The hunting of a hare which has been shot is exempt if it takes place on land —

    (a)   which belongs to the hunter, or

    (b)   which he has been given permission to use for the purpose of hunting hares by the occupier or, in the case of unoccupied land, by a person to whom it belongs.

Falconry

6   Flushing a wild mammal from cover is exempt hunting if undertaken —

    (a)   for the purpose of enabling a bird of prey to hunt the wild mammal, and

    (b)   on land which belongs to the hunter or which he has been given permission to use for the purpose by the occupier or, in the case of unoccupied land, by a person to whom it belongs.

Recapture of wild mammal

7   (1) The hunting of a wild mammal which has escaped or been released from captivity or confinement is exempt if the conditions in this paragraph are satisfied.

    (2) The first condition is that the hunting takes place —

      (a)   on land which belongs to the hunter,

      (b)   on land which he has been given permission to use for the purpose by the occupier or, in the case of unoccupied land, by a person to whom it belongs, or

      (c)   with the authority of a constable.

    (3) The second condition is that —

      (a)   reasonable steps are taken for the purpose of ensuring that as soon as possible after being found the wild mammal is recaptured or shot dead by a competent person, and

      (b)   in particular, each dog used in the hunt is kept under sufficiently close control to ensure that it does not prevent or obstruct achievement of the objective in paragraph (a).

    (4) The third condition is that the wild mammal —

      (a)   was not released for the purpose of being hunted, and

(b)   was not, for that purpose, permitted to escape.

Rescue of wild mammal

8   (1) The hunting of a wild mammal is exempt if the conditions in this paragraph are satisfied.

(2) The first condition is that the hunter reasonably believes that the wild mammal is or may be injured.

(3) The second condition is that the hunting is undertaken for the purpose of relieving the wild mammal's suffering.

(4) The third condition is that the hunting does not involve the use of more than two dogs.

(5) The fourth condition is that the hunting does not involve the use of a dog below ground.

(6) The fifth condition is that the hunting takes place —
    (a)   on land which belongs to the hunter,
    (b)   on land which he has been given permission to use for the purpose by the occupier or, in the case of unoccupied land, by a person to whom it belongs, or
    (c)   with the authority of a constable.

(7) The sixth condition is that —
    (a)   reasonable steps are taken for the purpose of ensuring that as soon as possible after the wild mammal is found appropriate action (if any) is taken to relieve its suffering, and
    (b)   in particular, each dog used in the hunt is kept under sufficiently close control to ensure that it does not prevent or obstruct achievement of the objective in paragraph (a).

(8) The seventh condition is that the wild mammal was not harmed for the purpose of enabling it to be hunted in reliance upon this paragraph.

Research and observation

9   (1) The hunting of a wild mammal is exempt if the conditions in this paragraph are satisfied.

(2) The first condition is that the hunting is undertaken for the purpose of or in connection with the observation or study of the wild mammal.

(3) The second condition is that the hunting does not involve the use of more than two dogs.

(4) The third condition is that the hunting does not involve the use of a dog below ground.

(5) The fourth condition is that the hunting takes place on land —
    (a)   which belongs to the hunter, or
    (b)   which he has been given permission to use for the purpose by the occupier or, in the case of unoccupied land, by a person to whom it belongs.

(6) The fifth condition is that each dog used in the hunt is kept under sufficiently close control to ensure that it does not injure the wild mammal.

SCHEDULE 2

Section 13

CONSEQUENTIAL AMENDMENTS

Game Act 1831 (c. 32)

1   In section 35 of the Game Act 1831 (provision about trespassers: exceptions) the following words shall cease to have effect: "to any person hunting or coursing upon any lands with hounds or greyhounds, and being in fresh pursuit of any deer, hare or fox already started upon any other land, nor".

Game Licences Act 1860 (c. 90)

2   In section 5 of the Game Licences Act 1860 (exceptions) exceptions 3 and 4 (hares and deer) shall cease to have effect.

Protection of Animals Act 1911 (c. 27)

3   In section 1(3)(b) of the Protection of Animals Act 1911 (offence of cruelty: exceptions) a reference to coursing or hunting shall not include a reference to —

     (a)   participation in a hare coursing event (within the meaning of section 5 of this Act), or

     (b)   the coursing or hunting of a wild mammal with a dog (within the meaning of this Act).

Protection of Badgers Act 1992 (c. 51)

4   Section 8(4) to (9) of the Protection of Badgers Act 1992 (exception for hunting) shall cease to have effect.

Wild Mammals (Protection) Act 1996 (c. 3)

5   For the purposes of section 2 of the Wild Mammals (Protection) Act 1996 (offences: exceptions) the hunting of a wild mammal with a dog (within the meaning of this Act) shall be treated as lawful if and only if it is exempt hunting within the meaning of this Act.

SCHEDULE 3

Section 13

REPEALS

Short title and chapter	*Extent of repeal*
The Game Act 1831 (c. 32)	In section 35, the words "to any person hunting or coursing upon any lands with hounds or greyhounds, and being in fresh pursuit of any deer, hare or fox already started upon any other land, nor".
The Game Licences Act 1860 (c. 90)	In section 5, exceptions 3 and 4.

Short title and chapter	Extent of repeal
The Protection of Badgers Act 1992 (c. 51)	Section 8(4) to (9).

Section A

1. What is the purpose of the Hunting Act 2004?
2. When did the Act come into force?
3. In what circumstances does it continue to be legal to hunt wild animals with dogs?

4. a) What is "hare coursing"?
   b) Does someone who goes hare coursing commit an offence under section 1?

5. Charles owns a large estate where there is a herd of wild deer. He has always enjoyed stag hunting.

   a) Advise Charles whether he can legally continue to do this.
   b) Would it make any difference if Charles used the meat to feed his dogs?

6. In what circumstances can a police officer (constable) stop and search someone whom he suspects of hunting?
7. PC Smith sees a group of men who he knows have connections with hunting loading a pack of hounds into the backs of several cars. He follows Mr Jones who drives home in one of the cars. When he reaches Mr Jones' home he sees Mr Jones park his car in a barn and enter the house with six hounds. Advise PC Smith whether he can—

   a) enter Mr Jones' house to search for evidence that he has been hunting with the dogs, or
   b) remove Mr Jones' car from the barn so that it can be examined for evidence of hunting.

8. Can a person be arrested if she—

   a) allows her land to be used for hunting with dogs/hare coursing?
   b) owns a dog that is taking part in a hare coursing event?

9. A pet dog has been diagnosed with rabies, a dangerous, infectious disease. There is concern that this dog could have infected wild animals (squirrels, rabbits and foxes, etc) living in the neighbourhood. Can the police use their dogs to hunt these animals so as to avoid the danger of a spread of rabies?

If you have access to a law library:

10. a) Find out whether any cases have been reported on the application of the Hunting Act 2004.
    b) Find out whether the Hunting Act 2004 been amended.

Section B

11. a) Is it legal to hunt any animals with dogs after the Hunting Act 2004 came into force?
    b) Why do you think Parliament did not ban all hunting with dogs?

12. a) What is the penalty for illegal hunting?
    b) Can a person who is charged with hunting be tried by a jury?

13. The House of Lords, acting in its judicial capacity, considered the Hunting Act 2004 on two occasions see *Jackson and others v Her Majesty's Attorney General* [2005] UKHL 56 available at *http://www.publications.parliament.uk/pa/ld200506/ldjudgmt/jd051013/jack-1.htm*

and

   R. (on the application of Countryside Alliance and others and others (Appellants)) v Her Majesty's Attorney General and another (Respondents) [2007] UKHL 52 available at *http://www.parliament.the-stationery-office.co.uk/pa/ld200708/ldjudgmt/jd071128/countr-1.htm*

   a) What were the claimants trying to establish in the *Jackson* case?
   b) What does the case tell us about the Parliamentary process when the Hunting Bill was considered by the House of Lords in its legislative capacity?
   c) What was the Countryside Alliance trying to establish?
   d) What does this case law indicate about public acceptance of the Hunting Act 2004?

14. Bristol Zoo owns some very clever monkeys. One night they managed to unlock their enclosure. Some of them are now at large within the zoo; others have climbed over the zoo walls and disappeared into the local area. There has been a report that a monkey has been hit by a car and was seen limping away through neighbouring gardens. The Director of the Zoo is worried because he has had to close the zoo to the public and about the risk of harm to the monkeys which have escaped from the zoo.
    Advise the Director of the Zoo whether the zoo keepers can use dogs to round up these monkeys.

Drafting exercises

15. Draft an amendment to the Hunting Act 2004 which allows fox hunting with dogs to take place either on specific days of the year (December 26th and January 2nd) or if a licence has been obtained from the local Chief Constable.

16. Draft a provision which exempts Stag Hunting from the provisions of the Act providing that it takes place on land owned by the Crown.

Exercise 3

CASE I

A   House of Lords

*TRM Copy Centres (UK) Ltd and others *v* Lanwall Services Ltd

[2009] UKHL 35

2009 March 30;   Lord Hope of Craighead, Lord Hoffmann,
B   June 17   Lord Rodger of Earlsferry, Lord Walker of Gestingthorpe,
                                     Baroness Hale of Richmond

*Fair trading — Consumer credit — Agreement — Agreement for installation of
photocopier in retail premises for use by customers — Retailer accounting
for sums collected from customers but making no other payment — Whether
bailment by way of hire — Whether "consumer hire agreement" — Consumer*
C *Credit Act 1974 (c 39), s 15 (as amended by Consumer Credit (Increase of
Monetary Limits) Order 1983 (SI 1983/1878), Sch, Pt II, art 4)*

The claimant companies installed leased photocopiers in retail premises on the
terms of agreements known as "location agreements". Under such an agreement
the retailer agreed to the installation of one of the claimants' photocopiers in a visible
and accessible place on his premises. If the retailer's customers used the photocopier
they were charged a rate specified in the agreement. The retailer accounted to the
D claimants for the sums collected less his commission. There was no obligation on the
retailer to make any other payment. The claimants discovered that the defendant,
which operated a competing business, had removed the claimants' photocopiers
from the premises of a number of retailers bound by location agreements and
replaced them with their own machines. The claimants brought proceedings against
the defendant for inducing the retailers to breach their contracts. In its defence the
defendant contended that a location agreement made with a retailer who was an
E individual was a regulated hire agreement under section 15 of the Consumer Credit
Act 1974[1] and therefore terminable in accordance with section 101 of the Act.
On the hearing of a preliminary issue the judge held that a location agreement was
not a regulated hire agreement. The Court of Appeal upheld that decision.
    On the defendant's appeal—
    Held, dismissing the appeal, that although the English definition of a consumer
hire agreement in section 15 of the 1974 Act appeared to apply to all kinds of bailment
F in which the possession of goods was given by one person to another upon condition
that, at the end of the agreed period, they were restored to the person by whom
possession was given or were dealt with as he directed, "bailment" within the meaning
of section 15 was confined to bailment by way of hire; that a bailment which was
gratuitous was outside the scope of the 1974 Act so that the effect of the definition of a
consumer hire agreement in section 15 was the same in England and Wales as it was in
Scotland; that the essence of hire was that the hirer acquired the use and possession of
G the hired goods in return for the payment of rent either in cash or kind; that the
location agreement lacked any obligation on the part of the retailers to pay anything in
cash or kind to the claimants for the hire of the photocopiers; that the payment of
commission by the claimants to the retailers on each copy made on the photocopiers
was consideration for the benefit that the claimants had obtained by having their
photocopiers located in a position where they were easily visible and accessible to the
retailers' customers; that in those circumstances the photocopiers were not being hired
H by the retailers; and that, accordingly, the location agreement was not a consumer hire
agreement within the meaning of section 15 (*post*, paras 10–12, 16–20, 23–25).
    Decision of the Court of Appeal [2008] EWCA Civ 382; [2008] Bus LR 1231;
[2008] 4 All ER 608; [2008] 2 All ER (Comm) 1021 affirmed.

[1] Consumer Credit Act 1974, s 15, as amended: see post, para 3.

1376

TRM Copy Centres (UK) Ltd v Lanwall Services Ltd (HL(E))   **[2009] 1 WLR**
Lord Hope of Craighead

The following cases are referred to in the opinions of the Committee:

A

Coggs v Bernard (1703) 2 Ld Raym 909
Eurocopy (Scotland) plc v Lothian Health Board 1995 SLT 1356
Galbraith v Mitchenall Estates Ltd [1965] 2 QB 473; [1964] 3 WLR 454; [1964]
   2 All ER 653

No additional cases were cited in argument.

B

APPEAL from the Court of Appeal
By leave of the House of Lords (Lord Phillips of Worth Matravers, Lord
Carswell and Lord Mance) granted on 30 October 2008, the defendant,
Lanwall Services Ltd, appealed from a decision of the Court of Appeal
(Sir Mark Potter P, Thomas and Hooper LJJ) on 17 April 2008 dismissing
the defendant's appeal from a judgment dated 18 July 2007 of Flaux J
[2007] EWHC 1738 (QB), who ruled on a preliminary issue that location
agreements entered into by the claimants, TRM Copy Centres (UK) Ltd,
Digital 4 Convenience plc and D4C Finance Ltd, with several retailers were
not consumer hire agreements for the purposes of the Consumer Credit
Act 1974.
The facts are stated in the opinion of Lord Hope of Craighead.

C

D

Jonathan Ferris (instructed by *Devereaux*) for the defendant.
Bridget Williamson (instructed by *Sherrards, St Albans*) for the claimants.

The Committee took time for consideration.

17 June 2009. **LORD HOPE OF CRAIGHEAD**
  1 My Lords, the appellant, Lanwall Services Ltd, supplies photocopiers
to leasing companies which lease them in return for a rental payment to,
among others, the operators of retail businesses in shops and sub-post
offices. It then services and maintains the photocopiers under a maintenance
agreement with the retailer. The respondents (for convenience I shall
refer to them collectively as "TRM") carry on business in competition with
Lanwall. They too deal in photocopiers, but they do so in a way that differs
from the business model used by Lanwall. They lease the photocopiers
from a finance company. They then install them in shops and sub-post
offices under an agreement, which is described as a location agreement, with
the retailer.
  2 TRM commenced these proceedings when they discovered that
Lanwall had removed their photocopiers from premises where they had
been installed under subsisting location agreements and replaced them
with equipment supplied by Lanwall. Their case is that Lanwall's actions
constituted the tort of inducing the retailers to breach their location
agreements with TRM. Lanwall's defence is that TRM's location agreements
are consumer hire agreements. Various consequences follow if Lanwall is
right on this point. The Consumer Credit Act 1974 provides that a licence
is required to carry on a consumer hire business, and that agreements of
that kind which are made by unlicensed traders are not enforceable against
the hirer. Lanwall says that TRM are not licensed, so their agreements are
unenforceable against the retailers. The Office of Fair Trading may make an
order that the agreements of that kind are to be treated retrospectively as if
the trader had been registered. So Lanwall also says that the agreements had

E

F

G

H

1377

A either been terminated or could be brought to an end by the retailers under that Act at any time.

3 On 2 May 2007 Master Rose ordered the trial of three preliminary issues. One of these was whether a location agreement, if made between TRM and a retailer who is an individual, is a regulated hire agreement for the purposes of section 15 of the Consumer Credit Act 1974. That section, as amended, provides:

B

> "(1) A consumer hire agreement is an agreement made by a person with an individual (the 'hirer') for the bailment or (in Scotland) the hiring of goods to the hirer, being an agreement which— (a) is not a hire-purchase agreement, and (b) is capable of subsisting for more than three months, and (c) does not require the hirer to make payments exceeding £25,000.
>
> "(2) A consumer hire agreement is a regulated agreement if it is not an exempt agreement."

C

Section 15(1)(c) will cease to have effect when section 2(2) of the Consumer Credit Act 2006 is brought into force, but no date for this has yet been identified. Lanwall's case is that TRM's location agreements are consumer hire agreements and that, as such, they are regulated agreements within the meaning of that section. Section 21(1) of the 1974 Act provides that a licence is required to carry on a consumer hire business. Section 40(1) provides that a regulated agreement is not enforceable against the hirer by a person acting in the course of a consumer hire business if that person is not licensed to carry on a consumer hire business of a description which covers the enforcement of the agreement. Section 40(2) enables a trader who is not licensed to apply to the Office of Fair Trading for an order that any agreements made during a period when he was unlicensed are to be treated as if he had been licensed as required. Section 101(1) of the 1974 Act provides that the hirer under a regulated consumer hire agreement is entitled to terminate the agreement by giving notice to any person entitled or authorised to receive the sums payable under the agreement. Contracting out of that protection is forbidden by section 173(1).

D

E

4 On 18 July 2007 Flaux J held that the location agreements were not consumer hire agreements within the meaning of section 15 of the 1974 Act: [2007] EWHC 1738 (QB). He decided the other two preliminary issues, as to whether on their true construction the two agreements that were before him were terminable at any time, against Lanwall also. Lanwall did not pursue those issues in the Court of Appeal. Its appeal against Flaux J's decision was directed only to the question whether the location agreements were regulated hire agreements for the purposes of section 15 of the 1974 Act. On 17 April 2008, the Court of Appeal dismissed the appeal: [2008] Bus LR 1231. The issue which is now before the House is whether the courts below were right to decide this preliminary issue against Lanwall. It raises the following questions. What are the essential elements of a consumer hire agreement within the meaning of section 15? In particular, do the terms of TRM's location agreement embrace those essential elements?

F

G

H

The location agreement

5 As Flaux J explained in para 3 of his judgment, two forms of location agreement were before the court. It had been possible to obtain a copy of only one of them, however. This was a form of agreement which took effect

1378

from 1 June 2002. So it was to its terms that he directed his attention. Under   A
this agreement the retailer agrees to the installation of a photocopier on his
premises and undertakes to provide a location for it which is easily visible
and accessible by the retailer's customers. The retailer's customers, and the
retailer too, may use the photocopier. If they do, they are charged the rate
per copy that is provided for in the agreement. The retailer undertakes to
collect all sums paid for copies made on the photocopier and to account for
them to TRM. He is entitled to deduct from those sums commission at a rate   B
which increases as a greater number of copies are made, together with the
VAT thereon. Accounting for these sums takes place monthly. No sums
other than the rate per copy, less commission, are payable by either party in
consideration of their undertakings to each other. The June 2002 location
agreement is for an initial period of 36 months. Thereafter, unless
terminated by either party on giving 90 days' notice, it is renewed   C
automatically for successive periods of 12 months.

6 The parties to the June 2002 location agreement are described as
TRM on the one hand and "the business" on the other. The standard form
assumes that the business will always be a company incorporated in
England. But in practice these agreements are also entered into with
individuals. As the agreement is described as a "UK Copier location
agreement" it appears to have been envisaged that they might be entered into   D
with companies incorporated in other parts of the United Kingdom too. For
present purposes, however, it is sufficient to note that in at least some of the
situations where TRM and Lanwall are in competition with each other they
were entered into with an individual. This has provided Lanwall with the
opportunity to argue that they can be brought to an end by the retailer under
the 1974 Act.   E

7 The relevant provisions of the June 2002 location agreement are as
follows:

"TRM and the business desire to allow TRM to locate a TRM owned
photocopy machine and related products (the 'equipment') and
proprietary promotional material at the retail locations owned and
operated by the business. The equipment will be available for use by the   F
business and its customers. TRM and the business agree as follows:

"1. *TRM's obligations*

"During the term of this agreement, TRM will: 1.1 deliver and install
the equipment and promotional material to the business's locations
owned and operated by the business as set out in Schedule 1 of this
agreement (store sites) and such other additional locations as TRM shall
agree; 1.2 supply the business with all the paper, toner and supplies   G
necessary for the operation of the equipment; 1.3 provide repair and
maintenance services for the equipment and promotional material;
and 1.4 provide appropriate training to the business for the operation of
the equipment.

"2. *The business's obligations*

"During the term of this agreement, the business will: 2.1 accept all the
supplies necessary to operate the equipment; 2.2 provide electrical power   H
to operate the equipment; 2.3 provide a clean, safe and orderly location
for the equipment, which is easily visible and accessible by the business's
customers; 2.4 provide adequate space for promotional material provided
by TRM; 2.5 collect all sums paid for copies made on the equipment and

A   account to TRM for all moneys received from customers using the equipment, less the business's commission in accordance with Schedule 2 below; 2.6 oversee the use and operation of the equipment by the business's customers making best efforts to maximise copier uptime by the timely refilling of supplies, removal of paper jams when possible, and contacting TRM promptly in the event of copier malfunction; 2.7 fulfil its duties, in accordance with its VAT status, to charge and remit all value

B   added tax (herein referred to as 'VAT') and any other taxes incurred with respect to copies made on the equipment; 2.8 promptly notify TRM in writing if the business's VAT status or VAT number changes; and 2.9 promptly notify TRM if the business changes ownership . . ."

"4. *Retail price and commission schedule*

"In consideration of TRM carrying out its obligations set out in this

C   agreement, the business will pay TRM monthly for all copies made on the equipment times the retail price specified in Schedule 2 (the monthly revenue), less the appropriate commission applied to all monthly copies as described in Schedule 2, together with VAT thereon. The amount which is payable to TRM shall be computed and paid as follows: TRM will calculate and invoice the business, monthly, for the amount due for copies made over the previous meter reading. TRM's invoice shall be

D   paid within thirty (30) days from the invoice date. A late payment charge of 1·5% per month, or a minimum of £0·50, shall be added to any unpaid balance. Further, in the event that the business fails to make such timely payment, TRM shall have the right to enter upon the business location and to terminate this agreement and remove the equipment and promotional materials from the business location at any time without

E   advance notice."

"11.*Use of equipment*

"The business shall at all times exercise reasonable care in using and supervising the use of the equipment and shall not remove the equipment from the business location, part with possession of the equipment, or allow the equipment to be used by anyone other than the business or its agents, employees and customers . . ."

F

Section 15 of the 1974 Act

8   The provisions of section 15 to which this case directs attention are to be found in the opening words of subsection (1). They state: "A consumer hire agreement is an agreement made by a person with an individual (the 'hirer') for the bailment or (in Scotland) the hiring of goods to the hirer . . ."

G   This is, as Professor Sir Roy Goode, *Consumer Credit Law and Practice*, looseleaf ed, vol 1, para 23.74, points out, an unnecessarily cumbersome provision. The definition might well have been expressed differently, had it not been for the precedents set by the Hire-Purchase Acts. Section 1(1) of the Hire-Purchase Act 1965, which applied to England and Wales, defined the expression "hire-purchase agreement" as "an agreement for the bailment of goods under which the bailee may buy the goods, or under which the

H   property in the goods will or may pass to the bailee". Section 1(1) of the Hire-Purchase (Scotland) Act 1965 defined the expression as meaning any contract whereby goods are taken on hire by one person from another in consideration of periodical payments, with an option to the person who takes them to become the buyer of the goods. Section 189(1) of the 1974 Act

uses the same concepts to define what is meant, in England and Wales or in   A
Scotland as the case may be, by the expression "hire-purchase agreement"
for its purposes. It then uses the same concepts to define the expression
"hirer". This is said to be a person to whom goods are bailed, or (in
Scotland) hired, under a consumer hire agreement.

9   The definitions in sections 15 and 189(1) are easy to apply in
Scotland. All one needs to know is that the statute has defined this type of   B
agreement as one for the hiring of goods. *Bell, Commentaries on the Law
of Scotland*, M'Laren's edition (1870), vol I, p 275 states that a contract
of hiring, or location, is a contract by which the temporary use of a subject,
or the work or service of a person, is given for an ascertained hire. At p 481,
he restates his definition in these terms:

> "The contract of hiring, or locatio conductio, is that by which the one   C
> party agrees, in consideration of a certain hire or rent which the other
> engages to pay, to give to that other, during a certain time, the use or
> occupation of a thing; or personal service and labour; or both combined."

For present purposes it is sufficient to note that it is the fact that the hiring is
in consideration of an ascertained hire or rent which the hirer agrees to pay
that marks this kind of contract out from others under which the temporary   D
use or possession of a thing is given to another.

10   The English definitions, which refer to an agreement for the bailment
of goods, require further analysis. They overlook the fact that bailment is
not synonymous with hire. It embraces all situations in which possession of
goods is given by one person to another upon the condition that they shall be
restored to the person by whom possession has been given, or dealt with as
he directs, upon expiry of the agreed period of possession: *Goode, Consumer*   E
Credit Law and Practice, para 23.74. Views have differed as to the classes
into which this legal concept may be arranged. In *Coggs v Bernard* (1703)
2 Ld Raym 909, Holt CJ said that there were six classes of bailment.
The most up to date discussion is in *Halsbury's Laws of England*, 4th ed
(2005 reissue), vol 3(1), para 2. It selects as the basic model the arrangement
in *Jones on Bailment*, 1st ed (1781) pp 35–36, which divides bailment into   F
five classes, as follows:

> "(1) the gratuitous deposit of a chattel with the bailee, who is simply
> to keep it for the bailor; (2) the delivery of a chattel to the bailee, who is
> to do something without reward for the bailee to or with the chattel;
> (3) the gratuitous loan of a chattel by the bailor to the bailee for the
> bailee to use; (4) the pawn or pledge of a chattel by the bailor to the
> bailee, who is to hold it as a security for a loan or debt or the fulfilment of   G
> an obligation; and (5) the hire of a chattel or services by the bailor to the
> bailee for reward."

11   Professor Norman Palmer, in his capacity as consultant editor of
Halsbury's Laws of England, "Bailment", observes in para 2 that modern
authority recognises many variations on these basic models, and that many
examples do not fit precisely into any particular category. But to understand   H
the kind of bailment that section 15 of the 1974 Act refers to, the
classification in *Jones on Bailment* is all one needs. This plainly, as Mr Ferris
for Lanwall accepts, is bailment by way of hire. That is to say, it is a
bailment under which the person who receives possession agrees to pay for

A   the use of the chattel in cash or kind during the period of his possession of it. A bailment which is gratuitous is outside the scope of the statute. On this analysis the effect of the definition in section 15 is, as one would expect, the same in England and Wales as it is in Scotland.

The effect of the location agreement

B   12 The location agreement lacks the most obvious badge of an agreement for hire. The obligations that the business undertakes, as listed in clause 2, do not include an obligation to pay anything in cash or kind for the hire of the photocopier. The only obligation which involves the making of payments by the business to TRM is that described in clause 4. In consideration of TRM carrying out its obligations under the agreement, the business undertakes to pay TRM monthly for all copies made on the

C   equipment multiplied by the rate per copy set out in Schedule 2. If no copies are made there is nothing to pay at all. If the copies made during the month are made only by customers using the equipment, the obligation is to account for the sums collected from the customers. If it has not used the photocopier itself during that month, the business does not have to pay anything at all to TRM out of its own money. The cash flow is all the other

D   way, as the business is entitled to deduct commission on the amounts that it has collected from the customers. Thus the financial returns that are obtained by either side relate entirely to the number of copies that are made by the photocopier. The greater the number of the copies, the better is the return to TRM on its investment. The greater the return to the business too, as the amount of its commission increases according to the number of copies made by the photocopier that it has agreed to locate on its premises.

E   13 Mr Ferris submitted that the effect of this unusual arrangement is that the photocopier is hired to the retailer. The essence of it, he said, was that the business obtained the right to use the photocopier in return for payment. The fact that the amount that had to be paid was related to the number of copies made was to be regarded simply as the business model for ensuring a return to TRM on its photocopier that the parties found most attractive. The fact that there was a stipulated amount that had to be paid

F   to TRM was all that was needed to bring the agreement under which possession of the photocopier was transferred to the business into effect so that it could make use of it within the scope of section 15 of the 1974 Act. The payment of this amount was to be regarded as referable to the use of the photocopier, as the expectation was that once it had been installed it would be used. The nature of the consideration that was to be given for the

G   opportunity to use it was immaterial. Any reward, whether monetary or otherwise, would do. He submitted that *Palmer on Bailment*, 2nd ed (1991), p 1209, note 12a confirmed this approach, as did the Supply of Goods and Services Act 1982, section 6(3), which provides that a contract can be a contract of hire for the purposes of that Act whatever is the nature of the consideration.

H   14 It seems to me however that this approach concentrates too much on one aspect only of the agreement. It overlooks the commercial reality of the transaction seen as a whole. As Thomas LJ put it in the Court of Appeal [2008] Bus LR 1231, para 31, following the approach of the First Division of the Court of Session in *Eurocopy (Scotland) plc v Lothian Health Board* 1995 SLT 1356, it is necessary to look at the commercial purpose of the

agreement. I think that, when the location agreement is looked at in this   A
way, it takes on an entirely different aspect from that suggested by Mr Ferris.

15   The preamble to the location agreement indicates that it was
conceived primarily as a means of maximising TRM's opportunity to
obtain a return on its investment in the photocopier by locating it in a
position where it would be used by as many people as possible. It refers
to the parties' desire to allow TRM to locate the photocopy machine,   B
including the promotional material, at the retail locations owned and
operated by the business. The photocopier is to be available for use by the
business, which undertakes to pay at the agreed rate for each copy that it
makes less the agreed amount of commission. But the fact that its use by
the business on these terms is not the primary purpose of the agreement is
demonstrated by clause 2.3 of the agreement, by which the business
undertakes to provide a clean, safe and orderly location for the equipment   C
which is easily visible and accessible by the business's customers. It is
demonstrated too by clause 2.6, by which the business undertakes to
oversee the use and operation of the equipment by its customers making
best efforts to maximise copier uptime. The commission schedule, which
provides for the commission or profit that the business is to earn from the
location of the equipment on its premises, tells the same story. It anticipates
the possibility of thousands of copies being made each month, on each of   D
which business commission will be paid, up to and beyond 14,000 copies.
Such volumes far exceed the number of copies that an individual retailer is
likely to make each month for his own purposes.

16   The question was asked in the course of the argument: who is paying
whom for this arrangement? Miss Williamson, in her brief address, adopted
that approach. To that question there can, in my opinion, be only one   E
answer. From the commercial point of view the emphasis is all one way.
TRM is paying the business commission on each copy made on the
equipment as consideration for the benefit that TRM has obtained by having
its machine and its promotional material located in a place where it is easily
visible and accessible by the business's customers. The business is under no
obligation to use the equipment for its own purposes. If it does, the cost per
copy is the same as that for everyone else, as is the rate of commission.   F
It does not have to pay anything for any benefit to its own business that may
result from the presence of the photocopier on its premises. The obligations
that it undertakes are all designed to maximise the use of the equipment
by its customers in order to promote the interests of TRM. This kind of
bailment does not fall precisely into any of the five classes listed in *Jones on
Bailment*: see para 10, above. It may be described as the delivery of the   G
photocopier to the bailee in return for a reward to the bailee, by way of a
commission on all sums paid for the copies made by it, for being permitted to
locate it on his premises. It is sufficient for the purposes of this case to say,
however, that the photocopier itself is not being hired by the bailee.

Conclusion

17   I agree with both the judge and the Court of Appeal that the   H
preliminary issue must be decided in TRM's favour. The location
agreement in TRM's standard form is not a consumer hire agreement
within the meaning of section 15 of the Consumer Credit Act 1974. I would
dismiss the appeal.

A ## LORD HOFFMANN

18   My Lords, I have had the advantage of reading in draft the speech of my noble and learned friend, Lord Hope of Craighead. For the reasons he gives, with which I agree, I too would dismiss this appeal.

LORD RODGER OF EARLSFERRY

19   My Lords, I have had the advantage of considering the speech of my
B noble and learned friend, Lord Hope of Craighead, in draft. I agree with it and, for the reasons he gives, I too would dismiss the appeal.

LORD WALKER OF GESTINGTHORPE

20   My Lords, I have had the advantage of reading in draft the opinion of my noble and learned friend, Lord Hope of Craighead. I agree with it,
C and for the reasons given by Lord Hope I too would dismiss this appeal.

BARONESS HALE OF RICHMOND

21   My Lords, I agree that this appeal should be dismissed, for the reasons given by my noble and learned friend, Lord Hope of Craighead. However, I do so with some unease. This happens to be a dispute between two rival providers of copying machines to post offices, shops and similar
D small businesses for use by the public or the businesses themselves. Neither needs any special protection from the other. But this might have been a dispute between the provider of such a machine and the small business to which it was provided. It turns on the application of a piece of legislation, the Consumer Credit Act 1974, which was designed to protect consumers such as these small businesses. It would be unfortunate if that protection were to turn on fine distinctions between the terms of particular contracts,
E which are usually in standard form and may not be carefully studied by the consumer. As the Crowther Committee, whose report led to the 1974 Act, put it, "The greatest weakness of the present law of credit, and that from which most of the other defects stem, is the failure to look behind the form of a transaction and deal with the substance": *Consumer Credit, Report of the Committee* (1971) (Cmnd 4596), para 4.2.2.

F 22   So it is worthwhile recalling why consumer hire contracts were included in the 1974 Act at all, despite the fact that they do not usually involve the provision of any credit (see Crowther Report, especially paras 1.1.9 and 6.2.53 to 6.2.59, and N Palmer and D Yates, "The application of the Consumer Credit Act 1974 to consumer hire agreements" (1979) 38 CLJ 180, 180). If a chattel such as a television set or a car is rented out for a long period, perhaps for most of its expected life, then the effect is
G much the same as a hire purchase or conditional sale agreement. The capital cost is spread out over the term and repaid by the consumer in the form of rental payments at the end of which there will be little if any value left in the item. The hirer who gets no ownership at the end of the term is even worse off than the hirer who at least becomes owner when all the instalments are paid. But he may be locked into the hiring for an unduly long time, perhaps longer than the useful life of the item hired. And there is a risk that he
H will not have understood the difference between hire and hire purchase: see *Galbraith v Mitchenall Estates Ltd* [1965] 2 QB 473. Hence the main protections recommended by the Crowther Committee were the provisions of information and a right of restitution in certain circumstances; the Act added the requirement that the supplier be licensed and gave the consumer

the right to terminate the hire: see White Paper, *Reform of the Law on*   A
Consumer Credit (1973) (Cmnd 5427).

23   Although the English definition of a consumer hire agreement in
section 15 of the 1974 Act appears to apply to all kinds of bailment (see the
concerns expressed by Palmer and Yates, above), it is common ground in this
case that it is confined to bailment by way of hire. The essence of hire is that
the hirer acquires the use and possession of the goods from the provider in
return for a rent, whether payable in cash or in kind. It is to be contrasted   B
with an agreement where the provider pays a person to keep, look after or
work upon his goods. So the issue in this case became: who was paying
whom for what? Were the businesses paying the provider of the copier for
the privilege of having the machine on their premises so that they and their
customers could use it? Or was the provider paying the businesses for the
privilege of locating his machine in a place where it might generate an   C
income for them both?

24   I do agree with Lord Hope that this agreement fell into the latter
category. Nothing had to be paid unless the copier was used. When it was
used, a set price per copy was payable to the provider. The business had to
collect this money and account to the provider for it. But the business earned
a commission on each copy made. It did not cost the business a rent to
have the copier there. Instead the business stood to gain from its presence.   D
And that gain came, not from profits which the business had earned with the
machine, but from profits which the provider had earned. One can imagine
consumer hire contracts in which a person hires a moneymaking chattel with
a view to putting it to profitable use. The classic example of hire purchase
was a sewing machine which the seamstress used to make or repair clothes
or other linens for reward out of which she was able to afford the rental   E
payments. But that is not what is happening here. The reward which the
business makes from having the machine on its premises is not from any
profitable use to which the business itself puts the machine. It is from the use
to which others put it. The fact that the business may be one of those users
makes no real difference. The business does not have to pay to have the
machine irrespective of its profitability.

25   This may look like a fine distinction but the arrangement does not   F
suffer from the main mischiefs which led the Crowther Committee and the
promoters of the 1974 Act to include consumer hire within its provisions.
Its worst feature is that the business is committed to housing (and insuring)
the machine for three years, but this is counterbalanced by the lack of any
commitment to pay for it. I am therefore persuaded that we need not be too
troubled by the fear that, as the Crowther Committee commented of the
common law, at para 5.1.4,   G

> "If the merits of the first dispute had been the other way, the court
> might well have formulated the statement of principle quite differently,
> and the whole direction of the law in that area might have been altered."

Appeal dismissed with costs.

S H   H

Section A

1. Who brought the initial complaint in the case of *TRM Copy Centres (UK) and others v Lanwall Services Limited?*
2. What was the issue before the judge at first instance?
3. Give a short statement of the issue raised by the *TRM* case before the House of Lords.
4. In which courts was the *TRM* case heard?
5. What was the decision in each of the hearings of the case?
6. Were these criminal or civil proceedings?

Section B

7. Has the case been reported in any other series of law reports?
8. Since Lord Hoffmann, Lord Rodger and Lord Walker merely agreed with and adopted the reasons given by Lord Hope, what purpose, if any, was served by then sitting on the case?
9. Baroness Hale agrees with the reasoning of Lord Hope but does so with "some unease" (p.1383). Why is she uneasy about an argument that she accepts, in this instance, is legally correct? What does this tell you about the things that judges think about before giving judgement?
10. Lord Hope refers to academic work by a number of authors including Professor Sir Roy Goode and Professor Norman Palmer (p.1380). Do these works have legal authority? If not, why not? If not, why does Lord Hope refer to them?

Exercise 4

CASE II

Fisher v Brooker and others

House of Lords

30 July 2009

SESSION 2008-09 [2009] UKHL 41, on appeal from:[2008]EWCA Civ 287

2009 WL 2207452

Appellate Committee Lord Hope of Craighead Lord Walker of Gestingthorpe Baroness Hale of Richmond Lord Mance Lord Neuberger of Abbotsbury

Thursday 30 July 2009

Opinions of the Lords of Appeal for Judgment in the Cause

Hearing dates: 22 and 23 April 2009

Representation

- Original Appellants: Iain Purvis QC Hugo Cuddigan (Instructed by Jens Hills Solicitors).
- Original Respondent: John Baldwin QC Jessie Bowhill (Instructed by harbottle & Lewis LLP).

Judgment

Lord Hope of Craighead

My Lords,

1 I have had the advantage of reading in draft the opinion of my noble and learned friend Lord Neuberger of Abbotsbury. I agree with it, and I also agree with the comments of my noble and learned friend Lord Walker of Gestingthorpe. For the reasons that Lord Neuberger gives I would allow the appeal and make the order that he proposes. I gratefully adopt his description of the factual background and his analysis of the issues that were before the courts below.

2 This is, as Mummery LJ observed in the Court of Appeal [2008] Bus LR 1123 , para 34, an extremely unusual case. One of its most striking features is Matthew Fisher's extraordinary delay in making his claim for a share of the musical copyright. In para 82 of his judgment Mummery LJ described the fact that Mr Fisher had waited for 38 years, with knowledge and without reasonable excuse, as unconscionable behaviour. Another, which is really a product of the first, is the fact that his claim is being maintained with a view to what happens in the future, not with a view to the past. The judge rejected his claim for a share of the royalties that were obtained in respect of the work during the six years before the issue of proceedings, and Mr Fisher did not appeal against that decision. Mummery LJ said in para 34 that what he was essentially seeking to do by insisting on his claim was to control the copyright for the future.

3 Remarkable though these features are, they need to be treated with some care as the law is applied to the facts of the case. Delay in itself is no bar to these proceedings. There is no statutory limitation period that applies in English law to claims to copyright, the duration of which has been laid down by section 12 of the Copyright, Designs and Patents Act 1988 , as substituted by the Duration of Copyright and Rights in Performances Regulations 1995 (SI 1995/3297): see section 39 of the Limitation Act 1980 . The position is less certain in Scotland. Section 8 of the Prescription and Limitation (Scotland) Act 1973 provides that if, after the date when a right to property has become exercisable or enforceable, a right has subsisted for a continuous period of twenty years unexercised or unenforced, and without a relevant claim having been made in relation to it, it is extinguished from the expiration of that period. Section 8(2) provides that the section applies to any right relating to that property, whether heritable or moveable, not being a right specified in Schedule 3 to the Act as an imprescriptible right, of which the most important is any real right of ownership in land. Intellectual property rights, such as

copyright, are not mentioned in that Schedule.

4 As David Johnston, Prescription and Limitation (1999), para 7.08 points out, it is not self-evident that the phrase "any right relating to that property" in section 8(2) of the 1973 Act includes ownership of that property. But he accepts that this seems likely to be so, and it has been suggested that a claim to recover corporeal moveables is lost by the negative prescription of twenty years: see Stair Memorial Encyclopaedia , The Laws of Scotland , vol 18, Property , para 567. Section 8 does not say that incorporeal property is to be treated differently from corporeal property. But both David Johnston, para 7.08 and Professor David Walker, Prescription and Limitation of Actions 5thed, (1996), p 85, indicate that an exception can be made in the case of the ownership of intellectual property which is regulated by other statutory provisions. Although the point has yet to be tested, I think that there is much to be said for the view that section 8 of the 1973 Act should not be read as extending to the ownership of incorporeal property the duration of which has been prescribed by another enactment. It would be anomalous if the period that section 12 of the 1988 Act prescribes for the duration of copyright throughout the United Kingdom (see section 157(1) of that Act) were to be subject to a provision about prescription that applies only to Scotland and the 1988 Act itself does not mention. It is common ground however that the provisions of the Limitation Acts 1939 and 1980 do not apply in this case. So it was to the prejudicial effects of the delay, not the mere fact that Mr Fisher has delayed for so long, that the respondents had to address this part of their argument.

5 As the judgments below have shown, this was not an easy task. The respondents' main defence to the claim when the case was before the trial judge was that Mr Fisher was not entitled to any share of the musical copyright at all. Having failed in that defence and in the related defence that because of the delay there could not be a fair trial, they now seek to rely on other aspects of the case that were not clearly focussed in the pleadings or were not fully explored in evidence. There were nevertheless some grounds for holding that the delay in itself was so unconscionable that any discretionary reliefs to which Mr Fisher might be entitled should, on equitable grounds, be refused to him.

6 It seems to me however that when they were considering the question whether the judge was right to grant all three declarations the majority in the Court of Appeal were, to a large extent, influenced by what they saw as Mr Fisher's motive for bringing the claim. He had, after all, sought an injunction before the trial judge. This led Mummery LJ, having referred to his object as being to control the copyright for the future and to dictate the terms on which he was to be entitled to share in its exploitation, to conclude that Mr Fisher was not entitled to the exercise of the court's discretion to enable him to enforce his joint share in the copyright: para 85. It was for this reason that the judge's declarations that he was a joint owner in the musical copyright with a share of 40% and that the respondents' licence to exploit the work was revoked when Mr Fisher commenced these proceedings on 31 May 2005 were set aside.

7 But there is a crucial difference in principle between the exercise of an undoubted right of property and resort for its protection to discretionary remedies. In so far as Mr Fisher may seek to restrain what the other joint owner may do in the exercise of its share of the copyright by means of injunctions, he will be subject to the court's discretion. Unconscionable delay may well have a part to play in the court's decision whether or not he is entitled to such a remedy. But it would be a very strong thing, in the absence of a proprietary estoppel, to deny him the opportunity of exercising his right of property in his own share of the copyright.

8 The law of property is concerned with rights in things. The distinction which exists between the exercise of rights and the obtaining of discretionary remedies is of fundamental importance in any legal system. There is no concept in our law that is more absolute than a right of property. Where it exists, it is for the owner to exercise it as he pleases. He does not need the permission of the court, nor is it subject to the exercise of the court's discretion. The benefits that flow from intellectual property are the product of this concept. They provide an incentive to innovation and creativity. A person who has a good idea, as Mr Fisher did when he composed the well-known organ solo that did so much to make the song in its final form such a success, is entitled to protect the advantage that he has gained from this and to earn his reward. These are rights which the court must respect and which it will enforce if it is asked to do so.

9 The second and third declarations which the trial judge made were directed to the exercise of rights, not the granting of discretionary remedies. The majority in the Court of Appeal were, for understandable reasons, reluctant to offer the court's assistance to someone who had delayed

for so long in asserting his claim. But it appears that, when they decided to deny him these further declarations which were designed to give effect to the rights that flowed from his co-authorship of the work which was found on unassailable grounds to have been established by the trial judge, they overlooked this fundamental distinction. I agree with my noble and learned friend that, leaving equity on one side as one must, there were no grounds in law for setting these declarations aside.

Lord Walker of Gestingthorpe

My Lords,

10 I have had the advantage of reading in draft the opinion of my noble and learned friend, Lord Neuberger of Abbotsbury. I agree with it, and for the reasons that Lord Neuberger gives I would allow this appeal and make the order that he proposes. Because of the interest and importance of this appeal I add some brief comments of my own, but they do not detract from my concurrence in Lord Neuberger's opinion.

11 In paragraph 81 of his judgment Blackburne J referred to the need, if the requirements for proprietary estoppel are made out, for any relief granted by the court to be proportionate to the degree of detriment suffered by the party (normally the defendant) asserting the estoppel. That balancing exercise may involve giving weight to any countervailing advantages that have been received by the defendant in the meantime. The clearest English authority for this is probably Sledmore v Dalby (1996) 72 P&CR 196 , where the defendant had already enjoyed nine years of rent-free residence and any equity that he might have claimed had already been satisfied: see the observations of Roch LJ at p 204 and Hobhouse LJ at p 209. This appeal would have been an even more striking example, if the requirements for an estoppel had been made out.

12 The appellant has successfully claimed to be legally entitled to a property right, that is a share of musical copyright. The respondents have failed in their attempt to fetter (or even extinguish) that right through the doctrine of proprietary estoppel. It would be remarkable, I think, if the court were nevertheless to produce a similar result by refusing to grant declaratory relief.

13 In an important passage which I read as introductory to his reasoning on this point Mummery LJ stated ([2008] Bus LR 1123 , para 79):

> "There is, in my view, a substantial distinction to be drawn between the right to attribution of authorship and the right to title and to the control of exploitation in the future. It does not appear that the practical significance of the very different effects of the three declarations was explained to the judge or even to this court in the skeleton arguments or the oral submissions. I confess that the full implications of the different declarations did not become clear to me until writing this judgment. The case was presented primarily on the basis that Matthew Fisher was not entitled to any relief, either because a fair trial of his claims was impossible or because he was prevented by his dilatory conduct and acquiescence from claiming any relief. If that was wrong, then it seems to have been assumed that all three declarations were appropriate."

14 This passage reflects the fact that (as often happens in complex litigation) the parties' positions went through something of a process of evolution as the case progressed through the courts. Mr Purvis QC, in opening the case to your Lordships, said that his client was interested purely in future royalties (transcript, day one, page seven). This implied that what he wanted was a change in the arrangements for distribution of royalties by the Performing Rights Society and the Mechanical Copyright Protection Society, while leaving intact the structure of the existing arrangements for exploitation of the musical copyright.

15 At trial, by contrast, the appellant did seek past royalties accrued during a six-year limitation period, and also an injunction in general terms restraining copyright infringement. He failed to obtain either of these heads of relief. The judge declined to grant an injunction because (para 88) he did not detect "any intention on the defendants' part to continue to exploit the musical copyright in the Work in defiance of any interest in it which Mr Fisher is able to establish." Neither of these heads of relief was pursued on appeal. Moreover, even at trial the appellant's primary aim seems to have been simply to obtain his proper share of the stream of royalties: his skeleton argument at trial stated (para 44):

"So far as the future is concerned, the declaration will ensure that C and his heirs will receive the royalties to which they are entitled from the PRS and the MCPS. The PRS and the MCPS will amend their records accordingly, so that C will in future receive his due share of the royalties collected from the performance, broadcasting and recording of the work."

16 Looking again at para 79 of Mummery LJ's judgment against this background, and also at the fuller discussion in paras 86-88 of his judgment, I am not sure whether Mummery LJ thought that the appellant wanted to upset the existing arrangements for exploitation of the copyright, or simply thought that he ought not to have that opportunity, whether he was likely to try to take it or not. In any event, I consider that the answer lies in para 75 of Lord Neuberger's opinion: if and when the appellant seeks an injunction to restrain an alleged infringement of his copyright, his application will have to be dealt with on its merit, including the merits of any equitable defences.

17 Where there is trespass to land or goods, or a comparable invasion of intangible property rights, the court's natural response is to grant injunctive relief, and not to leave the claimant to his remedy in damages. In Shelfer v City of London Electric Lighting Co [1895] 1 Ch 287 , 322, A L Smith LJ made a much-quoted statement of principle beginning as follows:

"Many judges have stated, and I emphatically agree with them, that a person by committing a wrongful act (whether it be a public company for public purposes or a private individual) is not thereby entitled to ask the Court to sanction his doing so by purchasing his neighbour's rights, by assessing damages in that behalf, leaving his neighbour with the nuisance, or his lights dimmed, as the case may be. In such cases the well known rule is not to accede to the application, but to grant the injunction sought, for the plaintiff's legal right has been invaded, and he is prima facie entitled to an injunction."

18 But, as A L Smith LJ went on to say, there are cases in which that rule is relaxed, particularly where it would be oppressive to the defendant to grant injunctive relief. The whole passage was quoted by Sir Thomas Bingham MR in Jaggard v Sawyer [1995] 1 WLR 269 , 277-278, and his judgment, and that of Millett LJ, contain a full exposition of these principles as they now stand. Jaggard v Sawyer was concerned with the refusal of injunctive relief for breach of a restrictive covenant, an equitable right, but the same principles have been applied in respect of legal rights such as a legal easement of light, or indeed legal freehold ownership.

19 Lord Neuberger makes it clear, but I would like to emphasise again, that your Lordships are not deciding anything, or even expressing any preliminary views, as to the grant or refusal of injunctive relief in some future situation. The restoration of the second and third declarations entitles the appellant to recognition as a co-owner of the musical copyright in the work, and enables him to start enjoying his share of royalties, but it does not anticipate any question that might arise if he were to seek injunctive relief in order to control future exploitation of the copyright.

Baroness Hale of Richmond

My Lords,

20 I agree that, for the reasons given by my noble and learned friend, Lord Neuberger of Abbotsbury, supplemented by those of Lord Walker of Gestingthorpe, this appeal should be allowed and the declarations made by the trial judge restored. As one of those people who do remember the sixties, I am glad that the author of that memorable organ part has at last achieved the recognition he deserves.

21 I wish only to add a footnote, prompted by the information which we were originally given, that Matthew Fisher was aged only 20 when Procol Harum recorded "A Whiter Shade of Pale" in April 1967. These days, it is easy to forget that the age of majority was 21, until it was reduced to 18 by section 1(1) of the Family Law Reform Act 1969 as from 1 January 1970. Any member of the band, or indeed their manager, who was under the age of 21 at the relevant time was therefore an "infant" to whom the complex and confusing rules relating to infants' contracts applied (see the discussion of the then existing law in the Law Commission, Working Paper No 81, Law of

Contract, Minors' Contracts , 1982, Part II; the changes made by the Minors' Contracts Act 1987 , as a result of the Law Commission's Report, Law Com No 134, 1984, do not affect the issues under discussion here and in any event apply only to contracts made on or after 9 June 1987).

22 The policy of the law was summed up by Lord Mansfield in the leading case of Zouch, d Abbot and Hallet v Parsons (1765), 3 Burr 1794, 1801, 97 ER 1103 , 1106:

> "… miserable must the condition of minors be; excluded from the society and commerce of the world; deprived of necessaries, education, employment, and many advantages; if they could do no binding acts. Great inconvenience must arise to others, if they were bound by no act. The law, therefore, at the same time that it protects their imbecility and indiscretion from injury through their own imprudence, enables them to do binding acts, for their own benefit; and, without prejudice to themselves, for the benefit of others."

23 Hence infants have always been permitted to make binding contracts of service, apprenticeship and for their performance of services, provided that these are for their benefit. They may therefore have to accept some terms which are to their disadvantage for the sake of the overall advantage which the contract brings. The question is whether the contract, taken as a whole is to the infant's benefit. Thus in Doyle v White City Stadium Ltd [1935] 1 KB 110 , a professional boxer was held bound by the terms of his licence from the British Boxing Board of Control, which allowed him to earn his living boxing but required him to keep the rules.

24 No doubt it was for this reason that the recording contract between the manager, on behalf of Procol Harum, and Essex Music opens with the words "This contract for your personal services …" Recording companies in those days will have been alive to the possibility that at least some of the young people with whom they were contracting were under the age of 21. But of course, the more unusual or disadvantageous the terms, the less likely it would be that such a contract would be held binding upon the infants involved. This, to my mind, is an additional reason for not construing the recording contract as an assignment of the musical copyright. The recording company very sensibly kept that as a separate matter to be dealt with by separate contracts.

25 Furthermore, the effect of even a contractual assignment of copyright by a minor is, to say the least, controversial. On the one hand, there is Lord Denning's dissenting judgment in Chaplin v Leslie Frewin (Publishers) Ltd [1966] Ch 71 , 89 where he observed:

> "The law of this country for centuries has been that if anyone under the age of 21 makes, or agrees to make, a disposition of his property by a deed or document in writing, he may avoid it at any time before he comes of full age or within a reasonable time thereafter."

Lord Denning cited the decision in Zouch v Parsons (above), at 1804, 1109, where Lord Mansfield accepted the law as laid down by Perkins, the full quotation from which is as follows:

> "… all such gifts, grants or deeds made by infants, which do not take effect by delivery of his hand, are void: but all gifts, grants or deeds made by infants, by matter in deed or in writing, which do take effect by delivery of his hand, are voidable, by himself, by his heirs, and by those who have his estate."

That rule was, as Lord Denning pointed out, accepted without question by the House of Lords in Edwards v Carter [1893] AC 361 , where it was held that if the infant chose to repudiate the disposition, he must do so within a reasonable time after coming of age. It finds a place in leading textbooks today: see, for example, *Emmet and Farrand on* Title , 19th ed (looseleaf from 1986) para 12.108.

26 However, Lord Denning's view may have been affected by his view that the contract in question, although a contract for services, was not for the benefit of the infant. The majority in Chaplin v Leslie Frewin , however, took the view that, at least if copyright were effectively assigned as part of a beneficial contract to supply services, then it was binding upon the infant and could not be avoided. However, they also expressed the view that, even if the contract had been voidable, the intellectual property had been transferred and could not be recovered. On this point, the editor of Cheshire, Fifoot and Furmston's Law of Contract 15th ed, 2006, p 559 suggests that Lord Denning's view is to be preferred.

27 None of this has been argued before us (the parties perhaps having forgotten when the age of majority was changed). There is no need for us to express a view on the point. When I raised this subject during the course of the hearing, we were told that Matthew Fisher was in fact 21 at the relevant time, so the question does not arise. But in this case the express assignments of copyright in the music and words were quite separate from the recording contract. The idea that an infant might be held validly to have made an implied and gratuitous assignment of his copyright would, I think, have astonished both Lord Mansfield and Lord Denning. Had Matthew Fisher been under the age of 21, therefore, this would have been an additional reason for rejecting the respondents' enterprising argument.

Lord Mance

My Lords,

28 I have had the benefit of reading in draft the opinions of all of your Lordships. For the reasons given by my noble and learned friends, Lord Neuberger of Abbotsbury, supplemented by those of Lord Walker of Gestingthorpe, I too agree that this appeal should be allowed and the declarations made by Blackburne J restored.

Lord Neuberger of Abbotsbury

My Lords,

29 This appeal concerns the ownership of the musical copyright in the song "A Whiter Shade of Pale", which was recorded by the band Procol Harum during April 1967 and first released as a single by Decca records under licence from Essex Music Ltd ("Essex") on 12 May 1967. As Blackburne J said in his judgment at first instance, it was "one of the most successful popular songs of the late 1960s", and it is "no exaggeration to say that with the passage of time the song has achieved something approaching cult status" - [2006] EWHC 3239 Ch, paras 1 and 3.

The factual background

30 The relevant facts, as found by the judge or were common ground, are as follows. The music in its original form was composed in early 1967 by the band's lead singer and pianist, Gary Brooker, around lyrics written by the band's manager, Keith Reid. Mr Brooker then recorded a demonstration tape of himself singing the song as he had composed it, accompanying himself on the piano. He played this tape to Mr Platz, the managing director of Essex, who told him that he considered it to be "a certain hit".

31 On the following day, 7 March 1967, Mr Brooker and Mr Reid entered into a written agreement with Essex ("the assignment"), whereby they assigned to Essex "all the Copyright as defined by the Copyright Act 1956 … in the words and music of the composition 'A Whiter Shade of Pale' [and another song] … absolutely". In the assignment, Essex agreed to pay Mr Brooker and Mr Reid specified percentages (normally 50% between them) of the sheet music and mechanical royalties, and of the synchronisation, performing, broadcasting and rediffusion fees, receivable in connection with the song. Mr Brooker and Mr Reid also recorded in the assignment that they would share the payments due to them thereunder equally. Around 17 March 1967, the song was registered with the Performing Rights Society ("the PRS") and with the Mechanical Copyright Protection Society ("the MCPS"). These two societies collect, and distribute, to the persons entered in their records as the copyright owners, any royalties due in respect of works registered with them.

32 Shortly thereafter, Matthew Fisher joined the band as organist, and, together with Mr Brooker and the other members of the band (Bobby Harrison, Ray Royer, and Dave Knight), he rehearsed and added to the music of the song, so that it evolved into its final form ("the work") which the band recorded in April 1967 ("the first recording"). Crucially for present purposes, Mr Fisher composed the familiar organ solo at the beginning of the work, and the organ melody which is a counterpoint throughout most of the four minutes during which the work lasts. The recording of the work was released on 12 May 1967 as a "single" record on the Decca label, under Essex's licence, and it became an instant "hit".

33 On 16 May 1967, the five members of the band, effectively acting through Mr Reid (therein "the manager") entered into a further contract ("the recording contract") with Essex. The effect of this contract was to enable Essex to exploit any recording made by the band over the period of a

year (subject to renewal by Essex a maximum of four times). In return, Essex was to pay the members of the band a specified royalty in respect of every record of any such recording which was manufactured. The main purpose of the recording contract from the point of view of Essex was that it operated as "the consent required by section 1 of the Dramatic and Musical Performers Protection Act 1958 " - clause 3(a). Unfortunately, there are two clauses with that assignation, so I shall refer to it as clause 3(ii)(a). By the first clause 3(a) - "clause 3(i)(a)" - the band members granted to Essex "the right to manufacture... sell, lease, license or otherwise use or dispose of ... records embodying the performances to be recorded hereunder ...". Further by what I shall for consistency's sake refer to as clause 3(i)(e), the members of the band also granted to Essex "the right to incorporate in records to be made hereunder instrumentations, orchestrations and arrangements owned by the manager at the time of recording them". It has been common ground that the recording contract applies to the first recording.

34 Thereafter, over the next two years or so, apart from enjoying great acclaim in connection with the work, the band recorded other songs (with words written by Mr Reid and music composed by Mr Brooker, sometimes together with Mr Fisher), whose musical and lyrical copyrights were assigned to Essex in the same form, and on the same terms, as the assignment.

35 In his evidence, Mr Fisher said that, during 1967, he had raised the question of his having a share in the rights in respect of the music with Mr Brooker and Mr Reid, but had been rebuffed or ignored by them. He explained that he had not wanted to push his claim as he feared that, if he did so, he would be asked to "say goodbye to a career in ... a number one pop group". In 1969, however, Mr Fisher did indeed leave the band, which by then had accrued certain debts. A relatively informal agreement was reached whereby the remaining members agreed to release (or, more accurately, I think, to indemnify) Mr Fisher from any liability in respect of such debts in return for his waiving any right to certain specified royalties (not including any copyright royalties in respect of the work).

36 Despite leaving the band, Mr Fisher was invited to play with them at various functions from time to time between 1969 and 2003. On a couple of occasions during that period, once in 1971 and once in 1991, Mr Fisher contended that he was entitled to certain royalties which he was not receiving, but he never suggested that he was entitled to any money in respect of the exploitation of the work.

37 In or about 1993, Essex's rights under the assignment and the recording contract were purportedly assigned to Onward Music Ltd ("Onward"), and Onward was registered with the PRS and MCPS as the owner of the copyright in the work. Meanwhile, the first recording was proving very successful, resulting in substantial royalties, which were collected by the PRS and MCPS and distributed to Essex (or their successors), as they were registered with the societies as owners of the copyright, and Mr Brooker and Mr Reid were then paid their shares under the terms of the assignment.

38 Quite apart from the first recording, the work has been extraordinarily successful over the 38 years since it was first released. It has been the subject of many articles and interviews, and has a dedicated following, as can be seen from the number of websites devoted to the work and the band. There are over 770 versions of the work performed by other groups, and themes of the work (especially the introductory bars) are available, and popular, as mobile telephone ring tones.

39 During April and May 2005, Mr Fisher, through his solicitors wrote to Essex and Mr Brooker (together "the respondents") notifying them of his claim to a share of the musical copyright in the work, explaining the grounds for his claim, threatening proceedings if his claim was not acknowledged, and putting forward terms of settlement. Those terms were rejected; accordingly, Mr Fisher began proceedings on 31 May 2005, and they came before Blackburne J, who gave a judgment which was largely favourable to Mr Fisher - [2005] EWHC 3239 Ch. However, on appeal, the respondents substantially succeeded: Mummery LJ and Sir Paul Kennedy set aside two of the three declarations made at first instance, although David Richards J dissented - [2008] Bus LR 1123 .

The Issues before the judge and the Court of Appeal

40 The judge had to decide a number of issues, only some of which are now raised in your Lordships' House. First, there was the question whether a fair trial was possible, bearing in mind

the passage of time between the composition of the work and the issue of Mr Fisher's claim. Although the judge rightly described Mr Fisher's silence about his claim between 1967 and 2004 as "remarkable" and "quite extraordinary", he concluded that a fair trial was possible - [2006] EWHC 3239 Ch, paras 16 and 17, and 24. This conclusion was strongly challenged by the respondents on appeal, but the Court of Appeal rightly upheld the judge on this point - [2008] Bus LR 1123 , para 43. There is no appeal on this point by the respondents.

41 Secondly, the judge had to determine whether, and if so to what extent, Mr Fisher could, in principle, claim any share of the musical copyright in the work. He decided that "Mr Fisher's instrumental introduction (i.e the organ solo ... as repeated) is sufficiently different from what Mr Brooker had composed on the piano to qualify in law, and by quite a wide margin, as an original contribution to the work" - [2006] EWHC 3239 Ch, para 42. Consequently, he held that "Mr Fisher qualifies to be regarded as a joint author of the work" - ibid. After considering various arguments raised by the respondents, the judge concluded that "Mr Fisher's interest in the work should be reflected by according to him a 40% share in the musical copyright" - ibid, para 98. Rightly, the Court of Appeal had little difficulty in dismissing the respondents' appeal on this issue - [2008] Bus LR 1123 , para 44. The respondents do not seek to appeal further on this issue.

42 The third issue was whether, nonetheless, Mr Fisher had no right to claim a share of the musical copyright owing to the circumstances in which he made his contribution to the work. In effect, the respondents argued that, given that the song in its original form had been recorded, and the musical copyright in it had been assigned to Essex, in March 1967, Mr Fisher impliedly assigned to Essex any interest he acquired in the musical copyright in the work. The judge rejected that argument - [2006] EWHC 3239 Ch, para 63. However, the Court of Appeal, or at least the majority, left the point open - [2008] Bus LR 1123 , para 100. This "implied assignment" argument is raised by the respondents by way of cross-appeal.

43 The fourth issue was whether Mr Fisher had lost his right to maintain his claim to an interest in the musical copyright by virtue of the recording contract. The judge held that the agreement "did not purport to take from Mr Fisher any copyright interest he had in the musical composition", and therefore rejected the argument - [2006] EWHC 3239 Ch, para 66. The Court of Appeal, or at least the majority, left the point open - [2008] Bus LR 1123 , para 111. The respondents maintain their case in this House on this issue by way of cross-appeal.

44 The fifth issue was whether Mr Fisher had lost his interest in the copyright as a result of estoppel, laches or acquiescence. The respondents failed on this issue before the judge - [2006] EWCA Civ 3239 , para 82. The Court of Appeal accepted that the judge was entitled to come to this conclusion, and that they could not interfere - [2008] Bus LR 1123 , paras 67 (Mummery LJ, with whom Sir Paul Kennedy agreed) and 117 (David Richards J). On this "laches, estoppel or acquiescence" issue, the respondents maintain their case by cross-appealing.

45 The sixth issue at first instance was whether Mr Fisher could claim his share of the monies paid out by the PRS and the MCPS in respect of the work during the six years before the issue of proceedings (it being rightly accepted by Mr Fisher that any claim going further back would be time-barred). The monies collected by the societies had been paid to Essex, or, since 1993, Onward, as the copyright owner registered with the societies, and the appropriate share in accordance with the assignment had then been paid to Mr Reid and Mr Brooker. The judge rejected this claim, on the basis that "for so long as Mr Fisher chose not to make ... his claim [and] allowed the societies to account to the [respondents], ... he must be taken to have gratuitously licensed the exploitation of his copyright" - [2006] EWHC 3239 Ch, para 94. The judge went on to find that this implied licence was revoked when the letter before action was sent to the respondents in May 2005 - ibid. There was no appeal to the Court of Appeal by Mr Fisher on this finding.

46 The final matter to be considered by Blackburne J was the nature of the relief to be accorded to Mr Fisher. The judge refused an injunction restraining Essex from exploiting the musical copyright in the work, as there was no evidence of the respondents seeking to do so "in defiance of any interest in it which Mr Fisher is able to establish" - [2006] EWHC 3239 Ch, para 88. There was no appeal by Mr Fisher on this issue.

47 However, the judge granted declarations in these terms:

"1. [Mr Fisher] is a co-author of ... 'A Whiter Shade of Pale' as recorded by ... Procol

Harum ('the work') and released as a single on 12 May 1967.

2. [Mr] Fisher is a joint owner in the musical copyright in the work, with a share of 40%.

3. The [respondents'] licence to exploit the work was revoked on 31 May 2005".

Allowing the respondents' appeal, the majority of the Court of Appeal held that it was unconscionable, in all the circumstances, for Mr Fisher to have revoked the implied licence, and that "the defences of acquiescence and laches operated to disentitle [Mr] Fisher from the exercise of the court's discretion to grant the second and third declarations" - [2008] Bus LR 1123 , para 85. Accordingly, they held that the licence continued and the second and third declarations should be set aside - ibid, para 89. David Richards J dissented - ibid, para 140. Mr Fisher's appeal against the setting aside of the second and third declarations raises a point which I regard as an aspect of the laches, estoppel, and acquiescence issue.

48 Accordingly, there are three matters to be considered, namely the implied assignment issue, the recording contract issue, and the laches, estoppel and acquiescence issue. In relation to the first two of these matters, it is right to mention that there was some discussion whether the rights granted to Essex under the assignment or the recording contract were assignable, at least without the consent of the other parties to the agreement. This point, which is of particular apparent force in the case of the recording contract (given that, as pointed out by my noble and learned friend, Baroness Hale of Richmond, it describes itself as concerned with "personal services"), was not decided by Blackburne J or by the Court of Appeal and was only lightly touched on in argument in this House. Although it would be desirable to resolve all issues between the two parties, I do not consider that this is one which we can properly determine at this stage. For present purposes I am prepared to proceed on the assumption that Onward effectively stands in the shoes of Essex.

Was there an implied assignment?

49 The respondents contend that the circumstances in which the work came into existence are consistent only with the copyright in the work becoming vested solely in Essex, and, in particular, with Mr Fisher having impliedly assigned his interest in the musical copyright to Essex. The essence of this argument is that Essex had taken an absolute assignment of the musical (and lyrical) copyright in the song in its original form, and was intending, and was intended by the members of the band, to exploit the song as developed for the first recording and released in May 1967, i.e. as the work. Accordingly, runs the argument, it must have been intended by Essex and by all members of the band, including Mr Fisher, that Essex would be the sole owner of the copyright in the work.

50 This argument is based on implication, which is normally invoked in order to give rise to an unexpressed term into an existing contract. However, it is clear, as a matter of principle, commercial reality, and indeed authority, that an unexpressed contract can arise by way of implication. In order to succeed in such an argument, it is, of course, necessary for the well established requirements for implication to be satisfied. Thus, in this case, the respondents have to show that, at the time of the alleged assignment, (a) it would have been obvious to Mr Fisher (as well as Essex) that his interest in the musical copyright was being, or had to be, assigned to Essex, or, which may amount to the same thing, (b) the commercial relationship between the parties could not sensibly have functioned without such an assignment.

51 In my judgment, this argument faces a number of insurmountable problems. First, it assumes that Mr Fisher knew that the song in its original form had been recorded and that the copyright had been assigned to Essex. He may have known these facts as at the time the work was recorded in April 1967 or when it was released in May 1967, but he did not say that he did and it was not put to him that he did. In this connection, it is relevant to mention that he had not, by that time, effected any assignment to Essex of copyright in relation to other musical works, so it could not be said that he must have been aware of Essex's usual practice. Where a party contends for an implied term or an implied contract, it is up to that person to establish the relevant factual foundation for his case. Indeed, the fact that these points were not put to Mr Fisher is scarcely surprising, as the contention was not pleaded, although it was advanced before the judge in argument, albeit in somewhat different terms from the way it is now put.

52 Secondly, the fact that the recording contract was only entered into on 16 May 1967, about a

month after the work was first recorded, and four days after the release of the recording, undermines the notion that, before that date, Mr Fisher had impliedly assigned his interest in the musical copyright to Essex. The date of the recording contract shows that, as one would have expected, the members of the band were content to leave it to Essex, an experienced record and publishing company, to produce the relevant documentation for them to execute as and when appropriate. That is scarcely consistent with the alleged implied assignment having taken place before 16 May 1967. The unattractiveness of the respondents' argument is reinforced by the fact, identified by Baroness Hale, that one is here concerned with five musicians, all of whom were in their early twenties, and a highly experienced music recording and publishing company, on whom they were no doubt relying.

53 Thirdly, having heard the evidence, the judge found that the question of what was to be done in relation to any interest in the musical copyright in the work as a result of additions to the original song "was left at large" - [2006] EWHC 3239 Ch, para 63. The question whether there was an implied contract is one of inference rather than primary fact, but it is a question which, at least in this case, turned to a significant extent on the precise factual circumstances, which were very much for the trial judge to evaluate. It is also true that those circumstances had arisen nearly 40 years earlier, and some of the important witnesses (in particular the relevant employees of Essex, including Mr Platz) were dead, but there was a significant amount of relevant oral evidence. In my judgment, there would have been no warrant for an appellate tribunal interfering with the clear and carefully considered conclusion reached by the judge on this issue.

54 Finally, there is the point that, even if there was some sort of implied contract, it is very unlikely to have been an outright free assignment of Mr Fisher's interest in the musical copyright. First, such an arrangement would have been more than was necessary to give business efficacy: all that would have been needed was a licence by Mr Fisher, as someone with a share of the copyright in the work, permitting Essex to exploit the first recording. Secondly, particularly in the light of the terms of the assignment, it would very probably have been appropriate to include provision for a reasonable payment, or quantum meruit, in respect of any implied assignment or licence. In the light of the other problems this argument faces, it is unnecessary and inappropriate to expand on this aspect.

The effect of the recording contract

55 There is no doubt that one of the main purposes of the recording contract was to ensure that Essex was able to exploit the first recording free from any rights which band members had in the sound recording itself - i.e. free the publishing right, as it is often called: hence clause 3(ii)(a). However, the more difficult question concerns the effect of clause 3(i)(e), when read together with clause 3(i)(a). For the respondents, Mr Baldwin QC, who appears with Ms Bowhill, (neither of whom appeared at first instance), places considerable reliance on paras (a) and (e) of clause 3(i). At one point, he appeared to go so far as to say that the effect of those provisions was to assign to Essex any copyright interests in the work owned by any member of the band.

56 The judge rejected this argument, on the basis that the recording contract was not concerned with copyright in the work - [2006] EWHC 3239 Ch, para 66. As he put it, the contract "merely gave to [Essex] the right to exploit the [April 1967] recording" and any other recording of the work played during the currency of the agreement.

57 In my view, the judge was right to reject the contention that, by executing the recording contract, Mr Fisher effectively assigned his share of the musical copyright in the work to Essex. Indeed, in the Court of Appeal, Mr Baldwin disclaimed any reliance on such a contention - [2008] Bus LR 1123 , para 107. However, I would be inclined to accept (indeed Mr Purvis QC and Mr Cuddigan, who appeared for Mr Fisher did not seem strongly to resist) the contention more strongly advanced by Mr Baldwin that clause 3(i)(a) and (e) operated as a licence to Essex from Mr Fisher, in his capacity as part owner of the musical copyright in the work, to exploit the first recording.

58 If this were not so, a member of the band with a copyright interest in the work would have been able to enjoin Essex from exercising its apparently unfettered rights under clause 3(i)(a), which seems inconsistent with the purpose of the recording contract. Further, it is hard to resist the contention that clause 3(i)(e) has precisely the effect which is contended on behalf of the respondents. Commercial sense suggests that Essex could well have been concerned to ensure that, although they had the benefit of the assignment from two of the five members of the band,

other members may have contributed to the work as it had been developed in the mean time and acquired intellectual property rights which might interfere with the unimpeded exercise of the rights granted by the recording contract. The notion that clause 3(i)(e) is concerned with such rights is supported by the use of the word "owned", as pointed out by my noble and learned friend, Lord Walker of Gestingthorpe.

59 On this basis, the terms of the recording contract may have the effect of depriving Mr Fisher of any royalties he might otherwise seek as a result of the exploitation of the work, in so far as it is through the medium of the first recording. However, even if that is right, it in no way impinges on the issue before your Lordships' House, namely whether the three declarations granted by the judge should be affirmed.

Laches, estoppel, and acquiescence

Preliminary observations

60 There are a few preliminary points in relation to the equitable arguments raised by the respondents and based on laches, estoppel, and acquiescence. First, a number of such arguments, which were raised and rejected at first instance, have not been raised before your Lordships. Save for the purpose of referring to them in connection with the points which have been pursued in this House, it is inappropriate to discuss them further.

61 Secondly, the equitable arguments raised by the respondents arise at three different stages, and, as my noble and learned friend, Lord Hope of Craighead, pointed out, there has been a tendency to conflate these stages, which has led to confusion. Having said that, it is only fair to add that the subsequent passage of time may, at least in some circumstances, reinforce (or even diminish) the unconscionability of a party raising a claim which he could have raised at an earlier stage. In this case, the three different stages are (i) during 1967, around the time the first recording was made and released; (ii) in 1969, when Mr Fisher left the band; and (iii) in 2005, when the current proceedings were started.

62 Thirdly, laches and estoppel are well established equitable doctrines. However, at least in a case such as this, I am not convinced that acquiescence adds anything to estoppel and laches. The classic example of proprietary estoppel, standing by whilst one's neighbour builds on one's land believing it to be his property, can be characterised as acquiescence - see per Oliver J in Taylor Fashions Ltd v Liverpool Victoria Trustees Ltd (Note) [1982] QB 133 , 151. Similarly, laches, failing to raise or enforce an equitable right for a long period, can be characterised as acquiescence.

63 Fourthly, in so far as the respondents' argument is put on the basis of estoppel, they would have to establish that it would be in some way unconscionable for Mr Fisher now to insist on his share of the musical copyright in the work being recognised. As Robert Walker LJ said in Gillett v Holt [2001] Ch 210 , 225D, "the fundamental principle that equity is concerned to prevent unconscionable conduct permeates all the elements of the doctrine" of estoppel. Given that their case at each of the three stages is based on the fact that Mr Fisher did not raise his entitlement to such a share, one would expect the respondents to succeed in estoppel only if they could show that they reasonably relied on his having no such claim, that they acted on that reliance, and that it would be unfairly to their detriment if he was now permitted to raise or to enforce such a claim. As was also said in Gillett [2001] Ch 210 , 232D, the "overwhelming weight of authority shows that detriment is required" although the "requirement must be approached as part of a broad inquiry" into unconscionability.

64 Fifthly, laches is an equitable doctrine, under which delay can bar a claim to equitable relief. In the Court of Appeal, Mummery LJ said that there was "no requirement of detrimental reliance for the application of acquiescence or laches" - [2008] EWCA Civ 287 , para 85. Although I would not suggest that it is an immutable requirement, some sort of detrimental reliance is usually an essential ingredient of laches, in my opinion. In Lindsay Petroleum Co v Hurd (1874) LR 5 PC 221 , 239, the Lord Chancellor, Lord Selborne, giving the opinion of the Board, said that laches applied where "it would be practically unjust to give a remedy", and that, in every case where a defence "is founded upon mere delay … the validity of that defence must be tried upon principles substantially equitable." He went on to state that what had to be considered were "the length of the delay and the nature of the acts done during the interval, which might affect either party, and

cause a balance of justice or injustice in taking the one course or the other, so far as relates to the remedy."

Estoppel based on Mr Fisher's silence in 1967

65 The respondents rely on the fact that, during 1967, Mr Fisher stood by and said nothing to Essex, and very little to Mr Brooker or Mr Reid, about his having a claim to a share of the musical copyright in the work, so that the respondents, and presumably Mr Reid, proceeded on the assumption that he had, or at any rate was making, no such claim. In particular, Essex spent money and effort in promoting and exploiting the work, on the assumption that the terms of the assignment reflected the copyright ownership in the work and the right to royalties thereunder. The respondents now argue that, had Mr Fisher raised his claim in April or May 1967, he would have been required to assign any share he had in the musical copyright in the work to Essex. Further, by waiting until the work became a great popular success, he has much greater bargaining power as a result of staying silent.

66 There are a number of problems with this argument. First, it does not reflect the respondents' re-re-amended defence. It was there pleaded that, if Mr Fisher had raised a claim in 1967 to a share in the musical copyright, the song would have been recorded and released without his contribution and/or he would have been expelled for the band. It was not pleaded that, had Mr Fisher raised such a claim, he would have assigned his share in the musical copyright to Essex.

67 Secondly, and no doubt as a result of this, there was no investigation before the judge as to whether there would have been such an assignment, what its likely terms would have been, or its likely financial consequences for the two respondents or Mr Reid, let alone as to whether they would have acted differently from how they did, over the ensuing years if there had been such an assignment, and how they would be prejudiced as a result of the point being raised only in 2005. Save in the most unusual case (and this is not such a case), it is inappropriate for an argument of this sort to be raised by a defendant for the first time on appeal, and impossible for the argument to succeed on appeal. The necessary factual investigation and findings will not have been made by the judge, and the claimant will not have been given an appropriate opportunity to investigate the relevant facts before and during the trial.

68 Thirdly, it seems to me likely that, if Mr Fisher had raised the issue in 1967, and had consequently assigned his copyright share to Essex, he would have received some share of the royalties. After all, Mr Brooker received some 25% of the royalties on the work for composing the original music, and Mr Fisher's subsequent contribution was significant, and, especially the introductory eight bars, an important factor in the work's success. In those circumstances, the respondents' estoppel argument would have had to take into account that, by delaying his claim for nearly forty years, Mr Fisher appears to have lost a great deal of money, which has been received by the respondents.

69 This was a point which the judge well appreciated. At [2006] EWHC 3239 Ch, para 81, he said that "it would... be a wholly extravagant and unjust result to deprive Mr Fisher for the [future] of his interest in the work's musical copyright on the basis of the estoppels that have been pleaded, ... when for almost 40 years the [respondents] have enjoyed the fruits of that copyright interest without the need to account for any part of them to Mr Fisher". That assessment (which exemplifies how the passage of time can have an effect on arguments relating to what happened in 1967) is self-evidently a conclusion with which an appellate court should interfere only if satisfied that it was plainly wrong or based on a mistaken understanding of established facts (which has not been demonstrated here).

70 The respondents contend that this assessment was arrived at in relation to estoppel arguments rather different from that now advanced by the respondents. Apart for the inherent unattractiveness of such a contention being raised by the respondents, it seems to me that the assessment is just as applicable to the estoppel argument advanced in this House as to those raised before Blackburne J. Mr Baldwin also points out that the judge did not consider the position of Essex and Mr Brooker separately, and suggests that it was only Mr Brooker, and not Essex, who would have benefited in the way described by the judge. That was not a point which appears to have been raised on the pleadings or in evidence or argument at first instance, and it is not right to entertain it on appeal. Its force depends on the terms upon which Mr Fisher would have assigned his share of the musical copyright, and what Mr Brooker and Essex (and Mr Reid) would have agreed in relation to their rights under the Assignment, all of which is pure

speculation at this stage.

Estoppel based on the events in 1969

71 The respondents argue that Mr Fisher's failure to raise his claim to a share of the musical copyright during the negotiations leading to the financial agreement when he left the band in 1969 deprive him of the right to raise it subsequently. It is well-nigh impossible to see how Essex or Onward could rely on these negotiations, as they were not involved in them in any way. Mr Brooker was a party to the agreement, but it is hard to see how it can give rise to any estoppel which assists him in these proceedings. No mention was made of the possibility or existence of any musical copyright interest which Mr Fisher might have had in the work, but that seems to me to add nothing to the point that Mr Fisher did not maintain his claim till 2005. It is not as if the agreement reached in 1969 was stated or implied to be in full and final settlement of all accrued rights which Mr Fisher had. I accept that the fact that the claim was not raised in 1969 could, in principle, have been relied on to cast doubt on the value of the contribution Mr Fisher made to the work, and that it would have assisted any argument the respondents had as to the reasonableness of any belief which they may have had that Mr Fisher had no such claim. Those might have been good arguments at first instance, but I cannot see how it takes matters any further now, in the light of the facts found by the judge.

The Court of Appeal's reasoning

72 As I have mentioned, the Court of Appeal upheld the judge's conclusion that the judge was entitled to reject the respondents' case on estoppel, but the majority went on to conclude that Mr Fisher was nonetheless not entitled to determine the licence which the judge found that he had impliedly granted. Mummery LJ's careful analysis, at [2008] Bus LR 1123 , paras 81 to 90, for reaching this conclusion and for setting aside the second and third declarations made by Blackburne J, seems to me to be encapsulated in the following two propositions. First, since May 1967, Essex, Onward and Mr Brooker had, to Mr Fisher's knowledge, continued "exploitation of the work on the basis that they owned all the copyright in it", and "it would be unconscionable for him [now], with a view to enforcing his property right by final injunction, to assert a joint share in the copyright and to terminate the implied licence under which he accepts the [respondents] have acted for very many years" (para 87). Secondly, Mr Fisher's delay in bringing his claim means that "he could dictate his terms and put the [respondents] in a weaker bargaining position than they would have been in, had he made his claim in, say, 1967 or 1969" (para 88).

73 As to the first of those reasons, it seems to me that, save in a very unusual case, it would be inconsistent to conclude that a claimant was not estopped from asserting his copyright interest, but then to refuse, on equitable grounds, to declare that the right existed. It is possible that there may be cases where such a course could be appropriate, but it would require wholly exceptional facts. As my noble and learned friend, Lord Mance said, if, as the Court of Appeal accepted, Mr Fisher originally had 40% of the musical copyright in the work and is not estopped from asserting it, then it is hard to see how he could be prevented from bringing proceedings simply for financial compensation or injunctive relief on the ground of copyright infringement. The refusal to grant him declaratory relief because he might seek an injunction on the back of it therefore seems to be questionable as a matter of principle.

74 In the present case, the majority of the Court of Appeal thought it appropriate to take such a course primarily because of the apparent inequity of Mr Fisher being able to seek an injunction to enforce his rights as the holder of an interest in the musical copyright in the work. Quite apart from the point made by Lord Mance, this point, as Mr Purvis argues, involves the tail wagging the dog. If the declarations set aside by the Court of Appeal are reinstated, then, were Mr Fisher subsequently to apply for injunctive relief to prevent unauthorised use of the work, such an application would be dealt with on its merits. If the court was satisfied that it would be oppressive to grant an injunction in the particular circumstances, for instance because of prejudicial delay, it would refuse an injunction to restrain the infringement, and leave Mr Fisher to his remedy in damages: see Shaw v Applegate [1977] 1 WLR 970 .

75 Mr Purvis contends that Mr Fisher was not primarily interested in obtaining injunctive relief, but was more concerned to establish his contribution to the work and to share in the future royalties. That may well be right, but he did seek an injunction before Blackburne J and there would be nothing to stop him seeking an injunction if the declarations set aside by the Court of appeal were

reinstated. However, the essential point is that, if and when Mr Fisher seeks an injunction to restrain an alleged infringement of his copyright, it should be dealt with on its merits.

76 Further, the decision of the majority of the Court of Appeal deprived Mr Fisher of the ability not only to seek injunctive relief, but also to claim any royalties in respect of the exploitation of the work, of which he owned 40% of the musical copyright. (That must follow from the conclusion that he could not determine the implied licence). It is hard to see how that could be right, simply on the basis that it would be inappropriate to grant him injunctive relief, given that Mr Fisher was not estopped from asserting his 40% interest in the musical copyright in the work.

77 As for the change in the bargaining position of the parties between 1967 and 2005, that was neither pleaded nor argued before the Judge. In any event, there was no evidence that Essex or the respondents would have acted any differently from the way in which they did if Mr Fisher had pressed his claim in 1967 or in the ensuing few years. Further, there is also the judge's finding at [2006] EWHC 3239 Ch, para 81, to which I have also referred, that Mr Fisher's very long delay in asserting his claim has been of considerable financial benefit to the respondents, effectively outweighing any disadvantage to them resulting from the delay.

The passage of time

78 As Lord Walker said in argument, the basic problem for the respondents is that there is no English law statutory equivalent in the field of intellectual property to the doctrine of adverse possession in relation to real property (although the Land Registration Act 2002 has made considerable inroads into that doctrine). Indeed, as Lord Hope mentioned, Mr Fisher would face considerable difficulties if he sought to maintain his claim in Scotland on the present facts, in the light of sections 7 and 8 of the Prescription and Limitation (Scotland) Act 1973 . Be that as it may, the position in this jurisdiction is that the mere passage of time cannot of itself undermine claims such as those raised by Mr Fisher in the current proceedings. The respondents therefore rely on laches.

79 The argument based on laches faces two problems. The first is that, as pointed out by David Richards J, laches only can bar equitable relief, and a declaration as to the existence of a long term property right, recognised as such by statute, is not equitable relief. It is arguable that a declaration should be refused on the ground of laches if it was sought solely for the purpose of seeking an injunction or other purely equitable relief. However, as already mentioned, that argument does not apply in this case. Secondly, in order to defeat Mr Fisher's claims on the ground of laches, the respondents must demonstrate some "acts" during the course of the delay period which result in "a balance of justice" justifying the refusal of the relief to which Mr Fisher would otherwise be entitled. For reasons already discussed, the respondents are unable to do that. They cannot show any prejudice resulting from the delay, and, even if they could have done so, they have no answer to the judge's finding at [2006] EWHC 3239 Ch, para 81, that the benefit they obtained from the delay would outweigh any such prejudice.

Conclusion

80 In these circumstances, essentially for the reasons given at first instance by Blackburne J and in the Court of Appeal by David Richards J, I would reject all the respondents' arguments based on equitable principles.

Disposal

81 It follows from this that I would allow Mr Fisher's appeal, dismiss the respondents' cross-appeal, and restore the two declarations set aside by the Court of Appeal save that the third declaration may require to be amended to keep open the issue whether Essex's rights under the recording contract have been validly assigned to Onward. I understand that your Lordships and Ladyship are of the same view, and accordingly I would suggest that the parties have 14 days to make submissions in writing as to the order that this House should make in relation to the costs in your Lordships' House and below.

The following questions relate to the law reports reproduced above for the case of *Fisher v Brooker*. When noting your answers to the questions, you should include reference(s) to the appropriate points in the judgment from which you have drawn your information.

Before embarking upon the questions below, use the internet to find the lyrics of the song "A Whiter Shade of Pale", which forms the centerpiece of these proceedings. You may also wish to search for contemporaneous video clips of the group "Procol Harum" performing the song.

[NB. On U-Tube, there are three video clips of this work being performed. The oldest, which is the original promotional video, is in colour, and evinces a sense of 1967 "style"; the second, in black and white, is a performance for the BBC on "Top of the Pops"; and the third is a solo rendition from a recent "revival" tour.]

Section A

1. What issues were before the House of Lords?
2. Were these the same issues as had been before the Court of Appeal and the High Court?
3. What declarations were made by the judge at first instance?
4. Why was the question of whether Mr Fisher was an infant in legal terms significant?
5. What reason had been given for suggesting that a fair trial was not possible in this case?
6. What was the effect of the House of Lords decision?

Section B

7. Has *Fisher v Brooker* been cited in any subsequent case?
8. Write a short statement of the ratio in *Fisher v Brooker*.
9. Three of the judges in *Fisher v Brooker* stated they agreed with the reasons put forward by Lord Neuberger, supplemented by those of Lord Walker. What significant extra arguments did Lord Walker put forward?
10. Baroness Hale looked at the position of contracts that had been made by an infant. Why do you think she thought it was significant that the point had not been argued by counsel before them?

Legal Reasoning in Judgements

THE HIERARCHY OF PRECEDENT

As we noted in Chapter 1 there is a hierarchy of courts with respect to precedents. Judgements of the Supreme Court are binding on all courts below it. However since 1966, when the then House of Lords issued a practice statement, judgements of the Supreme Court are not binding on itself. The Supreme Court will normally follow its own previous judgements in order to ensure consistency and predictability in the operation of the legal system but it is not legally obliged to do so. However, it may be possible to persuade the court that social circumstances have changed so that what it previously held to be the law is no longer good law. Equally it may be possible to persuade the court that its previous judgement was simply badly reasoned.

> 6.1

Judgements of the Court of Appeal, the court below the Supreme Court, are not binding on the Supreme Court. They are binding on all courts below the Court of Appeal. The Court of Appeal is said to normally be bound by its own previous decisions but there are a number of exceptions to this general rule. In the past several judges in the Court of Appeal have argued that the Court of Appeal should not be bound by its own previous decisions. They have suggested that the reasons for allowing the House of Lords to depart from its own previous decisions are equally valid when applied to the Court of Appeal. In addition to this in practice in many areas of law people cannot afford to take their cases to the Supreme Court; requiring the Court of Appeal to follow its own previous decisions therefore means that law cannot develop quickly enough in the light of changing social circumstances. Nevertheless, notwithstanding these arguments, the rule that the Court of Appeal is normally bound by its own previous decisions remains in place.

The court below the Court of Appeal is the High Court. Decisions of the High Court do not bind the Court of Appeal or the Supreme Court. They do bind all courts below the High Court. Decisions of the High Court, however, do not bind the High Court itself.

None of the courts below the High Court create precedents. Whilst their decisions are binding on the parties to the case they do not create rules of law that are binding on the courts in new cases.

RATIO AND OBITER

Even when a previous case is binding within the hierarchy of the courts, different parts of the judgment have to be treated in different ways. Lawyers distinguish two parts of a judgment: (a) the *ratio decidendi* and (b) that which is *obiter dicta* (*obiter dictum* in the singular). These two

> 6.2

	Importance in Precedence
Supreme Court (formerly House of Lords)	Binds courts below but not itself
Court of Appeal	Binds courts below and normally binds itself
High Court	Binds courts below but not itself
Crown Court	Binds no-one
County Court	Binds no-one

terms, ratio decidendi and obiter dicta, are commonly shortened to *ratio* and *obiter*. Put most simply, the ratio in a judgement is that part of reasoning in the judgment which is necessary in order to reach the conclusion that the judge arrived at. It is this that is *binding* on other courts in the hierarchy. Obiter dicta is a term that describes the remainder of the judgment. Examples of things that will usually be obiter dictum include reflections in a judgement on the historical development of a particular area of law or consideration of what decision the court would have made if the facts of the case had been different. Remarks in a judgement that are obiter are not binding on future courts. Thus, for example, in principle a magistrates' court could choose not to follow parts of a judgement from the Supreme Court that were merely obiter dicta, even though the Supreme Court is higher in the hierarchy of courts. However things that are obiter dicta in a judgement cannot simply be ignored; they are said to be *persuasive*. In the absence of a binding ratio the court may be influenced by obiter, particularly if that obiter is something that was said in a judgement in one of the higher courts within the legal system such as the Supreme Court or the Court of Appeal.

The basic distinction between ratio and obiter is clear enough. Three things are, however, more difficult. The first is deciding what the ratio of any particular case in fact is. The second is understanding exactly what is meant by saying that obiter is persuasive. The third is deciding to what degree, if at all, the judges actually follow the rules about ratio and obiter when they are arriving out their judgements. All these matters are areas of considerable controversy.

Judges do not, in their own judgements, say which part of the judgement is ratio and which part is obiter. The reader has to decide what the ratio is for themselves. However the decision is not simply a subjective one. What *you* are trying to do is to predict what future *courts* will say the ratio of a past case is. If you can do this then, you can predict what the courts will think the case tells them to do. In turn if you can do this you can you have more chance of saying what judgements future courts will produce. Because this is what you are trying to do it does not matter what you think the ratio is. If your view differs from that of the courts you will not know what the courts are going to do. You need to know what the courts will think. Equally, however, you do not know which judge will be deciding a case in the future. Thus what you are trying to do is to predict what an unknown judge in the future decides is the ratio of a past case. If you are to do this then it would seem that there have to be rules for determining the ratio that both you and the judge follow. If you use the same rules as the judge, and if you both use them correctly, you will arrive at the same answer.

Whilst there is general agreement between many academics and judges about the broad nature of the rules that surround the notions of ratio and obiter there is much disagreement about the detail. One starting point, however, is the observation that legal reasoning in the English courts is usually pragmatic in its nature. This means that the courts do not start with some general statement of legal principle but, instead, tend to begin with the facts of the case before them and then try to say what legal rules apply to those facts. Of course not all the facts in a case are important. The fact that the contract was made on a Friday will not usually matter. Whether or not somebody who is alleged to have conducted an assault was wearing a blue tracksuit or a red one might matter in terms of identifying the culprit but it will not affect how legal rules are applied. Legal reasoning thus begins with the facts of the case but it begins only with what some people have called the *material* facts of the case. These facts are, very roughly, the facts that central to the law in the case. The question then is how do we determine what are the material facts of a case. What rules help us decide?

The facts of the case are the facts stated in, or sometimes to be implied from, the judgement. It does not matter if the judge is plainly mistaken about those facts. If a judge makes a mistake about the facts of a case that might mean that the case will be taken to a higher appellate court. However, for the purpose of determining the legal rules that flow from the judgement, the facts are as the judge states them. If the judge says that a fact is material than it is so. Judges rarely do this. They usually talk about the facts in the case in their judgements but they often include many that are not material. There are certain presumptions about which are and which are not material facts. Facts about where something happened, when it happened and who it happened to, for example, are rarely material facts. However, the rules run out when it comes to deciding exactly what is a material fact and what is not. A material fact is a fact that is central to the reasoning the case, central to the line of argument that leads to the conclusion that the judge reached, but it is difficult to be more precise than that. The ratio is then the rule that arises as the result of the judge's reasoning about these material facts.

A ratio in a previous case only binds a court if it is addressing the same legal issue that arises in the new case. The fact that the Supreme Court has decided something about the law of murder will not usually matter if the current case before the court, whichever court it is, is about theft. In order to decide whether there is a binding precedent for a new case before the court it is necessary first to decide what the ratio of a previous case is and then to decide whether or not the previous case and the present case are sufficiently analogous. In deciding this, the notion of material facts is again said to be useful. Are the material facts in the two cases the same or similar? If so there will be a binding precedent. Deciding whether or not a previous case is sufficiently analogous with a new one so as to make a binding precedent is, in itself, a difficult task. Judges will sometimes draw a distinction, sometimes a very fine distinction, between two apparently similar cases. They are then said to *distinguish* the previous case.

All parts of a judgement need to be read because even dicta, although not binding, are persuasive. However, what persuasive means in this context is not entirely clear. "Persuasive" in ordinary conversation means something like "provides good reasons". However persuasive in the context of legal reasoning seems to mean something slightly different. The higher the court the dicta comes from the more persuasive it is taken to be. This could be for several reasons. First higher courts are appellate courts. Lower courts might find their judgements taken on appeal to those higher courts. Dicta from the higher courts might indicate how the higher courts will treat a particular issue when it becomes central to a case before it. Secondly the higher the court, in principle, the better and more experienced the judges should be. Dicta from such judges ought to have some kind of authority which stems from the knowledge of those who produce the dicta. Neither argument, however, is entirely convincing. Many, perhaps most, cases are not appealed even when they could be because of pressure of time or money. Why, then should lower courts worry about the prospect of appeal? More importantly, if cases are appealed, the appellate courts may change their minds about an issue, particularly when it becomes central to the trial and the argument that counsel put forward. Dicta are a far from perfect guide to what the authors of those dicta will decide in the future. Equally, even experienced judges make mistakes. A ratio that is clearly incorrectly argued is nevertheless a binding ratio. Is incorrectly argued dicta from a higher court still "persuasive"? It seems that it is but, then, what the word persuasive means is a little mysterious.

Everyone would accept that when the higher courts pass judgements they refer to previous cases. There are very few judgements of any length in the law reports that do not have copious references to past judgements. The traditional view is that the rules described above in chapter one about the hierarchy of the courts and the distinction between ratio and obiter described above in this chapter are sufficiently clear and sufficiently rigid so as to mean that most judicial decisions can be predicted before they are made. It is not just that there are legal rules. There are also rules and principles about how judges make law by referring to past cases and how they interpret statutes. Judges are bound by them. Thus, if you know what they are and if you read enough previous judgements, on most occasions, because of this, you will know what the court is going to decide. However many academics now view such a statement with some scepticism.

We have seen above that, even in a very elementary explanation of the notion of precedent, there are gaps in the rules that surround the notions of ratio and obiter. At the points where these gaps exist, the rules do not tell judges what they must decide. Choice or discretion is given to the judiciary. How large these gaps are is a matter for debate. However they are certainly there. When thinking about how precedent works we also need to take account of the fact that judges make many decisions each year. They make far more than they did in the past. This has created a great mass of previous judgements often offering a range of alternative views about the law in any one area. In trying to decide which precedents are applicable, in distinguishing or not distinguishing previous cases, the judiciary are also faced with choices. Here again the rules that are said to guide them might be thought to be vague and imprecise. Finally many modern judges and an even greater number of academics believe that some judicial decisions involve, at least in part, consideration of policy issues. Legal decisions sometimes involve decisions about things other than legal rules. Rules about ratio, obiter and the hierarchy of the courts are of little assistance in these instances. Here again judges are faced with discretion and choice.

To suggest that the traditional rules of precedent are of limited assistance in explaining how judges reach their decisions is not to argue that judicial behaviour is wholly unpredictable. Equally such a suggestion does not involve arguing that judicial decisions are mere personal whims or that cases that are found in the law reports are inconsequential when looking at legal rules. Instead it is to argue that judicial use of past cases is often more subtle than has previously been thought. Sometimes judges do talk about ratio and obiter in their judgements in the way described above. However this is infrequent. Even when they do not overtly refer to the rules above they may still be following them. Nevertheless what may be as important is a need that judges feel to justify their new decisions by references to what other judges have previously decided. In doing this they are seeking to show that their decisions are in keeping with the spirit of the legal system; they are not just their own individual preferences for what the law ought to be. This constrains what they can decide. Previous case law contains a wealth of views about the law but it is does push thought in particular directions and thus makes some decisions more likely than others.

The legislature plainly makes new legal rules. Whether or not, in an effort to meet new developments, problems, and shifts in society's values, genuine departures from established rules of common law actually occur, is a matter of debate. The traditional notion is that common law rules do not alter to meet the requirements of society (or "public opinion"); it is the role of the legislator to remedy this through statutory intervention with specific legislation, and not for the judges to create new rules. The legislature makes law; the judiciary merely apply it. However, many academics and some judges would now argue that the judiciary sometimes do more than simply apply existing law; that in looking for rules of law in previous cases the judiciary subtly change the rules, consciously or otherwise, so that they produce the conclusions that they seek. If this is correct the judiciary are, in this sense, just as much legislators as Parliament.

FURTHER READING

F. Cownie, A. Bradney and M. Burton, *English Legal System in Context,* 5th edn, Oxford ▶ 6.3
    University Press, 2010, Chapter 5.
R. Cross and J. Harris, *Precedent in English Law,* 4th edn, Oxford University Press 1991.
P. Goodrich, *Reading the Law: Critical Introduction to Legal Method and Techniques*
    WileyBlackwell, (1986) particularly Chapter 6.

▶ 7
Statutory Interpretation

JUDGES AND STATUTES

7.1▶ The traditional view, which has been accepted since at least the nineteenth century, is that the judiciary are bound by and, legally, must apply legislation, whether it is primary legislation or secondary legislation, no matter what its content. This is known as *the doctrine of parliamentary sovereignty*. This principle has the advantage that it separates clearly the role of the legislature, which is democratically elected to pass laws, and the judiciary, whose job it is to use their technical expertise to apply those laws. This, in turn, relates to a political concept, known as *the separation of powers*, under which the legislature, the executive and the judiciary have different but complementary roles in the political running of the country.

When the idea doctrine of parliamentary sovereignty is applied to the job of the judiciary one potential problem with this approach to the judicial role is that a statute might be passed that does something that is fundamentally objectionable. It might, for example, take away part of the population's right of access to the courts. A political principle, known as *the rule of law,* says, amongst other things, that everybody should be subject to the law and that the law should treat people equally. Many people see this as being fundamental to the maintenance of a liberal democracy. However the doctrine of parliamentary sovereignty in its traditional form does not guarantee that there will be adherence to the rule of law. If Parliament passes a statute saying all people with red hair will no longer have the right to vote the doctrine of parliamentary sovereignty says that the judges should enforce that law. Given that there is no written constitution for the United Kingdom, guaranteeing people's rights, this does not seem to be entirely satisfactory.

Not everyone is now convinced that, if a statute was passed that contravened the rule of law, judges should necessarily apply it. Some judges have argued that, at the very least, if a statute takes away the fundamental rights of the population as a whole, or a group of people in the country, it has to do so in very clear language before it could be enforced in the courts. Parliament has to make it plain that they intend to deny people rights that morally the population might think that they ought to have. The majority of people, including the majority of judges, still adhere to the traditional notion of parliamentary sovereignty. However, some people, including some judges, think this principle is too simplistic for the modern era. There should be some limits to what legislation Parliament can pass and expect the judiciary to apply. How we decide what those limits are is a difficult matter. Nevertheless we ought to agree that judges should not enforce every conceivable statute. However, even these people think that judges should normally apply primary or secondary legislation whatever it says, even if, privately, they disapprove of its content.

Even if you do take the view that judges should always apply legislation you have to accept that sometimes an Act or piece of delegated legislation may be unclear or ambiguous. In some cases the difficulty will be resolved by applying one of the general Interpretation Acts. These are Acts that give a definition of words commonly found in legislation. Thus, for example, one Interpretation Act, the Interpretation Act 1978, says that where a piece of legislation uses the word "he" or "she" this should be taken to mean "he or she" unless it is plain from the context that this should not be so. Some Acts have their own interpretation section, in which certain important words or phrases used in the Act are defined. However, if a difficulty cannot be resolved by such an Act or section, if the ambiguity or lack of clarity remains, it is for the judiciary to decide what the legislation means.

THE PRINCIPLES OF STATUTORY INTERPRETATION

In order to discover the way in which legislation should be applied, the judges have developed a complex network of principles for statutory interpretation, which are designed to assist in the proper application of the law. Although these principles are often called rules they are not rules in the strictest of senses. If you drive above 70 miles per hour, if caught and convicted, you will be punished. The rule is clear and when it is to be applied is clear. The principles of statutory interpretation are much more unclear. There is no definitive source for what any one of these principles actually says. When they should be applied is also a matter of constant debate. This is not to say that they have no substance at all. Judges sometimes talk about them explicitly when they are passing judgement. They are part of the language which many people use when they analyse what judges do. However some people would argue that these so-called principles cloak, in part or whole, what judges do when they interpret statutes. When we look at statutory interpretation, they would argue, we should put the emphasis on the word "interpretation". Judges may talk about these principles of statutory interpretation in their judgements, they would suggest, but what judges actually do is to make personal choices about how to read a statute. Their individual choices are influenced by things like their education and the legal culture in which they work. They are not simply personal whims. For this reason their choices are to some degree predictable. However, for some people, judicial decisions about how to interpret a statute are not really influenced by the principles of statutory interpretation discussed below.

The traditional starting point for statutory interpretation is *the literal rule*. The judiciary ought to look at the statute and apply its words literally. This principle accords with the doctrine of parliamentary sovereignty. Parliament decided what the law should be and expressed their wishes through the language of the statute. The courts must interpret those words literally. However, although the literal rule seems to offer an easy solution to the problem of statutory interpretation, in practice its application raises many difficulties. First words often, and perhaps even usually, have a number of different meanings. We may not be familiar with all of these meanings. In ordinary conversation we use only a limited range of meanings. However, if you look at the 22 volumes of the Oxford English Dictionary, the complexity of the English language immediately becomes apparent. It is also the case that sometimes words have ordinary, everyday meanings and also technical meanings. Equally words are usually read as parts of phrases or sentences. Rules of grammar tell us how to read such groupings but rules of grammar are not precise and are subject to argument.

▶ 7.2

On the face of it the literal rule seems to take away choice from the judiciary when they interpret legislation. They should just follow the words that Parliament used. But in many instances, and some would argue in almost all instances, language gives us a choice of meanings, with there being more than one literal meaning that could be followed. We have to choose between meanings, to choose between ordinary and technical meanings or to decide which rules of grammar apply to the construction of the particular phrase in the statute before us.

There is no doubt that in the past the literal rule had substantial support from the judiciary. They cited the literal rule as a reason for their judgements. In doing so they denied that they exercised any discretion when they passed judgement. However whether it actually adequately described their practices is another matter. In the present day both most academics and judges, because they acknowledge the complexities of language, will be uncomfortable with the idea that the literal rule will usually be of much assistance in deciding how to interpret a statutory provision. It may be used sometimes but usually it is too simplistic a principle to help when trying to work out what a statute means.

The second principle of statutory interpretation that can be used is *the golden rule* or *the purposive approach*. Following this approach the courts should look at a statute as a whole. Where there is more than one meaning that could be put to a particular provision, and where one of those meanings would lead to an "absurdity or inconvenience" in the context of the interpretation of the statute taken as a whole, then the courts should choose the other meaning, even if grammatically it seems to be the less appropriate choice. It is argued that such an approach, even when it involves not following the literal meaning of the words chosen by Parliament, complies with the notion of parliamentary sovereignty because it could not have been Parliament's intention to write a statute that contained a clear absurdity. In more modern language, when interpreting statutes courts ought to have an eye to the purpose of that statute. This approach does acknowledge that judges play a role in creating law, even when they are interpreting legislation, because they are making choices about what meanings they should apply. However, following this approach, their choice is constrained by the idea that they are making choices that would best fit with what must have been the intention of parliament when they passed the statute. The choices they make are not personal decisions about what policy they think ought to underlie the law. Moreover the judges are still following the language of the statute.

The final broad principle that is applied to statutory interpretation is *the mischief rule*. The mischief rule still adheres to the notion of parliamentary sovereignty. However the mischief rule says that sometimes parliament's choice of language in a statute is so poor that any sensible interpretation of the statutory provisions as they have been laid down will not lead to the desired change in the law that was clearly the intention of parliament. In such cases, following the mischief rule, the courts may be forced to read a statute as though it said something other than what it actually says so as to reach the result that parliament intended. The statute says X but the courts will read it as though it says Y. One problem in applying this principle lies in knowing how the courts will be sure what the intention of parliament with respect to an individual statute was. Since the 1990s the courts have increasingly looked to Hansard, the record of what is said in Parliament, to seek to ascertain the intention of statutes. As with the previous principle of statutory interpretation there is no straightforward clash between this principle and the notion of parliamentary sovereignty. The courts are still said to be following the intention of parliament. However the principle does give the courts considerable discretionary powers to create what is in effect new statutory language. Some will question how far such choices really reflect the court's knowledge of what Parliament actually intended, notwithstanding the contrary evidence of the language they used.

One final important influence on statutory interpretation is the Human Rights Act 1998. The 1998 Act incorporated many of the rights found in the European Convention on Human Rights into domestic law meaning that, in addition to the right that everyone has to take a case to the European Court of Human Rights, they are now enforceable within the domestic courts. When the courts are interpreting a statute they are now required, under the Human Rights Act, to interpret a statute, "so far as possible", so that it accords with the Convention rights. Once again this requirement does not contradict the notion of parliamentary sovereignty. The courts must look at the language of a statute and see whether it can be interpreted in a way that is in keeping with the Convention. This might involve an interpretation that is more strained than it otherwise would be. However Parliament, in the 1998 Act, has told them that is what they should do. Moreover, although there can be a strained interpretation of a statutory provision, the courts must still follow the language of the statute. Where it is not possible to interpret a statute so that it accords with Convention rights the courts can issue a *declaration of incompatibility*. Where this has been done that statute is still valid law but Parliaments and others have been alerted to the fact that the provisions of a statute are incompatible with people's Convention rights. In practice Parliament will amend the legislation so that it does not breach people's convention rights but it is not legally bound to do this.

FURTHER READING

F. Cownie, A. Bradney and M. Burton, *English Legal System in Context*, 5th edn, Oxford University Press, (2010), Chapter 6.

R. Cross, J. Bell and G. Engle, *Cross: Statutory Interpretation*, 3rd edn, Oxford University Press, (1995).

P. Goodrich, *Reading the Law: Critical Introduction to Legal Method and Techniques* WileyBlackwell, (1986), particularly Chapter 4.

▶ 7.3

8
Reading research materials

8.1 ▶ Chapter 4 explained that one way to answering questions about law was to use research methods taken from the social sciences and humanities. Because this kind of research is the only way in which some questions about law can be answered, it is important that those interested in law can understand it.

In order to understand research into law you have to understand how and why it is written in the particular way that it is. Once you can understand the structure of the material, you will be able to see whether or not it helps to answer the questions in which you are interested.

Haphazard approaches to research are likely to be unsuccessful, the information gathered being too unrepresentative of the world at large and, therefore, too inaccurate for any conclusions to be drawn safely. Good research is done systematically. Research methods are highly developed. There are three sources of information about how and why the law operates: records, people and activities. There are also three principal methods used in socio-legal research. The researcher may read records, interview people (or send questionnaires), or observe activities.

RECORD READING

8.2 ▶ The researcher reads the records and collects the required information, which is then either written down or noted on a prepared recording sheet. The researchers must ensure that the information collected from each record is as accurate and as complete as possible. This may involve searching through disordered files of letters and notes or simply copying the details from a form, such as a divorce petition.

INTERVIEWS AND QUESTIONNAIRES

8.3 ▶ Interviews are conducted in person, either face-to-face or by telephone. Questionnaires are given, or sent, to the respondents to complete. It is important, in so far as is possible, to ask the same questions in the same way each time so as to get comparable information. Questions may be "open- ended", allowing the respondent to reply in his or her own words, or be "closed", requiring selection of the answer from a choice given by the interviewer. The style and wording of the question is selected to fit the data sought. Whatever the questions, the interview must be recorded. This may be done by using a tape recorder or by the interviewer noting the replies. Interviews are most useful for finding out what reasons people have for what they have done and for exploring their feelings. If questions are asked about the future, the answers can only indicate what respondents currently think they would do. It has also been established that recollection of past events may be inaccurate, particularly about dates, times and the exact sequence of events. Interview and questionnaire design requires considerable skill, as does interviewing itself, if it is to reflect the respondent's views rather than those of the researcher.

OBSERVATION

The observer attends the event and records what occurs there. The observer may be an outsider; for example, a person watching court proceedings from the public gallery. Alternatively, the observer may be a person actually taking part in the events being described; for example, a police officer researching into the police force. Observation needs to be done systematically and accurately in order to avoid bias. Observers cannot record everything that they see. They must be careful that they do not record only what they want to see and neglect that which is unexpected and, perhaps, thereby unwelcome. One great difficulty in noting observations lies in deciding what to note down and what to omit. What seems unimportant at the time the notes were taken may take on a greater significance when a later analysis is made. It is important that the observer's record is contemporaneous, otherwise the data is weakened by what has been forgotten.

▸ 8.4

CHOOSING RESEARCH METHODS

For any particular piece of research, one method may be more suitable than another, because of the nature of the data sources or the approach that the researcher wishes to take. If, for example, you want to research into the reasons magistrates have for their decisions, there is little point in reading records of what those decisions were. Here, the best place to start would be to interview magistrates. No single method can be said to provide the truth about every situation; some would argue that no method can provide the truth about any situation, for no one truth exists. Each method provides information based on the perceptions of the people who provide it, the record keepers, the interviewers or the observers.

▸ 8.5

Choice of research method depends not only what information is sought but also on practicalities. The researcher may not be given access to records or permitted to carry out interviews. Professional bodies and employers are not always willing to let their members of staff participate in research. This may be because they consider the research unethical (perhaps requiring them to divulge information given in confidence), because they are too busy, because they do not see the value of the research or because they wish to conceal the very information in which the researcher is interested.

For many research studies more than one method is used to obtain a complete picture. However, practical matters, including budget and time limits, may mean that not every avenue of enquiry is pursued. What is important is that the methods chosen are appropriate to the subject of study, the approach of the researcher and the conclusions drawn.

SAMPLING

Looking at every case is not normally practical in research. Instead, the researcher takes a sample of cases. Thus, one may interview some lawyers or some defendants or observe, or read

▸ 8.6

records at some courts. If a completely random sample is taken, then it should have the characteristics of the population as a whole. A sample of judges should, for example, include judges of the different ages, backgrounds and experience to be found amongst the judiciary. However, if a characteristic is very rare a sample may not contain any example of having that characteristic. Thus, a 10 per cent sample of judges in the higher courts, (i.e. contacting every tenth judge) might well fail to include any women judges since there are very few of them. The size of sample and method of sampling must be chosen to fit with the study. In a study of attitudes of clients to lawyers there is clearly no point in interviewing only successful clients. The number of people refusing to take part in a study is also important. Researchers will try to obtain a high response rate (over 75 per cent) and also attempt to find out if those who refuse are likely to be different in any material way from those who agree to participate in the study.

RESEARCH FINDINGS

8.7 ▶ The account of any research will usually include some background information about the subject, the purpose of the study (the questions to be answered) and the methods used. Findings presented in words should cause no difficulty to the reader, but numbers may be quite confusing. Where comparisons are made, it is usually thought better to use *proportions* or *percentages* rather than actual numbers unless the numbers are very small. It is then important to be clear what the percentage represents: for example, was it 20 per cent of all plaintiffs or 20 per cent of successful plaintiffs. Some researchers do not give the actual figures, but prefer to use words such as "some", "most" or "the majority". This is not very helpful, since a word like "majority" can mean anything from 51 per cent to 99 per cent. If the numbers in a study are very small the use of percentages or proportions can itself be misleading. If a researcher looks at 10 people in their study and says 50 percent of their sample said X this might look more impressive than saying 5 people said X.

There is a variety of ways of presenting figures so as to make them clearer. Tables (lists of figures) are commonly used because they make it easier to compare two or more categories or questions. Graphic presentation, using bar charts (histograms), pie charts or graphs, can create a clear overall impression of a complex set of figures.

Figure 1 below is a bar chart. It shows clearly the different numbers of the three offences where guns were used. It also shows for each the relative proportion in which particular types of gun were used. As can be seen from this example, the greatest advantage of a bar chart is the way in which it makes a quick visual comparison of information easy.

Figure 2 is a pie chart. The whole circle represents 100 per cent of the particular group. The segments represent different percentages. In this example, the exact percentages represented in the different segments have been printed on to the chart. This is not always done. Different circles represent both different types of original sentence and different courts in which that sentence was imposed. The segments themselves indicate what happened to people who breached their original sentence: for example, by committing a further crime whilst on probation.

Figure 3 is a graph. This is probably the best way of showing a trend over time. The graph is designed to show the rise in the number of females found guilty of indictable (basically, serious offences). There are two major problems in doing this. One is that an increase in

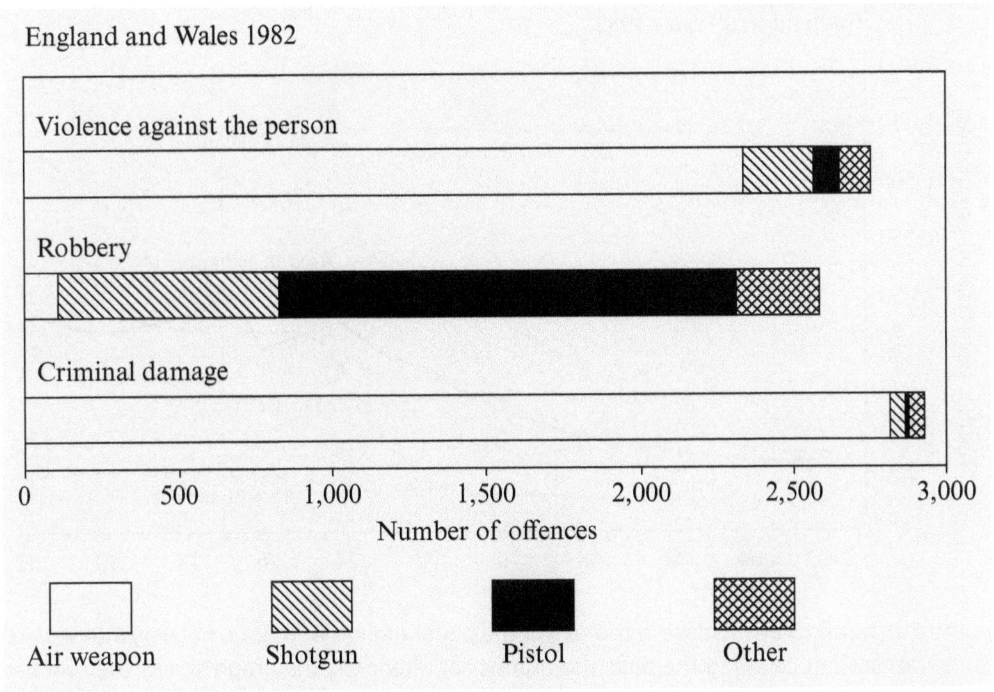

England and Wales 1982

Figure 1.
Notifiable offences in which firearms were reported to have been used, by type of offence and type of weapon.

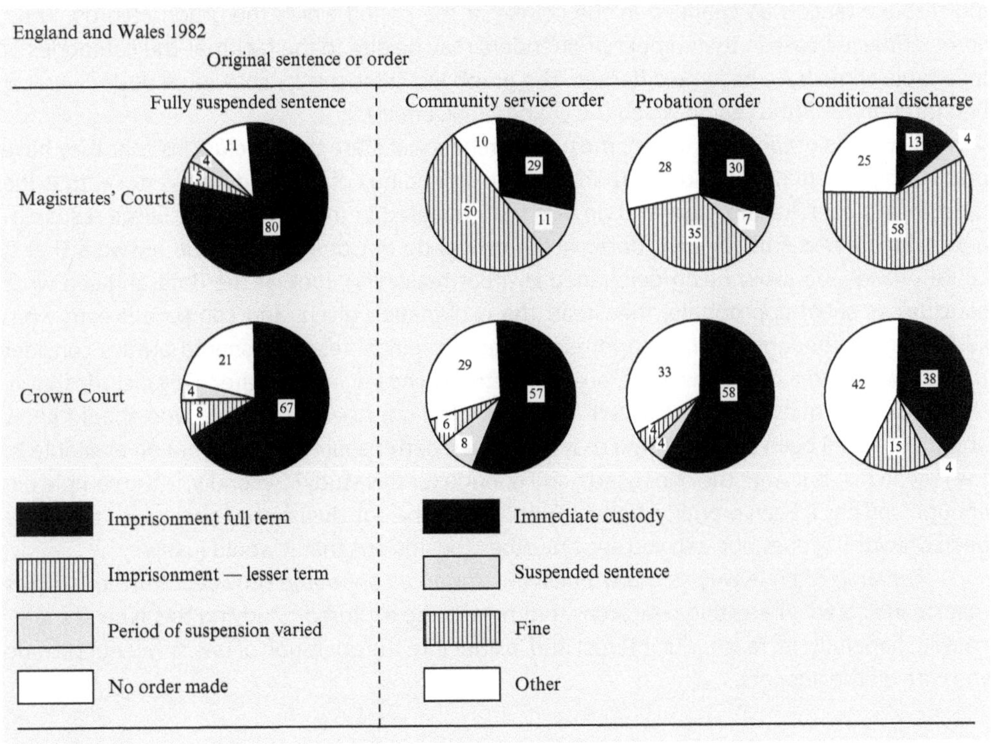

Figure 2.
Person breaching their original sentence or order by type of sentence or order imposed for the breach

Figure 3.
Females found guilty of, or cautioned for, indictable offences[1] per 100,000 population in the age group by age.

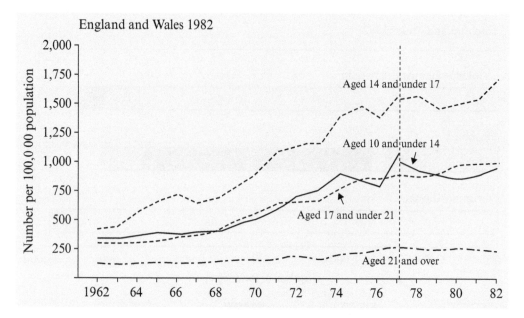

numbers caused by an increase in the size of the population as a whole is not very interesting. Thus, rather than counting the absolute number of offenders, the graph shows the number of offenders per 100,000 in the population. Secondly, the law relating to who is guilty of an indictable offence was changed in the course of the period which the graph records. Thus, some of the increase in the number of offenders may be due to the fact that the categories of indictable crime have become different. The graph indicates this by showing a dotted vertical line through 1977 (the year in which the change took effect).

As well as graphs and tables, most researchers will state the conclusions that they have drawn from the material and summarise the main findings of the study. It is crucial that the data should establish no more and no less than is stated in the conclusions. Some research-ers make great claims for their data, whilst others do not draw out all the answers that it could provide. To avoid being persuaded by poor reasoning, look at the data and see what conclusions seem appropriate, then read the explanation given, and compare it with what you originally thought. A critical approach to any empirical research should always consider the following three questions. First, are the methods chosen appropriate? This includes both, "have the right questions been asked" and "have the right people (people who should know about the topic) been asked". There may have been better sources of information available to the researcher, but were the ones used good enough for this study? Secondly, is the sample big enough and has it been properly drawn? Thirdly, does the data justify the conclusions that have been drawn? If it does not, can you see any other conclusions that it would justify?

Research often leaves as many questions raised as answered provided. Further studies may be indicated, interesting new areas that need to be explored. Studying this type of mate-rial will, hopefully, increase your interest and insight into the operation of law. It will not provide you with all the answers.

Exercise 5

READING RESEARCH MATERIALS

Reading and understanding research materials does not just involve seeing what conclusion ▷ 8.8
the author has reached. Understanding the evidence the author or authors has for the conclusion drawn is as important as understanding the conclusion itself. This section is intended to
improve your critical awareness of the materials that you are reading. Reading something critically means reading it to see what weaknesses there are in it. The fewer the weaknesses the
stronger will be the conclusion. When reading something, remember that there are flaws in all
articles and books. No author thinks their work is perfect. As a reader your task is to assess the
merit of a particular argument by being aware of its weaknesses as well as its strengths. With
practice critical reading will become an unconscious habit that you will bring to all your
reading. Start by reading *Women Solicitors as a Barometer for problems within the Legal
Profession–Time to Put Values before Profits?* by Lisa Webley and Liz Duff, the article reprinted
below. When you have read the article once go back and read it again making detailed notes.
When doing this, concentrate on trying to identify the strand of argument Webley and Duff are
trying to develop, paying close attention to the evidence that they present for the various
points that they make. Your notes should tell you both what the authors have written and what
you think the possible objections to the various details of their argument is. When you think
you understand the article, and have made your notes, try to answer the questions set out in
Section A below. Refer to the original article when your notes give you insufficient information
to answer the question. After you have finished the questions in Section A compare your
answers with those that we have given at the back of this book. If your answers differ from ours
you may need to go back and reread the article in order to get a better understanding of it.
Once you are sure you understand the answers to Section A go on and complete the questions
in Section B.

Section A
1. What issue do you think the authors are discussing?
2. What research method or methods are they using?
3. The article is concerned with what the authors say is "the culture of the [solicitors']
   profession [in England and Wales]" (p.376). They refer to, amongst other things, a
   number of research findings taken from the USA. Why do they use research about
   American lawyers? Can you think of any reasons why there may be a danger is using
   American material in this analysis?
4. The authors refer to the "masculinist cultures of the [solicitors'] profession" (p.384).
   What do you think they mean by "masculinist cultures"? Why do you think they do
   not use the simpler phrase "male cultures"?
5. What limitations are there to the evidence that the article presents for the proposition that solicitors' firms are losing their sense of professionalism?

Section B

1. The article suggests that there are two different reasons why one might be concerned about women leaving the solicitors' profession. What are they? Which one do you think is more important?

2. The article talks of the "commodification of the legal profession" (p.393). What do you understand this to mean? Why might the commodification of the legal profession be undesirable? Is commodification always undesirable?

3. What reasons are there for thinking that there should be diversity "in the higher levels of the solicitors' profession" (p.379)?

4. What problems do the author think there are with "work-life balance" arguments (p.400)? Do you think work-life balance considerations are important?

5. Any piece of research can be improved on. What areas that the authors look at do you think need further exploration? How do you think this work should be done?

Women Solicitors as a Barometer for Problems within the Legal Profession – Time to Put Values before Profits?

LISA WEBLEY* AND LIZ DUFF*

This article will consider the theoretical explanations for why women are not remaining within and progressing through the ranks of the solicitors' profession in England and Wales. It sets out the findings from a Law Society commissioned project to examine the reasons why women have had a break from practice or chosen to leave the profession. Finally, it considers whether one of the purported strategies used to empower women solicitors – the business case for equality of opportunity in the solicitors' profession – is actively working against women and the profession (more broadly), and that only a return to a wider values-based approach to professional identity will meet the criticisms raised by many of the women who participated in this research.

INTRODUCTION

The Law Society remains concerned about the rate at which and the reasons why women continue to leave the profession pre-retirement in relatively large numbers. The debate is wide ranging, covering issues from whether women should attempt to 'have it all' by combining a legal career with motherhood, to why there is a differential in promotion rates to partnership between male and female solicitors.[1] Even after three studies undertaken by

* School of Law, University of Westminster, 4 Little Titchfield Street, London W1W 7UW, England
webleyl@westminster.ac.uk   duffl@westminster.ac.uk

We would like to thank Professor Andy Boon and the three reviewers who commented on an earlier draft of this article, as well as Professor John Flood for his helpful suggestions on a later draft.

1 There is also much debate in the legal professional press. For an illustration of the competing views see: 'Having it All?', Letter to the Editor, *Law Society Gazette*, 31 July 2003, at 16; 'Balancing Act', Letters to the Editor, *Law Society Gazette*, 14 August 2003, at 16; F. Burton, 'New Ways to Work Towards the Work-Life Balance:

or for the Law Society, on average one per decade, and subsequent Law Society initiatives to improve the retention and advancement of women in the profession,[2] progress remains slow.[3] Within the period 1997–2002 1,568 solicitors failed to renew their practising certificates, which, when calculated by gender as a percentage of all solicitors who held practising certificates in 2002, represented non-renewal by 1.6 per cent of all male solicitors compared with non-renewal by 2.4 per cent of female solicitors.[4] Even thought these figures do not suggest an enormous difference in renewal patterns, it is the average age of renewal that highlights the differences. The mean male age of non-renewal is 52 years compared with 40 for women (three-fifths of women leave in their 30s). When Bradshaw and Thomas investigated the reasons why solicitors had not renewed their practising certificates, it became clear that men were more likely to allow their practising certificate to lapse because they had taken early retirement, whereas women's reasons were most likely to relate to child-related commitments. In addition, and perhaps related to this, female progression into senior positions appears to be a slow trickle up, rather than a constant and widening stream of advancement.[5] While the problems facing women as a group have been highlighted and studied repeatedly, problems of double discrimination – gender

The Compleat Women Lawyer or Closing the Rhetoric-Reality Gap', edited paper from the Annual Woman Lawyer Forum (2002). See, too, recent research on pay and promotion prospects in the context of parenthood by V. Wass and R. McNabb, *Discrimination and the Law: Pay Promotion and Parenthood* (2004) at <http://www.cf.ac.uk/carbs/econ/mcnabb/solspaper.pdf>, which indicates that women solicitors' earnings are on average only two-thirds that of their male counterparts and that only one-third of the difference in pay is attributable to a difference in career progression rather than other factors. For a recent exploration of the potential for positive change by the use of affirmative action in the legal profession, see D. Nicholson, 'Affirmative Action in the Legal Profession' (2006) 33 *J. of Law and Society* 109.

2 Sommerlad and Sanderson's research identified strategies that may be employed to retain women solicitors who had had children. See H. Sommerlad and P. Sanderson, 'The Legal Labour Market and the Training Needs of Women Returners in the United Kingdom' (1997) 29 *J. of Vocational Education and Training* 45. See, further, H. Sommerlad and P. Sanderson, *Gender Choice and Commitment: Women Solicitors in England and Wales and the Struggle for Equal Status* (1998).

3 The studies were conducted by A. Bradshaw and P. Thomas, *'Leaving the Profession': A Survey of Solicitors Not Renewing their Practising Certificates* (1995); Sommerlad and Sanderson, id.; J. Siems, *Equality and Diversity; Women Solicitors Research Study 48*, vol. 1 (Quantitative Findings) (2004); and L. Duff and L. Webley, *Equality & Diversity: Women Solicitors Research Study 48*, vol. 2 (Qualitative Findings and Literature Review) (2004).

4 Siems, id.

5 In a survey of the largest 100 firms conducted by the Young Women Lawyers group, only 25 per cent of new partners that year were women: C. McGlynn and C. Graham, *Soliciting Equality: Equality and Opportunity in the Solicitors' Profession* (1995). See, too, C. McGlynn, *The Women Lawyer Making the Difference* (1998) at 84–5 for a discussion of some women's experiences in this context.

intersected with race, sexual orientation or disability have not reached this level of critical examination.[6] Thus, while women have not yet reaped the full benefits of over two decades of equal opportunity initiatives, other marginalized or doubly marginalized groups face a long struggle even to reach this point.[7]

This article considers the theoretical explanations about why women are not remaining and progressing within the solicitors' profession at the same rate as men. It sets out our findings from a Law Society commissioned project to examine the reasons why women in the late twentieth and early twenty-first centuries have had a break from practice or have chosen to leave the profession. Finally, it considers whether one of the purported strategies used to empower women solicitors – the business case for equality of opportunity in the solicitors' profession – is actively working against women and the profession (more broadly), and whether only a return to a wider values-based approach to professional identity will meet the criticisms raised by many of the women who participated in our research. Concerns about the culture of the profession are not restricted to women, ethnic minority solicitors, and those from lower socio-economic groups.[8] Some men are also beginning to voice concern that the culture within the profession is acting against their interests too. It appears that the commercialization of legal practice may have led to a commodification of the professional project that actively undermines the value placed on all solicitors.

---

6 For a discussion of the United States experience of double discrimination, see N. Dowd, 'Resisting Essentialism and Hierarchy: A Critique of Work/Family Strategies for Women Lawyers' (2000) 16 *Harvard Blackletter Law J.* 185; S. Sturm, 'From Gladiators to Problem-Solvers: Connecting Conversations about Women, the Academy, and the Legal Profession' (1997) 4 *Duke J. of Gender, Law & Policy* 119; E. Gorman, 'Work Uncertainty and the Promotion of Professional Women: The Case of Law Firm Partnership' (2006) 85 *Social Forces* 865.

7 See, further, Dowd, id. There is certainly evidence to suggest that other groups suffer as attention turns on the attempt to redress gender imbalance in the law. See C. Menkel-Meadow, 'The Comparative Sociology of Women Lawyers: The "Feminization" of the Legal Profession (1986) 24 *Osgoode Hall Law J.* 987, at 901. For a discussion of gender resegregation within law firms, see F. Kay, 'Flight from Law: A Competing Risks Model of Departures from Law Firms' (1997) 31 *Law and Society Rev.* 301. See, too, R. Abel, 'Comparative Sociology of Legal Professions: An Exploratory Essay' (1985) 1 *Am. Bar Foundation Research J.* 1; K. Clanton, 'Glass Ceilings and Sticky Floors: Minority Women in the Legal Profession' (2001) 49 *University of Kansas Law Rev.* 176.

8 See A. Boon, 'From Public Service to Service Industry: the Impact of Socialisation and Work on the Motivation and Values of Lawyers' (2005) 12 *International J. of the Legal Profession* 229.

376

I. EXPLANATIONS FOR WOMEN'S POSITION IN THE SOLICITORS' PROFESSION AND STRATEGIES TO AID ADVANCEMENT

Some have argued that any barriers that women face are of their own making, as former President of the Law Society Martin Mears once famously said: 'There are no barriers to the advancement of women apart from those they choose themselves or those that are inherent in their biology.'[9] This 'human capital' theory of female choices, in which it is argued that women invest less in their education and their career and thus get less out by way of pay and promotion, is used to explain why women are not promoted at the same rate and speed as men, why women feel less enchanted with their workplace, and why, it has been argued, women ultimately leave the profession or choose to put their role as a parent, or carer, before that of solicitor.[10] Human capital theory, the dominant theory that seeks to explain how women are responsible for their own lack of progression and promotion, claims to unpack why women are not at parity with men in terms of status or pay. It also conveniently provides a solution to women – invest more heavily in your career and you will reach the higher echelons of the profession. The difficulty, however, is that for women to be perceived as making a similar commitment to men, they must 'choose' not to have children, as the status of mother appears to be automatic evidence of reduced commitment in a way that being a father is not.[11] For those women who are willing and able to take this stance, human capital theory would appear to be gender neutral and offer the opportunity of equal status, equal pay, and equal promotion. However, there is evidence to suggest that equal investment does not guarantee such a prize, as the potential to take maternity leave is seen as a future potential risk of reduced commitment.[12] Consequently, as McGlynn points out, human capital theory is a mask for discrimination – the potential for motherhood is inherent in women as a class and thus there is always the potential for a reduced commitment in the eyes of the profession. Being female is enough to

---

9 Martin Mears, President of the Law Society, 1995–1996, *Times*, 16 April 1996. See, in contrast, C. McGlynn, 'A Different Voice' (1996) 146 *New Law J.* 816; C. McGlynn, 'The Business of Equality in the Solicitors' Profession' (2000) 63 *Modern Law Rev.* 442 and, for a discussion of the role of cultural capital, see Sommerlad and Sanderson, op. cit. (1998), n. 2.

10 See C. McGlynn, 'The Status of Women Lawyers in the United Kingdom' in *Women in the World's Legal Professions*, eds. U. Schultz and G. Shaw (2003). See, further, J. Hagan and F. Kay, *Gender in Practice – A Study of Lawyers' Lives* (1995).

11 As Collier explains, fatherhood does not tend to make up such a strong part of core identity by comparison with paid employment: R. Collier, 'A Hard Time to be a Father? Reassessing the Relationship Between Law, Policy and Family (Practices)' (2001) 38 *J. of Law and Society* 520, at 530. See, too, C. Smart and B. Neale, '"I Hadn't Really Thought About It": New Identities/New Fatherhoods' in *Relating Intimacies: Power and Resistance (Explorations in Sociology)*, eds. J. Seymour and P. Bagguley (1999) at 530.

12 See McGlynn, op. cit. (2000), n. 9, at p. 447.

377

be perceived as having less commitment; equal opportunity cannot ever be achieved under the terms of human capital theory.[13]

By contrast, much of the feminist academic literature has focused on attacking assumptions of equality of opportunity for women and men, in part because male and female roles within the family continue to be distinctive,[14] and in part because apparent gender neutrality in the work place is less neutral than gendered.[15] Many articles have been written on the problems facing women within the legal profession. Holmes categorized the problems as those of 'overwork; hierarchy, bureaucracy and specialisation; moral conflict, and the difficulty of combining work with childrearing',[16] as well as the fact that the profession was structured by men for men.[17] Much of the discussion has focused clearly on issues of sex differentiation or, rather, sex-based prejudice within the profession, although the nature of the discrimination appears to be rooted less in overt sexism and more focused on covert gender discrimination – the charge that the current professional structure is both gender neutral and operates gender neutrally. Indeed Collier has highlighted:

> the powerful economic, political and cultural shifts which have transformed, and are transforming understanding of employment, 'family life' and ... the 'work-life relation'

and it is this which seems to be at the core of disjunction between women solicitors' expectations and experiences within the profession.[18] There is an

13 id.
14 In addition to those cited elsewhere in the article, see H. English, *Gender on Trial: Sexual Stereotypes and Work/Life Balance in the Legal Workplace* (2003) at 203; K. Hull and R. Nelson, 'Gender Inequality in Law: Problems of Structure and Agency in Recent Studies of Gender in Anglo-American Legal Professions' (1998) 23 *Law and Social Enquiry* 681; M.-J. Mossman, 'Challenging "Hidden" Assumptions: (Women) Lawyers and Family' in *Mothers in Law: Feminist Theory and the Legal Regulation of Motherhood*, eds. M. Albertson Fineman and I. Karpin (1995) at 290; Smart and Neale, op. cit., n. 11, at p. 118; Dowd, op. cit., n. 6; C. Fuchs Epstein et al., 'Glass Ceilings and Open Doors: Women's Advancement in the Legal Profession' (1995) 64 *Fordham Law Rev.* 291. See K. Gerson, *No Man's Land: Changing Commitments to Family and Work* (1994) for a discussion of the difficulties associated with categories such as men and women, the notion of family and work. See R. Collier, ' "Nutty Professors", "Men in Suits" and "New Entrepreneurs": Corporeality, Subjectivity and Change in the Law School and Legal Practice' (1998) 7 *Social and Legal Studies* 27.
15 For a discussion, see D. Rhode, 'The Profession and it Discontents' (2000) 61 *Ohio State Law J.* at 8-9. See, further, Collier, op. cit., n. 11 and Collier (1998), id.
16 D.K. Holmes, 'Structural Causes of Dissatisfaction among Large-firm Attorneys: A Feminist Perspective' (1990) 12 *Women's Rights Law Reporter* 9, at 13.
17 See the discussion in Canadian Bar Association, *Touchstones for Change: Equality, Diversity & Accountability* (1993) at 85 and, further, M. Thornton, *Dissonance and Distrust – Women and the Legal Profession* (1996) at 157.
18 R. Collier, 'The Changing University and the (Legal) Academic Career – Rethinking the Relationship between Women, Men and the "Private Life" of the Law School' (2002) 22 *Legal Studies* 1, at 3-4 for a discussion of reconceptualizing gender and, in

expectation of gender neutrality both by men, for whom the expectation is more usually met, and by women whose expectations of gender neutrality are met less often as they advance through their career.[19] Many commentators, including the Association of Women Solicitors, consider that the answer to continued concerns about gender neutrality is reliance on a business-efficiency or a profit-maximization model within the legal profession as this should be gender neutral. The argument goes that the profession should be appraised of 'the business case', as it is often named, for equal opportunities policies and strategies.[20] It has been argued that by according women and minority groups full and equal status within the profession, profits will rise and the profession will benefit. The positive secondary benefit for the profession, it is claimed, is equal advancement for women. Thus, equal opportunities for women are attractively sold as higher profit margins for large commercial firms, a wider range of skills and thus organizational efficiency for smaller firms, and a way to reap the benefits of high training investment costs.

If the human capital theory provides little comfort for women in the profession, what of the business case for equality of opportunity? The business case for female advancement has been made, and continues to be made, to provide a market-based rationale for the need to implement equal opportunities policies. It has been made for over ten years, and yet the Law Society continues to express concern about the lack of diversity in the higher levels of the solicitors' profession, and has introduced yet more initiatives (such as the Diversity Access Scheme) in order to boost the numbers of solicitors from diverse backgrounds entering the profession.[21] It has also

particular, our understanding of the masculine. Interestingly Collier also points to these problems in academic life in general in his review of Bradney's analysis of the changing face of academic life: A. Bradney, *Conversations, Choices and Chances: The Liberal Law School in the Twenty-First Century* (2003). For his discussion of Bradney's analysis, see R. Collier, 'The Liberal Law School the Restructured University and the Paradox of Socio-Legal Studies' (2005) 68 *Modern Law Rev.* 475, at 491–492. See, too, Dowd, op. cit., n. 6.

19 M. Costello, 'Women in the Legal Profession: You've Come A Long Way – Or Have You?' (1997) *Detroit College of Law Rev.* 909, at 917:

> They [women] do not believe or want to believe that they are almost certain to encounter gender bias at some stage in their careers that will have the potential to adversely affect their advancement. Because of their complacency, they are unprepared when reality strikes, and often react by changing jobs or careers, or simply dropping out of the work force – in too many cases, depriving the legal profession of their skills and talents.

20 For example, the Women Lawyers' Forum held in London in March 2005 focused on these issues.

21 As McGlynn indicates, the face of legal practice is changing rapidly, with increased female representation and greater interest being placed on the role and experience of women in the legal profession, after years of neglect. However, the interest is relatively recent and initiatives have yet to lead to a joined-up strategy to assist in fully supporting women solicitors. See McGlynn, op. cit. (1998), n. 5, at p. 2. See, too, the Law Society Diversity Access Scheme, *Diversity in Action – A Guide for Solicitors* <http://www.lawsociety.org.uk/becomingasolicitor/careerinlaw/equalityanddiversity.lawas>.

recognized that this good work will be undermined if women, and solicitors from lower socio-economic groups and from ethnic minority backgrounds, leave the profession in disproportionate numbers post qualification.[22] The business case has also been undermined, not least because, by definition, it does nothing to challenge the economic imperative of the business model, and does not strive for equality as of right, but rather because it is economically rational to do so. It is based on the economic efficiency of markets and of firms that do not discriminate on economically irrational grounds, such as gender. McGlynn succinctly summarizes the three central tenets of the business case to be:

> ... the implementation and effective enforcement, at firm level, of equal opportunity policies will improve employee morale to an extent that is positively reflected in the productivity of the firm ... The second element ... suggests that it makes financial sense for employers to capitalise on any investment made in their employees, that is they make the best use of their human capital ... The third aspect ... is directed at frightening employers into adopting and enforcing equal opportunities policies in order to obviate expensive sex discrimination claims.[23]

McGlynn then provides a persuasive argument for why the business case may not advance women in the workforce. If the business case is ultimately shown to be economically suspect, then the rationale for adopting equal opportunities policies would be diminished, and thus the gains that women had made in the legal profession may be lost.

She admits that the business case may, in the short term, improve the position of women in the profession, and much has been written on the need for firms to capitalize on the human capital of their women solicitors. However, women solicitors are still leaving the profession in greater numbers than men, even after Law Society initiatives that flowed from three studies to examine why this may be so. The literature still points to the pay gap between male and female solicitors and the slower promotion prospects of women. Some gains may have been made, but the business case has not led to wholesale change, and McGlynn would argue that the business case masks the problems that many women are facing. Basing equal opportunity arguments on the market perpetuates the solicitor as a unit of production, a

---

22 This is certainly not a new phenomenon and has been recognized in the United States literature for some time. Nelson and Trubek note that studies in the late 1980s suggest that, although a larger proportion of women and lower socio-economic law students and those from minority groups are entering the legal profession compared to previous decades, they are also the associates who are most likely to leave large law firms. R. Nelson and D. Trubek, 'Introduction: New Problems and New Paradigms in Studies of the Legal Profession' in *Lawyers' Ideals/Lawyers' Practices: Transformation in the American Legal Profession*, eds. R.L. Nelson, D. Trubek, and R. Solomon (1992) 1, at 9. Further references to United States literature on this area may be found in Nelson and Trubek's chapter.

23 McGlynn, op. cit. (2000), n. 9, at pp. 447–8.

form of human capital to be employed in the most efficient manner to maximize profits for the firm. It does not, nor does it purport to, deconstruct the structures and practices in law firms to examine the extent to which they act against women and other groups, and to seek to reconfigure the whole notion of legal practice and legal identity to promote genuine equality of opportunity for people of different cultural, social, and sexual backgrounds. Instead it seeks to fine-tune the existing model, without further reflection on its nature. In short, it reinforces the view that the legal profession is constructed in a manner that is gender neutral, if slightly less accommodating of women who have children, than of men or childless women. It is the antithesis of reflective practice.

Having said that, many of the proponents of the business case do seek to improve the lot of women in the profession, and in making some gains, may in time make more radical ones. If sufficient women rise to positions of power within the traditionally masculinist world of partnership, perhaps in time that world will be increasingly feminized and the identity of the profession will also shift.[24] That has certainly been the hope expressed by many – that, in time, the profession will change as women make up a larger percentage of senior staff. However, the business case is still not bearing much fruit even in the mid-2000s. The human capital theory appears to proffer the opportunity of equality on the basis of equal effort, equal commitment, and equal work for equal pay and promotion, as long as one is able to convince the partnership that one is not female. The business case appears to extend the opportunity of equality as long as it remains economically rational to do so.

In the meantime, during our recent research commissioned by the Law Society considering the experience of women solicitors who had had a break in their practising certificate in recent years, it became clear from our discussion that women solicitors were noting that their male colleagues were experiencing some of the same problems that they too had faced, but that men were more unwilling to leave or to speak up about the problems.[25] Collier too has noted many of the same concerns by male solicitors as we did with women solicitors.[26] This led us to consider whether in fact Sturm's analogy of the canary in the miner's lamp may be operating in the United Kingdom solicitors' profession – that women's progress within a sector is a barometer for how the profession is faring across its spectrum.[27] Her hypothesis is that the failure of women to thrive in a profession may be

24 However, see Menkel-Meadow, op. cit., n. 7, who considers that such gains have not been made on this basis in the United States.
25 Duff and Webley, op. cit., n. 3.
26 R. Collier, 'Male Lawyers and the Negotiation of Work and Family Commitments', paper given at SLSA Annual Conference 2004 on his research findings from the British Academy funded project.
27 Sturm, op. cit., n. 6.

381

evidence not simply of gender and other forms of discrimination, but evidence of whether the profession is wholly dysfunctional. She notes that women are more likely as a class to experience discrimination than men; they are more visible than many other minority groups because of their greater numbers and provide more accessible indicators of problems within the profession. This is largely due to the more frequent examination of their position than that of solicitors from ethnic minorities, lower socio-economic groups, gay solicitors or solicitors with disabilities. If this were true, if women's experience were symptomatic of a wider problem facing the whole profession (albeit one that affected disadvantaged groups more substantially), then is it possible that the increasing drive towards business efficiency, the commodification of legal services, and profit maximization may now be adversely affecting the profession in the round? Problems affecting the whole profession are more likely to receive attention, and thus reach a resolution, that those only affecting marginalized groups. The next section of this article considers some of the main findings from our research into women solicitors' experience of legal practice.[28] It then considers the extent to which the business case for equal opportunities may in fact be actively undermining the position of women in the profession, and now also perhaps its more traditional constituency – men.

II. FINDINGS FROM THE LAW SOCIETY WOMEN SOLICITORS RESEARCH

1. *Methodology*

The Law Society commissioned us to undertake qualitative research to explore the current reasons why women were leaving the solicitors' profession,[29] to follow on from its own quantitative research, through which they had contacted all women who had had a break in their practising certificate at some time during the previous five years.[30] The Law Society's

28 It is admitted that using the term 'women' is a difficult one due to the risk of essentialism. We allowed women who participated in the study to define whether they considered the issues they faced to be ones that were individual to them or were issues that they believed to be specific to particular groups or to women more generally. The findings reflect their views on this rather than, necessarily, our own. We have tried to provide more specific detail on the women's own circumstances where they believed that the issues they raised related to their own characteristics rather than to all women solicitors. For a discussion of the difficulties associated with categories such as men and women, the notions of family and work, see Gerson, op. cit., n. 14. See Collier, op. cit. (2002), n. 18, on reconceptualizing gender and, in particular, our understanding of the masculine.

29 A full account of the research and research method may be found at Duff and Webley, op. cit., n. 3.

30 For findings see Siems, op. cit., n. 3.

382

quantitative telephone interviews provided a group of women who expressed a willingness to take part in our qualitative research.[31] The qualitative research was conducted using six focus groups, run in London, Leeds, and Manchester, of women solicitors with a recorded break or non-renewal of their practising certificate at some stage during the previous five years. The number of women in the focus groups we conducted ranged from three to six. Women were self-selecting – those that were willing and able to take part in the focus groups that were arranged in each of the areas were welcome to participate and childcare was provided when needed. The research did not include a control group – we did not interview women who had not had a break in their practising certificate, nor did we interview men. Research on male solicitors' views was already being undertaken by Collier at this time, and much previous research had been undertaken on women solicitors more widely. This research has been discussed in the preceding section and is returned to later in this article, where we believe there to be important comparisons.

Although we had originally categorized the participants as either 'returners' to or 'leavers' from the profession, in keeping with the Law Society's classification for their earlier quantitative research, some spanned both categories. Some of the women had subsequently returned to the profession, while others considered themselves as having left the profession for good. Some of the 'leavers' felt that in the future they might return to legal practice. Others who were 'returners' believed that in the future they might leave legal practice. Having said that, the 'returners' tended to have career breaks for two main reasons: child-care (rather than continuing employment with maternity leave) or to travel. Many 'returners' had taken the career break opportunity to return to a different type of legal practice, for example, to move in-house or to move into public sector or government based legal employment. Two participants had retired and one had been forced to leave on grounds of ill health. A small minority of participants had worked part-time in legal practice, however, the number who felt that it was successful was even smaller. In fact only three women felt that their part-time working was a really positive experience. The 'leavers' most often gave the reason that they had chosen a career change due to their dissatisfaction with legal practice.

31 The Law Society identified 529 women as the population of 'returners to the profession' or 'leavers from the profession' during the previous five years, based on information in the practising certificate records. This categorization is by no means clear cut, see Duff and Webley, op. cit., n. 3, at p. 15. Of these, 82 per cent (439) were interviewed in the Law Society quantitative research, and 341 stated that they were willing to take part in our research. Potential participants were identified using a stratified random sampling technique in respect of these 341 women. The sample was divided into those with addresses in the north and those in the south. We should have preferred to adopt a more sensitive sampling technique; however, this was not possible within the confines of the research.

The issues to which the women repeatedly returned were lack of flexibility in the workplace, the long hours culture, the difficulty of fitting their work patterns into a male working paradigm, less favourable promotion prospects compared with male colleagues, poor management practices, and dehumanization of the individual by the firm. These were not universal, but were shared by the majority. The research did not seek to be representative of all women solicitors' views and we understand that our participants cannot represent women as 'a class' – essentialism is a difficulty in qualitative studies of this size, particularly when the participants comment on whether they believe that their experience is particular to them or one which they have seen, or they believe to be shared by other women. Their views are outlined below, and where we have considered their characteristics or firm characteristics to be important (or where they noted their importance) we have included those, along with any minority views, to illustrate our findings.

2. *The culturally masculinist office*

It is recognized by many commentators that masculinist cultures within many law firms make it difficult to retain women solicitors, as the appearance of gender neutrality masks the gendered traits privileged in the recruitment and promotion of staff.[32] According to a consultant with a City firm:

> There is an outpouring from law firms of the brightest and best (women), often to company legal departments, which, through sophisticated personnel and appraisal policies, are more likely to be meritocracies in which women do well.[33]

This accords with the views of many of our participants; indeed, a number of them had taken the same route themselves, leaving private practice not to work in a completely different field, but to become in-house lawyers. They had since found that their assumptions of better management and terms and conditions had been borne out. The majority of our participants felt that women solicitors in private practice were expected to fit in to a masculinist working paradigm.

> 5F2: I still think it's very much a man's profession.
> 5F2: I think it's changing and there are an awful lot of women in the profession but I still think you're looked on as you're not as capable as they are. I still feel that, even when I finished...

The masculinist cultures of the profession have led to assumptions about what constitutes an ideal lawyer. These assumptions revolve around perceived masculinist characteristics rather than feminist ones, and therefore,

---

32 McGlynn, op. cit. (2000), n. 9. See, further, Dowd, op. cit., n. 6; Fuchs Epstein, op. cit., n. 14.; Menkel-Meadow, op. cit., n. 7, and Sturm, op. cit., n. 6.
33 Denise Kingsmill, in the *Law Society Gazette*, 4 February 1998, 152.

while women may aspire to be the ideal and idealized lawyer, it is rare that they will ever be able to achieve the ideal.[34] The image of authority is masculine, yet perceived as gender neutral – as Collier explains:

> assessment of women against a normative 'ideal' employee, a figure understood simultaneously (and somewhat paradoxically) to be both distinctively gendered (as male/masculine: assertive, rational, competent, unemotional and so on); and, equally, to be somehow gender-neutral in terms of the commitments and dependencies which are seen as 'outwith' the field of paid employment.[35]

The woman of authority is therefore other than the norm, the exception.

There was a widespread perception among our participants, from large and small firms, commercial, general practice and legal aid, that women solicitors must act like men if they want to achieve progression at the same rate as male solicitors. In other words, they argued that women are required to behave differently, to become someone they are not, in order to progress quickly.[36] This does not appear to be a finding unique to United Kingdom legal practice. Rhode's research reveals that female characteristics and the characteristics expected of successful solicitors – assertiveness and competitiveness – are often perceived to be in contradiction.[37] Seron has gone further to suggest that to be a successful lawyer in a commercial context one needs to be a good entrepreneur, bringing in business and turning over a high volume of work and income, whereas it is difficult to find women who would be viewed as 'very entrepreneurial' because that implies the ability to 'hustle' and take risks that are often not typical female traits.[38] Thus, the characteristics of a good lawyer are the characteristics of an entrepreneur, and men are viewed as having these in greater measure than women. The vast majority of our participants, regardless of legal practice type or specialism, commented that traditionally masculinist traits were valued over feminist ones. The commercial and corporate law solicitors' concerns principally related to the need to 'hustle' to bring in more business.

> F31: '... I don't mean it's a peculiarly male thing but there's an awful lot of men who can talk a good a job but they don't necessarily *do* it and it has always riled me that a lot of my female colleagues, people who are really good

---

34 Thornton, op. cit., n. 17, at pp. 10–40.
35 See Collier, op. cit. (2002), n. 18, at p. 10.
36 H. Sommerlad, 'Women Solicitors in a Fractured Profession' (2002) 9 *International J. of the Legal Profession* at 215, stated by a finance lawyer in one of the Magic Circle firms.
37 D. Rhode, *The Unfinished Agenda: Women and the Legal Profession*, the ABA Report on Women in the Profession (2001) at 6
38 C. Seron, 'Managing Entrepreneurial Legal Services: The Transformation of Small Firm Practice' in Nelson, Trubek, and Solomon, op. cit., n. 22, at pp. 71–2. See P. Patton, 'Women Lawyers, Their Status, Influence, and Retention in the Legal Profession' (2004–5) 11 *William and Mary J. of Women and the Law* 173, at 182–3 for a discussion of the sociological literature on these traits.

at what they do and really efficient and get good outcomes are often ignored and passed over for promotion in favour of men who are frankly hopeless and the weakest people in the organisation but in front of the right people they've put on the right sort of front ...

This fits with Goriely and Williams's findings on the traditional approach to evaluating newly qualified solicitors, which relies more on measuring solicitors against the characteristics of the suitable 'chap' than on a rational and standardized approach to evaluation and appraisal.[39] It accords too with Sommerlad and Sanderson's and Kanter's discussion of cultural capital within legal practice, and with Gorman's statistical analysis that the greater the uncertainty in outcome in a case or transaction, the more likely that managers will return to cultural capital as a indicator of potential success than any past performance measure.[40] Many of our participants felt that they were being evaluated against the wrong criteria, and that the criteria used were not those that women as a group could meet as readily as their male counterparts – the classic definition of indirect discrimination. Nor did they believe the criteria to be inherently desirable as they were focused on individualistic tendencies such as competitiveness within the firm, rather than criteria that fostered positive team working environments that built long-term relationships with clients.[41]

Working patterns, styles, and skills were reported by most of the participants as other sources of inequality of opportunity for many women solicitors. They highlighted good communication skills, excellent client care, diligence, and a sense of responsibility as the key skills that they brought to the profession,[42] but also felt that they were steered into areas of work that were considered to utilize these skills but were perceived to be women's work and consequently lacked status, promotion prospects or strong financial reward. Many believed that team working was seen to be a weakness rather than a strength. Some believed too that this difference in working patterns explained why male managers found it impossible to see how job and file sharing could work effectively as, for them, this would require a substantial change in working style as compared with many female staff who were more naturally inclined towards a collaborative style of working.[43]

---

39 See T. Goriely and T. Williams, *The Impact of the New Training Scheme. Report on a Qualitative Study* (1996) at ch. 10 for a discussion and, in particular, at 124–5.

40 R. Kanter, 'Reflections on Women and the Legal Profession: A Sociological Perspective' (1978) 1 *Harvard Women's Law J.* 1, at 7. See, further, E. Gorman, 'Work Uncertainty and the Promotion of Professional Women: The Case of Law Firm Partnership' (2006) 85 *Social Forces* 865.

41 For a discussion of how teaching partisanship pervades attitudes to legal practice and of the dehumanization and commodification of solicitors, see Sturm, op. cit., n. 6.

42 For a discussion of gender differences, skills, and leadership, see S. Hegelsen, *The Female Advantage: Women's Ways of Leadership* (1990).

43 Discussions around flexible and part-time working featured prominently in the focus groups. For reasons of space, and because they need more detailed discussion, they are not discussed in this article.

3. *Competition and the market versus values and the private sphere*

The long-hours culture and the lack of satisfaction with that, as well as the impact this has on women with caring responsibilities,[44] and the merger of the professional with the social in respect of business and networking events after work alienate some women solicitors.[45] Women in our research did not note their concerns about the sexual capital of women in marketing opportunities, but did point to the elision between sporting events and business development opportunities, along with a heavy drinking culture, that all the participants found at best difficult to keep up with and at worst alienating and exclusionary:

> F3: That was a lot of evening drinks . . . and I'm pleased to be out of that . . . I mean some of them were quite fun, . . . the clients we had were lovely . . . the evenings in themselves weren't normally dull, just the number of them and the fact that you couldn't really say no, and the senior partner would organise it and you were expected to be there. There might be 2-3 in a week and there's a terrific drinking culture that's associated with it as well and so they go on until closing time and then where are we going now? If you say, well, actually I'm going home, they all look at you as if you're a lightweight. Ridiculous.

Sporting trips appeared to be by invitation only, were often during the working day, and were usually not open to women in the department. The after-work marketing events with clients were near compulsory, did not fit well with responsibilities outside work, and took up a lot of time in the evenings; they begrudged spending this time on what is after all, yet more work. Yet again, they felt that the goal of profit maximization was placed above the welfare of the firm's employees.

There was also a belief that a substantial proportion of their male colleagues relished the late nights and the feeling of working to tight deadlines, and that those solicitors who did not display similar traits were considered to be less than loyal to the professional project and the firm. But, this was not an exclusively male preoccupation; as the quote below suggests, it becomes part of the firm's culture:

---

44 The increased negative impact of long working hours on women solicitors who were primary child carers was noted by Sommerlad, op. cit., n. 36, at pp. 217–22, as long hours tend to militate against flexible working practices. See, further, C. Epstein and R. Saute, *The Part-time Paradox* (1998) for a discussion. This was noted in the early 1990s in the United States by Fuchs Epstein, by Hochschild and, in the 1990s, Nelson and Trubek. See Nelson and Trubek, op. cit., n. 22, at pp. 9–11.

45 McGlynn, op. cit., n. 10, at pp. 103–4. Exclusion from mentoring and networking opportunities were noted as a concern by participants who believed these were beneficial to promotion prospects as well as important to professional development. For a discussion of the importance of networking and mentoring, see R. Dinovitzer and J. Hagan, 'Lawyers on the move: the consequences of mobility for legal careers' (2006) 13 *International J. of the Legal Profession* 119.

> 3F6: ... and I know this has been said about men going for drinks after work and that sort of thing but it's no different when you work in an office full of women. If you're there late at night you know, you get ... a kind of blitz spirit ... let's order a pizza ... and quite naturally those sort of bonds begin to develop but unfortunately it means that if you're not in a position to compete on the playing field ... you become more outside of the group and I don't know what the answer is to that.

Others noted that their male colleagues were equally unhappy about the long hours that were expected of them. Further, our participants all agreed that long hours in the office was seen as a 'good', regardless of productivity level or necessity. In addition, they believed that the long hours spent in the office were worn as a badge of honour, an expression of machismo, and that those who opted out of this culture were sidelined away from interesting work and work that was likely to lead to promotion.[46] It was suggested by some that the partners in their firms encouraged long working hours because they believed this would increase the firm's profit margin. However, the reverse may be true. Parsons argues the business case for reducing working hours, quoting 'The Quality of Working Life' report by the Institute of Management that shows that by reducing the hours that staff work, their business can become more profitable and also a more enjoyable place to work.[47] He provides evidence such as moves by companies like Bass that have inserted terms into their contracts for legal services that require firms to comply with a maximum 50-hour week for their lawyers.[48] Apart from anything else, fresher staff are more likely to produce better quality work, he argues. In addition, they are less likely to be away from work due to ill-health. Research conducted in 1999 by Solcare for Bygott Biggs, the legal recruitment agency, found that: 70 per cent of those who took part in the research were completely exhausted; 70 per cent were worried about the amount of work they had to do; 67 per cent worked long hours to get the job done; 30 per cent of male lawyers and 20 per cent of female lawyers were drinking to excess; alcohol-related deaths in the legal profession are twice the national average.[49] The vast majority of women that we talked to believed that firms could improve their productivity simply by cutting working hours and valuing their staff as people rather than renewable resources. The long-hours culture was universally condemned as a threat to health, enthusiasm and

---

46 This bears out Thornton's findings, op. cit., n. 17, at p. 163.
47 Institute of Management, *The Quality of Working Life: 1998 Survey of Managers' Experiences*, cited by R. Parsons, *The Heart of Success: Making it in business without losing in life* (2002) at 30. See p. 26 for a humorous yet chillingly accurate comparison drawn between a city lawyer and a prisoner – the prisoner is considered to be in a better position than the lawyer, as the prisoner will be held captive for 15 rather than 40 years, even if the lawyer does get to leave the office on occasion.
48 Parsons, id., at p. 28, citing a report in the *Times*, 22 January 2000.
49 id., at p. 34.

commitment, family relationships, work efficiency and quality, client service, access to justice, and professionalism.

Sommerlad describes moves by some firms to push aside the impression that a long-hours culture is expected of lawyers and indeed to replace this with a 'nice place to work' ethos.[50] The rationale for this is that the firm is more likely to retain staff and to retain female staff than if it is perceived as working solicitors into the ground. Three of the women who participated in our research, all of whom had children, reported that they had been treated very well by their firms and enjoyed working in that environment, even though they too had at times worked long hours for their firms. Only one of them was based in London and she was very senior within that firm. However, this appears to be the exception rather than the norm, isolated instances rather than the beginnings of a whole shift in culture. Similar findings were reported in the quantitative study; of those solicitors who had considered leaving the profession, half of the females said they had considered leaving due to long hours and pressure compared to only a third of the males.[51]

Billing targets were another source of concern, although less so than is suggested by much of the United States literature. It was generally accepted that there was the appearance of parity in billing targets between them and their male peers, but that the way in which work was allocated meant that targets were harder to achieve for some than for others. One woman reported that her billed hours were 'stolen' by a senior male colleague while she was away on maternity leave. Many reported an overly aggressive culture associated with billing targets:

> 3F4: I think in some ways cost targets are quite good, you focus on what you're doing, you know, you earn good fees, you get a good salary, it's very clear but there's all sorts of shenanigans that then go on because of cost targets, I mean we used to have the most incredible office politics over good cases and he was stealing good cases and he was allocating work and it was the head of department's secretary so of course she was creaming off anything that she thought was going to pay well to, you know, her solicitor and all that sort of nonsense which I think is very destructive and it makes people not want to help each other out because you don't want to help one of your colleagues because you're thinking, well, I'm losing my billing time and I'm going to now have to stay late to make up my billable hours.

This quote relates to an exchange between women who had worked in City firms, high-street firms, and legal aid practices and was mentioned in the context of a legal aid firm rather than a large City practice. The participants all agreed with the problems inherent in billing targets, although one women who was a partner in a large commercial firm believed that billing targets were not inherently problematic as long as they were managed properly by the partnership. In particular, some women felt that they were given 'softer'

---

50 Sommerlad, op. cit., n. 36, at p. 221.
51 Siems, op. cit., n. 3, at pp. 62–3.

work, or more administrative duties that detracted from their billable hours or their ability to meet the target, although others felt this was the case in some firms, but not their own.

> 2F3: women traditionally do sometimes do soft work, don't they, that bills, you know, that is less profitable, and sometimes women may take on more work ... on more administration within the firm and then their targets would be less. I mean our targets were always quite odd because some areas of the law pulled in the money and some didn't and actually again I was very lucky to be in a firm that didn't place too much emphasis on that. I say that slightly tongue-in-cheek, it's probably different in bigger firms ...

Thornton has highlighted the role differentiation between men and women in legal practice, suggesting that women have been viewed as handmaidens who support male lawyers in their career progression rather than carve out a career of their own.[52] She goes further to suggest that women are now accepted and may even be preferred to male colleagues in certain roles, as long as they are acting under supervision, supporting senior male colleagues by 'reproducing conventional legal knowledge' as women work hard, can be trusted, will not take too many risks, and will seek advice if they feel they need it. These women, who act as backroom workers, provide an excellent service to senior men, without demanding career progression at the same pace as their male counterparts.[53] This had implications for their promotion prospects, for the type of work they were given, and also for the extent to which they felt valued for the work they did.

The majority of our participants believed that promotion prospects for women, particularly those who go on to have children, are lesser than those for comparable and even less well qualified and less hard-working men. This was perceived to be due to concerns by firms about promoting people who may ask for part-time or flexible working arrangements, which tends to be more associated with female colleagues. Others had experienced blatant discrimination once they had had a child, and sometimes from female rather than male colleagues, as this rather brutal quote illustrates:

> 1F1: ... it's as if you're always compensating for the fact that you might break your career, the fact that you were at high risk as a partner in case you had children, that's how they would have seen it. And ... when I went to an interview with my departmental head, ... who was a partner, at the end of my maternity leave when I'd had my first child, before I'd even sat in the chair she said don't even ask for part-time because there's no way that we'll consider it, she said, everybody knows where your loyalties will be and therefore we're not prepared to entertain it, and before I'd left the room she was phoning up the office that I worked at to ask about who could take my place before I'd even left the room. So, you know, there is that, there is such a big element of being prejudged.

---

52 Comments made by a senior barrister in Thornton, op. cit., n. 17, at p. 149.
53 id.

390

And so, while for many women, they felt their experience was one of indirect sidelining within the firm, for others it was clear that a choice had been made about whether they would be totally loyal to the firm or not, and, if found wanting, they would be pushed aside.[54]

Human capital theory would suggest that women were seeking less out of their work life than their male counterparts and that they did not invest the same mental and emotional energy into work as male solicitors do. This is in stark contrast to the views of our participants who had taken a career break.[55] Most of the women solicitors who had returned after a break were positive about their return to work because they found the work challenging and interesting. They particularly enjoyed the mental stimulation that work afforded them, especially those that had been on maternity leave. This group felt more self-confident on return to work, as they felt they were doing something in their own right and were being judged on this, although the feeling of confidence was in part attributed to working in a supportive environment. The women who did not feel supported on their return lost enthusiasm for the job and confidence in their abilities as a result. Participants also enjoyed the social interaction afforded by working outside the home. Some women came back to work reinvigorated and enthusiastic about practising as a solicitor, which seems at odds with the lack of identification between self-image and work. They perceived themselves to be more productive and more committed than their peers who had not had a career break. The return to work after a period away from the environment did highlight for many of the participants that while they were pleased to return to professional life, the culture that pervaded it felt very alien to them.

Although most explained that they were positive about their return to work, and regardless of the type of firm that they worked in, dissatisfaction began to creep in to the discussions when some of the women talked about conflicting work and family commitments. Some of our participants had only recently returned to work and had not yet found difficulties in juggling work and childcare, but over time some had found it very difficult to manage particularly after the birth of a second child. Galanter and Palay's research established that as female participation in law firms increased, they were less satisfied with legal practice than their male peers, and in law practice generally. In part, their dissatisfaction stemmed from the interplay between work and their family responsibilities.[56] The ABA Young Lawyers Division Survey[57] also suggests that younger lawyers, who it is contended were less

---

54 See, further, Patton, op. cit., n. 38, at pp. 181–2.
55 Most of the career breaks were as a result of maternity leave, however, for others it was to travel, to work abroad, or to undertake other caring responsibilities.
56 See M. Galanter and T. Palay, 'The Transformation of the Big Law Firm' in Nelson, Trubek, and Solomon, op. cit., n. 22, at p. 54 and their review of earlier United States research in the area.
57 B. Melendez, *ABA Young Lawyers Dvision Survey: Career Satisfaction* (2000) at <http://www.abanet.org/yld/satisfaction_800.doc>.

391

likely to have family responsibilities, were more satisfied than other surveys have suggested, such as the Boston Bar's research, which found that the difficulty of balancing home life, work life, and community service was one of the main barriers to professional fulfilment.[58] It is the lack of recognition of a life outside of the office that appeared to cause the greatest dissatisfaction, rather than the long hours that were required. Long hours in the office do not necessarily correlate with dissatisfaction, but it may be symptomatic of how little firms think of their staff and their lives. In our research, the extent to which our participants felt that their firm valued them as autonomous people made an enormous difference to their feelings of worth and their feelings towards their job. Four of our participants made it clear that they felt valued and enjoyed their work life as a result.[59]

It could be argued that some models of the business case may not require people to enjoy their jobs, as long as they are prepared to continue to work at a level that makes financial sense to the firm. Other models may consider that enjoyment and productivity go hand in hand to maximize profit. However, one anathema to the business model must surely be poor management practice, as trained managerial level staff are required to make rational business decisions and manage their staff in the business interest.[60] Three of the four who enjoyed their working environment explained their satisfaction in part because they had tremendously supportive mangers and this fostered their loyalty and commitment. However, the majority of women were concerned that some of the poor practice in the firms that they had worked in was a result of poor management rather than a deliberate attempt to exploit staff. A solicitor, who had formerly worked as a housing law specialist undertaking legal aid work, felt that many of the 'management' strategies were counterproductive, if unconsciously driven:

> 2F2: I think my main negative aspect was probably although in one way I quite liked being left to work on my own, in other ways I think I was quite often thrown into situations which I wasn't trained for or prepared for in any way

58 Boston Bar Association Task Force on Professional Fulfillment, *Expectations, Reality and Recommendations for Change* (1997) at <http://www.bostonbar.org/prs/reports.htm>.

59 One was a partner in a large City firm, one was an associate in a large provincial firm, another had just retired from a high-street practice specializing in non-contentious work, and the final one had worked 'at her husband's' firm as she described it. The other participants talked extensively about the stress they endured, at times at the expense of their physical and mental health, their family life, from the enormous burden of responsibility they felt towards their clients and their firms. There is insufficient space to discuss this in detail here, but it was one of the reasons why two of our participants had left work as a solicitor to become school teachers. Both reported lower levels of stress as a result, and noted that their personalities had reverted to their pre-law, more carefree days.

60 This is not a finding limited to the United Kingdom experience. See Rhode, op. cit., n. 15, at p. 11, and J. Henning, *Maximising Law Firm Profitability: Hiring, Training and Productive Lawyers* (1993).

392

and I think in the long term that has an effect on your deep core of confidence because you're constantly dealing with situations where you think I shouldn't be doing this and somebody more superior should be assisting or guiding me and they're not, I'm just being dumped.

Others too highlighted the fact that managers in private practice rarely receive management training and this showed in the interaction between those managers and their staff:

4F: One of the things you used to hear, mostly as a joke, is that how good lawyers make bad managers.

Those who worked in-house believed that managerial practice was more enlightened in their current positions than in previous private practice employment, although there was one exception to that which was explained as one very poor manager rather than a lack of a good management system. They were also happier in their work and consequently felt more positively towards their work place. Perhaps the lack of management expertise leads solicitors to feel devalued in the work place, and dissatisfied with their professional lives?

4. The dehumanizing office – the commodification of the legal profession?

A long list of factors appear to affect a solicitor's satisfaction in the workplace including the extent to which they feel valued for the work that they do and the extent to which they considered themselves to be part of a profession that performs an important function in society. In the United States, the Boston Bar concluded that the list of factors that detract from feelings of worth and professionalism included: the increasing measurement and pressure for increased productivity, the increased commercialization of legal practice, the move towards lawyers as technicians rather than professionals, a decrease in the politeness and civility of members of the legal profession, particularly among litigators, the lack of mentoring, increased law student debt, feelings of isolation and alienation in legal practice, negative perceptions of lawyers, resources issues, and lack of practice management training.[61] Many of these factors were noted by our participants, although not increased student debt (this may change in coming years), nor lack of civility in the litigation environment. It has been argued that large law firms and corporate legal departments rely on staff notions of legal professionalism to ensure that the work undertaken by their staff is of a high quality.[62] This could equally be said to be true in smaller firms, legal aid firms, and law centres that rely heavily on the professionalism of their solicitors to work

---

61 Boston Bar Association, *Report of the Boston Bar Association Task Force on Professional Fulfillment* (2003) at <http://www.bostonbar.org/prs/fulfillment.htm> 6–7.
62 R. Nelson and D. Trubek, 'Arenas of Professionalism: The Professional Ideologies of Lawyers in Context' in Nelson, Trubek, and Solomon, op. cit., n. 22, at pp. 208–9.

393

often long hours, for low pay and in difficult circumstances.[63] However, across the legal profession there have been moves toward routinization of work and the adoption of corporate values that may either have the effect of deskilling staff, or at least giving the impression to staff that they are being deskilled and thus deprofessionalized.[64] As one of our participants explained:

> 3F4: the worse thing for me was the Legal Aid Board or whatever they call themselves now, I mean the amount of ridiculous nonsensical bureaucracy that's ... pointless and really quite insulting to your professionalism ... on top of everything else you have to do, to have to deal with the Legal Services Commission was a nightmare ... all our phones had a loudspeaker thing on them because you get put on hold by the Legal Services Commission for up to an hour and a half at a time and you'd walk round our office and you could just hear the Four Seasons because that's their hold music, coming out of every room.

Solicitors in the large and small firms, commercial, legal aid, City, and provincial all mentioned status as an important draw to the profession, but also their perception that the profession was losing its professionalism either through outside intervention (in the case of legal aid firms) or through pandering to the unrealistic demands of clients in the commercial sphere. A number of our participants were concerned that the profession was also losing its status and would soon become Supermarkets-R-Us-Law writ large, as a result of call centres replacing law offices and the professional ethos jettisoned for a consumer service ethos.[65] This dented their self-image and feelings of status. Solicitors in smaller firms and not-for-profit organizations felt that the lack of resources was hampering their ability to act as professionals for their clients. All our participants felt, to a greater or lesser extent, on a treadmill that they could not get off while staying in the profession, and it was one that did not value their experience or their skills, and did not wish to or was not able to value them as people.

Sommerlad's research identified the perception that working in a law firm may be a dehumanizing experience.[66] There was unanimous agreement from our participants, unprompted by us and in six separate focus groups, that firms did not to value their staff nearly enough, even from the four private practice staff who believed themselves to be valued by their most recent employer:

---

63 R. Moorhead, 'Legal Aid and the Decline of Private Practice; Blue Murder or Toxic Job?' (2004) 11 *International J. of the Legal Profession* 159.
64 However, see R. Abel, 'Constructing the Professional Commodity' in his *American Lawyers* (1989) for a fuller discussion about the factors that create the notion of legal professionalism.
65 See D. Clementi, *Report of the Review of the Regulatory Framework for Legal Services in England and Wales* (2004), downloadable at <http://www.legal-services-review.org.uk/content/report/index.htm>.
66 Sommerlad, op. cit., n. 36, at p. 217.

394

> 1F2: I agree with that totally and I also think that value, value the human resources you've got, there are so many people with so much commitment and enthusiasm, but it needs to be nurtured and not just switched off and burnt out ...

It was argued that firms could increase loyalty and also productivity by valuing their staff. Not only that, but each group stated that it was economically nonsensical to lose staff through lack of value or neglect. Once more, some of the participants were referring to the business case for valuing staff:

> 1F3: Again I agree that having developed people and nurtured the talent and put people through training contracts at some expense, I think the firm has an interest in getting the right people in the right jobs, working in the right way for everybody and if there's a way to achieve that I think it would show dividends.

Others considered it more a matter of human decency. The lack of value was felt particularly strongly on return to work after a career break or maternity leave. This was evidenced as a perception that they had somehow lost their years of acquired skill and knowledge as a result of, in some instances, a relatively short period away from work.

Some of the anecdotes from our focus groups were so shocking that they brought focus groups to a complete standstill for some time, as the other women in the group first tried to take in what they had heard, and then offered support to the teller and finally burst into laughter at the absurdity of the situation. The next quote illustrates the extent to which one woman not only felt like she had been reduced to a number by her firm, but had indeed been so reduced:

> F1: well, it's ... one of the biggest firms and it is anonymous, you're very much anonymous. You're viewed as a means of making income and very often nobody knows who you are anyway apart from that. I mean you get memos to sort of employee number 693, you know, they haven't learnt that skill of a name – [laughs] – so I think that's right, I think there is a big difference between small firms and big firms ...

It is difficult to say how this large law firm can consider that it values its solicitors as professionals, when it addresses them in such a fashion. Nor is it surprising when, as a result, solicitors feel that they have no choice but to move on. Mercifully this extreme situation did not appear to have been replicated amongst the other firms at which our participants had worked, nor did any of our participants find it anything other than shocking.

It has been suggested that women consider that they can compensate for the downsides of working in a masculinist culture with 'psychic income',[67] including working for the public good, creating a better quality of life for

---

67 See A. Gellis, 'Great Expectations of Women in the Legal Profession, a Commentary on State Studies' (1991) *66 Indiana Law J.* 941, at 962.

themselves and their families, and other such non-monetary, 'softer' trade offs.[68] This certainly appeared to be the case for some of our participants. Some had traded money for a public sector legal job in the hope that this would increase their psychic income and consequently their quality of life, although some had found that with the move towards private sector ethics in the public sector, their hopes of increased psychic income were decreasing over time:

> 2F1: So it's a work culture thing and unfortunately it has drifted from commercial practice into the public sector in a way that the public sector is obsessively measuring itself.

There was concern expressed by those working in legal aid firms and law centres that the softer benefits that they had traded for less money and less status, were being eroded by the need to bring in more money, the move towards business efficiency, and the need to justify one's working practices to outside agencies. They felt that this could only get worse over time. Some had had to move out of the legal field entirely to find a more human environment and to regain an acceptable quality of life, and one even believed that retraining as a school teacher had been a major improvement.

The literature concedes that men are also afflicted by the masculinist cultures and also by the subordination of the employee to the demands of the firm. Whether subordination of the person, or dehumanization, and masculinist cultures are one and the same is a moot point; they may be products of the current rather unsophisticated business model that appears to be operating in many firms. A number of our participants explained that their male colleagues felt equally if not more trapped as they could not use the 'excuse', as one of our participants called it, of maternity leave to think about where next in terms of career, or use the break as an exit strategy for a new way of life.

> 3F1: ... the reaction of a lot of my male colleagues when I said I was leaving was that they would like to but then it was out of the question for them because they had families and they're still the main providers.

This differs from Thornton's view that the social pressure on men to succeed is so strong that:

> [M]en are therefore encouraged to strive to suppress humanistic sentiments in order to slough off the feminised seeds of invidiousness associated with subordinate status. Women have rarely been perceived as serious careerists ...[69]

although it may make it more difficult for men to leave work or change career. Collier's research into the views of male solicitors, carried out at a similar time as our own, would suggest that many male solicitors experience many of the suffocating effects of the legal culture, which have been dubbed

---

68 For a discussion see Thornton, op. cit., n. 17, at pp. 158–62.
69 id., at p. 153.

396

EXERCISE 5 ● 139

masculinist traits, and yet they too feel powerless to resist them.[70] However, women lawyers have been reporting the dominance and difficulties associated with the masculinist cultures in very similar terms for close to twenty years, with little evidence that the cultural shift is moving in the direction of women at all.[71] They continue to do so, as this quote from a solicitor who moved in-house having trained at a City law firm and then worked at a niche practice in the West End explains:

> 3F3: I think it's probably something that's true of the characters of a lot of individuals in the law, particularly men I have to say, but I just found a lot of them incredibly aggressive and not particularly productive or helpful in getting things done and maybe I'm a particularly unaggressive person, I don't know, but it was something that I just, I shuddered at the thought of having to go back and deal with some of those people ... I wasn't prepared for [it] when I went into the profession in the first place, I really didn't expect people to be such bullies. I mean I'm not a wimp or anything but there was some people ... it's their aim just to get one over on you all the time and it just makes for unpleasant working ...

It may now be biting against male solicitors as well, and this may prompt change in the profession, whereas women's concerns seem to have affected little change over that period. The business case, as adopted by the legal profession at present, may be nemesis for professionalism and also for solicitor satisfaction with their work, for both women and men.

III. A VALUES BASED MODEL OF LEGAL PRACTICE?

There is good evidence from the United States that women are disproportionately affected and that alienation may be sufficient to cause women to leave the profession, and similar evidence is mounting in the United Kingdom. United States research conducted by Catalyst indicated that large numbers of women go to law school and yet women represented as little as 15.6 per cent of partners and 13.7 per cent of general counsels in Fortune 500 companies. The study[72] found that women intended to stay with their current employer for three years fewer than the men in the study, and that women who were younger or from ethnic minority groups (women of colour as described in the United States report) intended to leave their present

---

70 Although see research by Richard Collier indicating that male solicitors also feel under pressure with the difficulty of balancing family and work: Collier, op. cit., n. 26. See, too, R. Collier, 'Work-life balance: ladies only?' *The Lawyer*, 23 May 2005, 33.

71 See Menkel-Meadow, op. cit., n. 7.

72 See Catalyst, *Women in Law: Making the Case* (2001) research undertaken by Catalyst and sponsored by Columbia University School of Law, Harvard Law School, the University of California at Berkley Law School, the University of Michigan Law School, and Yale Law School.

employer sooner still. But alienation was not restricted to women, nor was the desire to leave their current positions. If alienation results in women leaving the profession, then it may lead men to leave too. The findings suggest that employers are more likely to retain solicitors if they provide them with opportunities for promotion and advancement as well as opportunities to develop themselves personally and professionally by making mentors available and allowing them control over their work.[73] The United States findings were similar to suggestions made by participants in our study, who also felt that career advancement, mentoring, and opportunities for personal development were important for retaining women in the profession. They also concluded that with the amount of time, money, and effort expended in training solicitors to full fee-earning potential, it was economically inefficient to then allow them to leave if there were ways in which their employment could be retained. Again, the business model was harnessed as a way to canvas support for equal opportunities policies.

It cannot be said that our participants found working as a solicitor to be an entirely negative experience and on that basis there is hope. All participants expressed positive aspects about their work as a solicitor; none felt that their career choice had been a complete mistake, nor that the profession was irredeemable. The great positives of working as a solicitor were the intellectual challenge and the variety of work that they carried out. For many, the satisfaction of working for and interacting with clients was an important, positive aspect of their role and for some, the status associated with being a solicitor was important. Some women enjoyed the interaction of office life, found teamwork to be a positive element of their work while retaining their independence as professionals. As one now retired member of the profession noted:

> 5F2: But I think it is a very good profession and I know it's harder now but it has given me an awful lot of pleasure and I hope I've given people what they wanted because I think your clients are important and I think it's something that you get a great deal of satisfaction from, if you're doing the job correctly, which hopefully we all do.

Participants also provided examples of the negatives about leaving work as a solicitor. For some it was the drop in pay (particularly those who had worked in commercial law practice), for others it was the loss of status or the feeling that they had lost part of their identity by leaving legal practice. Some women even went as far as to say that they felt a sense of failure for leaving the profession, for not being able to fit in with the established system of work within the profession:

---

73 The research was conducted through a detailed survey of 6,300 graduates from the participating schools from the classes of 1970–1999 with a response rate of 24 per cent. The research also involved interviews and focus groups with 21 lawyers from a representative sample.

398

1F2: I think to some extent a feeling of disappointment, that you'd achieved something, I felt I'd achieved something by qualifying and then feeling that you had put it on one side, that that part of your identity had gone.

A number of those that had felt compelled to leave still wished that they had been able to find a way to make working as a solicitor work for them.

The participants spoke constantly about the need for the 'establishment' in law firms to look to working practices in other sectors, to embrace difference and to value talent rather than conformity or the exclusive drive for short-term profit.[74] The women were passionate believers in the role that the profession could play in society and the importance of women solicitors in that project, but many felt that as long as their talents went under-recognized, women would continue to leave and these opportunities would be lost. Those few who spoke in support of their working environment expressed gratitude that their firms had treated them well. For the remainder, it was not concessions they wanted, it was working practices that made good economic, ethical, and social sense.[75] It is not so much that the profession has a choice as to whether it tackles these concerns, it is more that sooner or later it will have to. If not, the culture will continue to deteriorate, and solicitors, regardless of gender, colour, creed or sexual orientation, will be forced to chose between legal practice or life.

How best to reconceptualize professional identity and the professional project in order to further the advancement of women, and of other marginalized groups in the profession? A market-based business approach, as currently configured, has not succeeded to any great extent and as Radin and McGlynn explain, it continues to prize the economic above self. For those of us who believe that equality of opportunity is a social and moral right, as opposed to a means to the end of short-term profit maximization, it is difficult to conceive of a way to persuade a profession that is still relatively homogeneous in the senior ranks to reconsider its role and its identity in this way.[76] They may be swayed by long-term profit concerns, which would permit a more sophisticated business model to triumph, but ultimately this may not help those smaller firms and law centres and nor would it address the issue of values as fundamental rather than subordinate to the market. Sommerlad and Sanderson's research provides a good insight into why this may be so: the theory and the practice of cultural capital explains why the profession remakes itself in its own image, but what arguments may be advanced, or what strategies may be employed to enlighten the profession

---

74 Sommerlad and Sanderson have suggested strategies in this respect, op. cit. (1997), n. 2. See, too, Duff and Webley, op. cit., n. 3 for further details of strategies suggested by participants in this study.

75 For reasons of space we have not included our participants' views on part-time and flexible working practices. These may be found in Duff and Webley, id. and in a subsequent article that will focus on this issue.

76 See R. Korzec, 'Working on the "Mommy Track": Motherhood and Women Lawyers' (1997) 8 *Hastings Women's Law J.* 117, at 136.

so that true progress may be made towards equality of opportunity?[77] The answer may lie in the findings of Collier's research into the experience of men and the dissatisfaction and the hurdles that many of them reported that they face during their working lives.[78] The work-life balance discussion, advanced by professionals and in the literature more usually in the context of women and, in particular, in the context of working mothers, appears to be gaining momentum with male professionals as well. Work-life balance debates are not exclusively market driven, although the business case is now being used in this context as well, in terms of increased enthusiasm and increased focus leading to greater productivity and quality of work. The work-life balance may, however, hold the key, to refocusing the profession as it focuses on the human experience both in work and outside work, rather than the needs of the firm as a purely profit-making enterprise.

There are obvious difficulties with this approach, not least that the work-life balance debate or 'theory' remains rather ill-defined.[79] It falls within the field of 'we know it when we see it', along with gut reactions, many of which have plagued the advancement of women in the profession in the past. It could be argued that work-life balance is really another branding for feminist cultures, but a less obvious and less threatening one for the legal establishment to consider. Work-life balance may be seen as code for having less commitment to the workplace, which has dogged part-time workers' (often women) promotion prospects.[80] Equally, unless law partners appear to see a benefit, to soften the blow of potentially lesser profits each year, then it is unlikely that law firms will take such theories seriously. There are, we are sure, many more arguments against raising the work-life balance debate as a counter to the current business case, not least the assumption that all firms are profit-making, or profit-focused, or that all firms are sufficiently financially viable to take non-financial considerations into account in the short term. Sadly, the threat that women will continue to leave the profession in large numbers, taking with them their valuable experience and the money that the firm has invested in their training and development, has not improved retention of women solicitors.

One wonders whether the threat of men leaving in similar numbers may galvanize firms into changing their approach to working practices, promotion decision making, and the culture of long hours and presentism that pervades the sector. The tide may be turning, if only as a result of male demands rather than female ones. A genuine acceptance of the need to reach

---

77 Sommerlad and Sanderson, op. cit. (1998), n. 2.
78 Collier, op. cit., n. 70.
79 See Collier, op. cit., n. 15. See, further, English, op. cit., n. 14.
80 See, further, Fuchs Epstein et al., op. cit., n. 14; E. Burton, 'More Glass Ceilings Than Open Doors: Women as Outsiders in the Legal Profession' (1996–7) 65 *Fordham Law Rev.* 565; C. Fuchs Epstein, 'Women in the Legal Profession at the Turn of the Twenty-First Century: Assessing Glass Ceilings and Open Doors' (2000–1) 49 *Kansas Law Rev.* 733.

a work-life balance may well advance the position of women in the profession, although it may take men to demand the changes before it does. A more feminist culture may develop at the request of men, who are also feeling dehumanized and devalued, rather than from female intervention. It is unlikely to restructure the profession to such an extent that it will assist in developing a culture of equality of opportunity that will take down barriers affecting other marginalized groups.[81] That will only be possible if the profession is genuinely prepared to examine its cultural capital foundations, and there is little evidence in our study and those of many others, to suggest that this is likely to occur in the near future.

CONCLUSIONS

Work-life balance debates bring the profession back to the issue of values, as opposed to one central value – law as business, law as profit. As Rhode discusses in the United States context:

> most lawyers want not only a comfortable lifestyle, but also a supportive practice environment and socially useful work. Ironically enough, attorneys' success in achieving the first objective has limited their ability to achieve the others.[82]

The pursuit of the current business model of law, which appears to lack sophistication or long-term focus and does not yield to basic ethical principles of equality and human value, pursues efficiency through routinization across all sectors, and profit in many. In the process, it has squeezed out the opportunity to undertake challenging and valuable (in a personal sense) legal work, has led to a management structure that removes much of the control from individual solicitors over workload, work type, and work patterns. It has also increased the dominance of the public over the private sphere to the extent that many once public-sphere activities have been moved to the private (voluntary work, pro bono activities), at a time when the private sphere is already under pressure in respect of family and other personal commitments.[83] The solicitor as a unit of production has become a reality in some firms. Until the pursuit of business efficiency and profit are relegated to the status of one value – but not the core value – of the profession, it is unlikely that the status of women, of minority groups, and for that matter of fathers, will improve substantially.

The research has demonstrated that many of the problems that have been reported in earlier studies on women in the legal profession, both in the

---

81 See Mossman, op. cit., n. 14, at p. 293.
82 Rhode, op. cit., n. 15, at p. 13. This lecture, published as an article, provides a detailed analysis of the profit versus wider values tension in the United States legal profession.
83 For a discussion, see D. Myers, *The Pursuit of Happiness* (1993) at 133–4. This point is also raised by Rhode, id., at p. 6.

401

United Kingdom and in the United States, persist. The research participants were all women who had had a break in their practising certificate and their insights explained that the lack of a successful work/life balance, the institutionalization of the long-hours culture and, for some, the deprofessionalization of their work had an impact on whether they wished to remain in the profession. They believed that many of the problems were associated with the current business model adopted by firms, whether this was profit-driven or audit-driven. They also suggested that the negative effects were not isolated to particular groups of women but were being experienced to some extent by both genders and across all firms, even if they were more acute for traditionally marginalized groups. It will be interesting to see whether men are more able to effect institutional change in the profession and whether the change improves work/life balance for all solicitors regardless of gender.

▶ 9
Studying at University

University isn't all about studying. Most students want to make friends and have a good social life, as well as getting a degree. Many have lots of other goals, such as participating in sporting activities, travelling or earning some money. However, getting a good degree, and thereby opening up a really wide range of employment possibilities, often features quite highly on many students' wish-lists. In order to achieve your full academic potential, and graduate with a degree that you really think reflects your true abilities, it helps to think about the study skills you might need to acquire, or develop, to help you. The purpose of this chapter of *How to Study Law* is to help you fulfil your academic potential. It suggests some strategies that are intended to help you study law more effectively, not only so that you can improve your academic performance, but also so that studying law may become a more enjoyable and satisfying experience, and one which leaves time for all the other things you want to do while you are at university.

▶ 9.1

Successful study does not simply involve spending a lot of time working. Students who spend a lot of time on their work do not necessarily receive high marks (although clearly there is some correlation between the effort you put in to your academic work and the results you can expect to achieve). The purpose of this chapter is to suggest some techniques which you can apply to the tasks which law students are asked to carry out, such as writing essays or participating in seminars, which will enable you to get the most out of the degree you have chosen to study.

LEARNING INDEPENDENTLY

As a student in a college or university, you will be expected to take responsibility for your own learning. Your tutors will assume that you can work on your own without supervision, develop your research skills, complete assessment tasks and hand them in on time. You are likely to spend a much smaller proportion of your time on timetabled activities than you did at school. Your tutors will generally be helpful, but they are not school teachers, and they will not expect to guide your day-to-day learning in the same way as your teachers may have done. You will be responsible for ensuring that you know what lectures and small group sessions you need to attend, where they are held and at what time. You will be expected to know whether you have to prepare work in advance of a seminar or tutorial, and to do it in time. You will also be responsible for meeting any deadlines set for coursework or assessment tasks. The freedom to learn in your own way is very rewarding, but some people find this approach very challenging, because it is extremely different to the one they were used to before they came to university.

▶ 9.2

It is up to you to organise your time and plan it so that you can get everything done which you need to do, both in terms of your academic work and your social life, as well as any paid employment you might be engaged in. The next section of this chapter is devoted to time management, because it is one of the most useful skills you can learn. It will not just be useful whilst you are a student; it is one of the skills that are commonly called "transferable", because it can be used not just while you are a student, but also throughout the rest of your life.

MANAGING YOUR TIME

9.3 ▶ As a law student, you will be expected to do a number of different things: attend classes or lectures, prepare work for discussion in tutorials, seminars or classes, write essays and sit exams. At the same time, there will be other things you want to do, such as go out with your friends, go shopping or play sports. There will also be things that you pretty much *have* to do (unless you can get someone else to do them for you) like buying food and doing the washing. In order to fit everything in, it's best to work out a plan, so that you don't forget to do something or start getting behind with your work.

- **Buy a diary or use the calendar on your mobile device**
  You can use your diary or electronic calendar to plan your time. To be effective, it needs to contain a complete record of what you have to do. You need to carry it with you and add new appointments as you make them. You could start by putting in all your academic commitments—lectures, tutorials/seminars, deadlines for coursework and so on. Then add in social engagements and other things you want or need to do. Get into the habit of writing other commitments into your diary as soon as they come up.

- **How much time should I spend on my law degree?**
  No-one would suggest that you spend all your time studying. The whole point of managing your time is to have enough time *both* to study effecrively *and* to do all the other things you want to do. It is impossible to tell anyone precisely how much time they need to spend studying. Everyone is a unique individual and has different rquirements. But, if you are a full-time student, then think of working for your degree as being similar, in terms of time, to a full-time job—around 40 hours a week. At certain times, if you have an assessment to prepare, or exams to revise for, you will find you need to spend considerably more time. The important thing is to work out how much time you personally need to spend in order to fulfil the requirements of your course of study.

- **Become good at prioritising**
  Much of the time you will have multiple things you need to be making progress with—seminar preparation, buying lunch, meeting friends, listening to music, attending lectures and so on. You clearly can't do everything at once. Many people find it helpful to make lists, covering what they want to get done on a particular day or in a certain week. Get used to prioritising items on your list—highlight those that you absolutely MUST get done, and fit the others in around them.

● **Find out if there are hidden institutional time constraints**
Even if you are good at time management, your plans can be upset by the arrangements made by your institution. It is all very well planning to do lots of research for an essay during the vacation, but not if the library is going to be closed for building alterations for three weeks. Equally, you may come across the problem of "bunched deadlines", where several of the courses you are doing require assessed work to be handed in on the same day. You can alleviate these problems by finding out about the library, computers, and other support services well in advance and by asking tutors to give you assignments in good time, but you may not be able to overcome such difficulties completely. If you are planning your time well in advance, however, that should give you sufficient flexibility to deal with the resulting pressure on your time, and you will be in a much better position than someone who has given no thought to such problems.

● **Be realistic when planning your time**
Although you will often be working to deadlines imposed by your tutors, it will be up to you to organise your time around those deadlines. Be realistic about how much time you need to set aside in order to complete your essays or tutorial preparation. It is counterproductive to set yourself a deadline that you cannot possibly hope to meet. Many activities will take longer than you think; for instance, most law students are surprised how long it takes them to do the research for an essay!

When you are planning your time, you need to be realistic about your own strengths and weaknesses, too. If you are the sort of person who can stay in and write your essay on a Saturday afternoon when all your friends are going out together, that's fine. On the other hand, if you are the sort of person who cannot wake up before midday, it is unrealistic to plan to write your essay at 8.30 in the morning. If you do not allow yourself sufficient time to do something, you may start to feel depressed and frustrated. If your schedule is realistic, you will gain satisfaction from knowing that you have achieved what you set out to do. Of course, everyone underestimates the time they need sometimes, but you should try to avoid this happening to you too often.

● **Don't leave things until the last minute**
This especially applies to preparation for tutorials and seminars, and the research you will need to do for assignments. If you leave things to the last minute, you may well find that most of the books and articles you need to use have already been borrowed by other students. You can sometimes rescue the situation by finding the information you need elsewhere, but it takes a lot of thought, time and energy to discover alternative sources of information. Your tutors are unlikely to be sympathetic if you miss deadlines simply because you left everything to the last minute.

MAKING LECTURES WORK FOR YOU

Lectures usually last 1–2 hours, and are delivered to large groups of students at once. They allow the lecturer to explain the main ideas in an area. Often, lecturers will also take the opportunity to tell students about the latest developments in an area, and to explain any particularly

▷ 9.4

complex parts of a subject. Lectures are often regarded as forming the backbone of a course and it is usually assumed that most students will attend them. The content of lectures, and the handouts or powerpoint slides that often accompany them, also form the basis for further independent study.

Lecturing style is closely related to the personality of an individual lecturer, so you are likely to come across a wide variety of lectures delivered in many different styles. Some will be excellent, some less so. As a student, you will need to develop a good technique for dealing with lectures, which you can then adapt to cope with the different lecturing styles you come across. Don't forget that while most lecturers want to be good at what they do, and deliver lectures of a very high standard, you are ultimately responsible for your own education. You must make lectures work for you. Here are a number of suggestions which will help you to do that.

● **Arrive in reasonably good time**
Handouts and important announcements are often given out at the beginning of lectures; you may be very confused if you miss them. Equally, the first few minutes of the lecture itself are important, as the lecturer will often summarise the main points of the lecture, or remind you where they have got up to in their coverage of a topic.

● **Listen actively**
Listening to a lecture can be a very passive experience. Students are not generally expected to interrupt a lecture by asking questions or making comments (although some lecturers will include interactive elements in their lectures). In a standard lecture, it is very easy to "switch off" and lose the thread of the lecture. To avoid this, take notes to help you to concentrate. Do this even if you are permitted to record the lecture: you may never get round to listening to it again, but your notes will be very important for revision when you come to do your exams. When you are listening to the lecture, try to relate what you are hearing to your existing knowledge of the subject and think how the new information fits into it. A lecture can be very boring if the lecturer has a monotonous delivery, but as an effective listener, you need to train yourself to ignore poor delivery, and concentrate on the content of what is being said, which you can briefly record in your notes.

● **Eliminate distractions**
In order to help you concentrate in lectures, you need to eliminate as many distractions as possible. Switch your mobile phone off; texting your friends might appear more fun than taking notes in the short term, but it won't help you when you are revising for exams. Make sure you are comfortable; use a clipboard if there is no desk. Use a convenient size of paper, which gives you enough space to set out your notes clearly. If you have a series of consecutive lectures you may become uncomfortable because you are sitting for long periods; try to move your limbs slightly during the lecture and use any brief gaps between the lectures to get out of your seat and move around a bit.

● **Take notes to aid concentration**
Since one of the main purposes of taking notes is to use them in the future, it is important to devise a system of note-taking which produces a clear set of notes which you will

understand when you come to look at them again, weeks or months after the original lecture. Handouts or powerpoint slides that support the lecture can make the task of note-taking easier, if they are well used; they should show you the broad structure of the lecturer and the main topics which will be covered. The lecturer may help you by summarizing their main points; they may also try to aid your understanding by including examples or illustrations; these are good to include in your notes, as they will help to remind you of the workings of the arguments. Note the names of cases, statutes and academic writers who are mentioned; if there is a lecture handout, this should help you as it will contain names of cases and statutes and other technical legal terms, so you don't need to get all these perfectly during the lecture; you can insert them when you review your lecture notes.

● **Take notes which will be useful in the future**
There is no single "best" way of taking notes. Some people will take quite detailed notes; others will take down the key points in a diagrammatic form. Many people find it helpful to use headings and sub-headings to emphasise the main points made, and to indicate changes in topics. Numbered points can provide a quick way of noting a large quantity of information. Underlining and the use of different coloured pens can direct your attention to particular points.

The most important factor here is to establish a style of note-taking which results in a useful set of notes for you to refer to after the lecture has finished. Since law degrees generally rely on lectures as the main source of information, you may feel you need to write down quite a lot in order to be sure that you have everything you need. However, don't attempt to write down everything the lecturer says, as you won't be able to do this, and you will lose the sense of what they are saying. When you have taken some notes in some lectures, it is worth stopping to ask yourself if they will be useful to you in the future. If they are too messy, too short or too confusing, you can take steps to improve your note-taking technique. If you are unsure about the best way in which to take notes, you should consult one of the study guides that are listed in the "Further Reading" section at the end of this chapter.

● **Review your notes as soon as possible**
It is important to review your notes while the lecture is still fresh in your mind. You may need to expand what you have written, or add headings, or do a little research on a point which you have not understood. Some people like to summarise their notes in diagrammatic form at this stage.

TUTORIALS AND SEMINARS

Tutorials involve small groups of students who meet regularly with an academic tutor to discuss questions that have generally been set in advance by the tutor. Seminars are similar, but usually involve larger groups of students; sometimes seminars may be led by one or more of the students. These names for small group work are often interchangeable, so you may find something labelled "tutorial" which is attended by 30 students. The title is not important; it

▶ 9.5

merely indicates a "teaching event" which is usually smaller scale and more interactive than a lecture. In both tutorials and seminars, all the students are generally expected to have prepared the topic under discussion in advance and tutors usually expect that all the students involved in the group will participate, by joining in the discussion. The following points will help you get the most benefit from these sessions:

● **Ensure you know what is expected of you**
Many tutors set specific work for tutorials and seminars. Ensure that you obtain this in good time, so that you can prepare the topic properly. If you are unprepared, and unfamiliar with the subject matter, you won't get much out of the session, because you won't be able to participate in the discussion and you will find it hard to understand what is going on. Different tutors will run these groups in very different ways. You will need to be adaptable, to fit in with different teaching styles. Some tutors will make this easy for you, by having explicit "ground rules"; with others you will have to work it out for yourself.

● **Try to participate**
Often, you will attend tutorials and seminars with the same group of people for a whole module. Clearly, the experience will be more pleasant if the members of the group get on with each other, but this is essentially a learning experience, so you have to balance your desire to be friendly with your learning needs. No one wants to make a fool of themselves in front of a group of other people, but if you do not try out ideas in discussion, you are not going to develop your thinking, so a little bravery is called for. Try not to be so worried about what the others will think that you do not participate at all. Everyone is in the same situation, so people are generally sympathetic to contributions made by others.

● **Consider making a contribution early in the discussion**
If you make a contribution to the discussion at a fairly early stage, it is likelier to be easier than if you delay participating, for a number of reasons. In the early stages of discussion, it is less likely that other people will have made the point you have thought of. Tutors who are keen to involve the whole group may single out people who have not said anything and ask them direct questions; this is much less likely to happen to you if you have already made a contribution. If you are less confident about talking in front of other people, the longer you wait to say something, the more difficult you may find it to join in.

● **Think about the art of polite disagreement**
The aim of academic discussion is to try to develop the ideas you are considering. Often, this involves members of the group disagreeing with one another's ideas. Remember that you are challenging the argument which is put forward, not the person who is advancing it. It is also important to remember this when your ideas are challenged.

● **Expect to be challenged**
During group discussions, tutors will try to teach you not to make assumptions. Their aim is to help you to think critically and precisely. They will therefore challenge many of the things you say. Most people are not used to being challenged in this way, and the ability

of tutors to question almost everything you say can seem unduly negative. However, if you are going to succeed in thinking rigorously, you need to be able to question your own ideas and those of other people, and tutors whose sessions are the most challenging may turn out to be the best ones you have.

● **Do not expect to take notes all the time**
If you take notes of everything that goes on in a tutorial or seminar, you will be so busy writing that you will not be able to participate in the discussion. Not only will you not be able to say anything, but note-taking also detracts from your ability to think about the points that are being made. Try to limit your note-taking to jotting down the main issues raised and the outline of any answer given. You can then read over your notes later and follow up any points of particular interest.

● **Learn to take advantage of small group learning situations**
It is much easier to learn in small groups than in large lectures, because small groups should give you the opportunity to ask questions about aspects of the subject under discussion that you do not understand so well. Clearly, you do not want to dominate the discussion, or interrupt with too many questions, but small group situations do give you an opportunity to raise issues that are of particular concern to you.

RESEARCHING A TOPIC FOR AN ESSAY/PROBLEM, TUTORIAL OR SEMINAR

When you are preparing for a tutorial or seminar, or preparing to write an essay or problem answer, you will need to carry out some research in order to find the information you need. In the case of tutorials and seminars, you will often be given specific reading lists, so some of the research has been done for you, but you will still need to use the information to the best advantage. Here are some suggestions to help you research effectively. ▶ 9.6

● **Read the question carefully**
Before you start gathering materials, you need to be clear about what you are being asked to do. Titles that invite you to "discuss" or "critically analyse" mean that you are expected to engage in reasoned argument about the topic; you are not being invited merely to describe something. One of the easiest traps to fall into is to fail to answer the question which is set because you are concentrating on conveying as much information as possible about the general area of law, rather than focusing on the specific aspect which is the subject of the question you are answering. Keep the question in mind the whole time; write it out and keep it in front of you while you are researching.

● **Identify your key words**
First, define the area you are interested in. Think of the key words which you can use to identify relevant materials. You may need to re-define your key words if, for instance, you find that the first few words you think of bring up too many references. In that case, try to think of much more specific terms which you can search.

● **Use the references in the text**

Academic writing contains a lot of references and footnotes. At first, this can be confusing, and you may tend to ignore them. However, when you are researching a topic, footnotes and references are an important source of further information. A good way to start your research on a topic is to look in the footnotes or references of any textbooks or specialist books that you have found; they often contain references to journal articles, and once you have found the title of a relevant journal article, you can return to your library catalogue and find out whether your library keeps copies of that journal. Footnotes and references can direct you to other relevant material in a number of different ways:

(a)   They can give full references to articles or books that are just mentioned or summarised in the text. This is useful if the material referred to is relevant to your work, because you can then read the full text.

(b)   They can give references to other books or articles on the same topic, which put forward a similar argument (or the opposite one often indicated by the word "contra" in front of the reference). Again, you can extend your knowledge by following up the references.

(c)   They can give further explanation about points made in the text.

All these types of reference can provide you with further information about the topic which you are researching. That is why footnotes and references are so useful.

● **Use a variety of sources**

Searching the library catalogue will generally direct you to books with titles that include your key words. But library catalogues will not generally direct you to articles in journals. To find these, you will have to use a different research strategy. One good way to start, as finding articles is to look in the footnotes of any textbooks or specialist books that you have found. Once you get an idea of the journals which are the most important in a particular area of law which you are interested in, you can locate them in the library and look through the contents pages of the latest issues to find the most up-to-date articles.

You can also locate books and articles by using any relevant electronic databases that your library subscribes to. Your library should have instructions about how these work; if it doesn't, you can ask one of the librarians to explain them.

You can use specialist law databases, such as Lexis and Westlaw, to locate both cases and statutes on a particular topic; they also contain references to some journal articles. However, there are a number of specialist databases, such as Heinonline, which concentrate on providing access to journals, and these are the best place for you to locate journal articles.

If you are researching a statute, you may also find it helpful to consult the website of the Government department which is responsible for the area of law covered by the statute, since Government websites often contain copies of consultation papers and other official documents which can provide useful background information and help you to understand the statute more easily.

There are a number of hard copy publications that give details of all British books in print, arranged by subject, as well as by author and title. The Index to Legal Periodicals will help you to find articles in legal journals and there are similar publications relating to social science literature, often called "Abstracts". Using these sources will help you find a wider range of materials than those referred to on your reading lists. You may then be able to use these as alternatives to the ones that everyone else is using or which are unavailable when you wish to consult them.

● **Be time-sensitive**

Start with the most recent literature on your chosen topic, i.e. the latest books and the most recent issues of relevant journals. These items may not appear on reading lists, so may have been missed by others.

If you are using a legal textbook (usually at the beginning of the research process), remember that new editions are produced quite frequently, so you need to be sure that you are using the latest edition. You can usually check this by looking on the publisher's website. Even if you have the latest edition, do not rely on it as your sole source of information; there may have been a lot of recent developments in that particular area of law, which are not referred to in the textbook, because they have occurred since it was written. Similarly with articles in journals: remember that the law changes frequently; check that any legal points made by the author are still valid.

● **Make the best use of your library**

You need to ensure that you are using your library as effectively as possible. There may be leaflets designed to help readers find their way around the different catalogues, or there may be a resource page for law on the internet homepage of your law department or the homepage of the library; see if any of these can help your research. Some libraries have specialist librarians who are immensely knowledgeable and helpful. Try to help yourself first, but do not ignore the experts whose job it is to help you.

● **Use the internet appropriately**

Many students find the internet a very convenient source of information. However, it is unlikely that you can rely on the internet as your only research tool. And when you do use it, you need to use it appropriately. Many students just rely on Googling a topic, and think that this is sufficient. Google is often a useful place to BEGIN your research, but it is unlikely that you will find sufficient material if you just rely on Google, and do not use any other sources of information. You need to be aware that much of what you find using Google will not be appropriate for use in an essay or assignment which you submit at university. A lot of material on the internet is journalism, which is interesting, but not authoritative enough to be used in an academic essay. You should only rely on journalism or opinion pieces if that is the ONLY information you can find on a topic (which will rarely be the case). Thus it will only be very occasionally that you can directly use a newspaper article, or the opinion of a pressure group, which you have found on Google, to back up your arguments in a piece of academic writing. You will need to use the specialist electronic resources provided by your university, or look at a government website, or that of the Law Commission, to <u>follow up</u> the leads you have found on Google and build on those leads by retrieving academic articles and books on the topic you are researching.

However, if you go beyond just using Google, the internet can be a useful research tool. In addition to following up leads you find on Google itself, you can use Google Scholar to locate academic materials, and you can also use the internet can to find a range of official publications, published by government departments, or by official bodies such as the Law Commission, and such documents can be very useful for research purposes.

● **Researching for different approaches to law**
Bear in mind the perspective you need to adopt in order to answer the essay or problem question you are working on. Problem questions focus on a "black-letter" or "doctrinal" approach to law; they demand that you use decided cases and statutory materials to justify the points you make. In general, it is not appropriate to include references to other materials, such as academic articles, when writing a problem answer.

When you are answering an essay question, you may have the opportunity to introduce a wider range of materials; in addition to any relevant cases and statutes, you may be expected to discuss Law Commission materials, consultation papers and reports from relevant government departments, academic articles and books, and materials from other disciplines, such as criminology, sociology, economics or politics. You need to find out from your lecturers and tutors which approach you will be expected to adopt when you are writing your essay.

● **Be prepared to search other nearby libraries**
Sometimes you may find that your library does not have sufficient information on a topic that you are researching. Perhaps everyone else in your year has been set the same essay, and there just aren't enough books and journals to go round. Think of other libraries in the area that you could use and have a look in their catalogues to see if it would be worthwhile visiting them. Perhaps their students are not all doing the essay on offences against the person that your year has been set. Often, universities have schemes which allow students of other universities to have limited borrowing rights; it is often worth finding out if one of these schemes applies to a nearby university library other than your own which you might wish to use.

● **Find things out for yourself**
When you are gathering and using written materials, remember that you must always find out things for yourself. The insertion of a footnote in a piece of academic writing that has been published in a journal or book does not necessarily mean that the footnote is accurate. Sometimes, when you find the article or case report that is referred to, you discover that it cannot possibly be used as justification for the proposition which you have just read. In order to find out whether a footnote is accurate, you will need to look up the reference for yourself. You should never merely replicate a reference without looking it up for yourself.

● **Enjoy Research!**
Although researching is hard work, it can also be very enjoyable. It is immensely satisfing when you find some material which backs up a point you want to make, or you discover

lots of information about a topic that you are going to write about. Researching is like many other things in life—the more you put into it, the more you get out. Give yourself a chance to enjoy your research by allowing sufficient time to do it and developing your research skills as much as you can—ask your librarian for help if you need it, so that you can learn how to find materials as quickly as possible.

RECORDING YOUR RESEARCH

Research can be very enjoyable and interesting, and it helps you discover the subject of law for yourself, but if you don't write down accurately the sources you find when you are researching, you can waste a lot of time. You will need to give full references to anything you want to rely on when you write an essay or answer to a problem question. If you do not write down the details of the material you find, it's very tedious to have to go back and try to find them again.

▶ 9.7

- **Always write down a full reference**
  Whenever you read something which you think might be useful, you should write down its full reference; this not only means you will be able to find it again quickly, it also means you have all the information you will need if you want to refer to it in a footnote and/or bibliography.

  For a book, you will need the author, title, edition (if it is not the first edition), publisher, place of publication and date of publication. You may also like to make a note of the catalogue reference so that you can retrieve the item from the library easily; this will usually be a Dewey decimal reference number. Your reference should look something like this:

  Bradney et al. *How to Study Law* (3rd edition) Sweet & Maxwell, London, 1995. (340.07 HOW)

  If you are recording a journal article, your reference will be something like this:

  Addison & Cownie "Overseas Law Students: Language Support and Responsible Recruitment" (1992) 19 JLS p.467 (PER340 J6088)

  It is important to write down references in such a way that you can easily distinguish between references to books, and references to articles. The system that has been used here is to italicise the titles of books, but put titles of articles inside inverted commas.

- **Make concise notes**
  Always begin by asking yourself why you are taking notes. Refresh your memory as to the question you are trying to answer. Remember that you can take different types of notes on different parts of a text — detailed notes on the directly relevant parts, outline notes on other parts, while sometimes you will be able to read through without taking any notes at all.

- **Make clear notes**
  Your notes will be more use to you if they are reasonably neat. Try to develop a standard way of recording the source you are taking the notes from, perhaps always putting it at the top right-hand corner of the page, or in the margin. You can use this reference for your bibliography, or for footnotes, or for your own use if you need to clarify a point at

some later stage. In order to make it even easier to find your way around the original text, you might like to make a note of the actual page you have read, either in the margin, or in brackets as you go along. Here is an example of some notes on the first few pages of a chapter of a book:

H. Genn (1987)
Hard Bargaining
Oxford Uni. Press, Oxford.
(344.6 GEN)

Chapter 3 "Starting Positions"
Structural imbalance between the parties (p.34).
One-shotter pl. v Repeat-player def. See Galanter 1974.
Repeat players — advance intelligence, expertise, access to specialists, economies of scale. See Ross 1980.
Distribution of personal injury work (p.35)
Pls huge variety of firms.
Defs-insurance co/specialist firm
Defs solicitors allowed few mistakes (p.36 top)
Defs solicitors nurture relationship w insurance co.
Contrast position of general practitioner.

The student who wrote these notes has not only noted the full reference to the book they are working on, and the main points made in chapter 3 of the book. He/she has included a couple of references to work by other researchers (Galanter and Ross) which can be followed up later to see if those experts have anything to say which is relevant to the essay the student is writing. The student has also been careful to note down the page number in Genn's book that contains the points which are important..

● **Do you need to photocopy the bibliography?**
When you are taking notes, you will often note down references to other articles or books referred to in the text you are reading. You will have to decide later whether you need to look these up, but many people find that it disturbs their train of thought to look up the full reference for each of these as they occur in the text. If that is the case, it is important to photocopy the bibliography of your source, so that you have a copy of the full reference in case you need to refer to it later. In the example above, the student would need to photocopy the bibliography of "Hard Bargaining", otherwise they wouldn't know what they meant by references to "Galanter, 1974" or "Ross 1980".

● **Keep notes and comments separate**
It is a good idea to think critically about the content of what you are reading. However, if you want to make comments, keep these separate in some way, on a different sheet of paper or in the margin. Otherwise, when you come back to the notes, you might find it impossible to distinguish your great thoughts from those of the original author.

● **Good presentation is important**
Remember that clear presentation of your notes is just as important when you are taking notes for an essay or seminar as it is when you are taking lecture notes. Use headings and sub-headings, and remember that underlining and the use of different-coloured pens can direct your attention to particular points.

READING FOR RESEARCH

It is important to develop a strategy for dealing with the large amount of reading you will have to do. All students have to face this problem, but if you are studying law, you have a particular problem, because studying law requires you to read a great deal of material quickly. In addition, although by this stage you are an expert reader, you are unlikely to have had much experience, if any, of reading legal materials, such as case reports and statutes, so in this respect you are a novice again. When you are researching, you need to be able to read quickly through the material you locate, so you can decide whether it is sufficiently relevant to look at in more detail, and perhaps make some notes from it.

▶ 9.8

    The chapters in this book which deal with reading cases and statutes will help you develop an effective method of reading these new types of text, and once you have practised, you will find that you can process them as quickly as other types of text, such as articles or textbooks, with which you are already familiar. There are many different ways of reading; for example, you can skim quickly through something, or you can read it slowly and carefully. In order to decide what kind of reading you should be doing at any particular time, you need to think about the purpose of your reading. You also need to be aware of the different techniques of reading and be able to use each type as it becomes relevant.

● **Scan the text first**
To check the relevance of a text, skim through it, looking for the key words and phrases that will give you the general sense of the material and enable you to decide whether it is relevant for your purposes. When looking at a book, the title and contents pages will give you a broad outline of the information you will find. Sub-headings within an article perform the same function. You can use these headings to decide whether or not to read a piece of text in more detail.

● **Approach the text gradually**
Even when you have decided that a particular chapter of a book or an article is relevant, check it out before you begin to take notes; you may not need to take notes on the whole chapter, but only a part of it; similarly, with an article. It is often suggested that you should read the first sentence of each paragraph to find out more precisely what the text is about.

● **Reading statutes**
As you have discovered in Chapter 5 of this book, statutes must be read carefully and precisely. At first, they can seem very complicated to read, because they are so detailed. When you read a section of a statute, try to establish the main idea first, then you can re-

read it and fill in the details on the second reading. You might find it helpful to photocopy the parts of the statute that you have to read, so that you can use a pen or highlighter to mark the main idea. There is an example below:

Sale of Goods Act 1979 Section 11 (3)
   Whether a stipulation in a contract is a condition, the breach of which may give rise to a right to treat the contract as repudiated, **or a warranty**, the breach of which may give rise to a claim for damages but not to a right to reject the goods and treat the contract as repudiated, **depends in each case on the construction of the contract**; and a stipulation may be a condition, though called a warranty in the contract.
   The main point that is being made is quite simple, and can be identified by reading the phrases in bold type "Whether a stipulation in a contract is a condition or a warranty depends in each case on the construction of the contract". Having established what the section is basically about, you can now go back and find out what the section says about the effect of a stipulation in a contract being classified as either a condition or a warranty.

● Reading cases
Although reading a reported case might seem more straightforward than reading a statute, it is important to remember that reading the judgments in a case and extracting from them both the facts and the decision requires practice.
   Sometimes you will be able to get an indication of the important aspects of a decision from a textbook or from a lecture. However, if you are faced with a decision about which you know very little, you can read the head-note first, which will summarise both facts and judgments for you. Many students are tempted to regard reading the head-note as sufficient, but this is not a good strategy; you need to read the whole of the leading judgment to understand the ratio of the case properly. (You will be able to tell which is the leading judgment by noticing from which judgment most of the points in the head-note are taken.)
   Reading dissenting judgments is also helpful. It is a good way to understand the complexities of a legal argument. Often, your tutors will ask you to think critically about decisions; reading dissenting judgments are a good source of ideas about the strengths and weaknesses of a decision.

WRITING ASSIGNMENTS (ESSAYS AND PROBLEM ANSWERS)

9.9 ▶ During your law course, you will be set various types of assignment to submit to your tutor. The most common of these are essays and problem questions, and it is with these types of assessment on which this section of *How to Study Law* is focused. Writing an assignment is a challenge, but it is also one of the most rewarding aspects of studying law. When you focus on a particular area of law for the purposes of writing an assignment, you bring together a lot of the skills you are developing; you need to research, organise the material, reflect on the question and engage in some critical thinking.

● **Clarify the task**

Before you do anything else, read the question carefully. Identify which area of law it is asking you about. This may not be immediately apparent, particularly in a problem question. Read the whole question through carefully to help you understand which area(s) of law are involved. Then make sure you understand exactly what the question is asking you about the area of law involved. It is highly unlikely that it will just ask you to write down all you know about, for example, the tort of negligence. It is much more likely to ask you to criticise a particular part of the law of negligence, or explain the strengths and weaknesses of an aspect of the law of negligence.

● **Make a plan**

The next stage of the writing process is to make a plan. A plan provides a structure for your argument and allows you to organise your arguments into a coherent whole. It is a vital stage of the research process and you need to produce one as soon as possible. You may want to do a bit of basic reading first, but generally, the plan should be one of your first tasks. Plans for problem answers are easier to produce than those for essays, because the events that make up the problem give you a structure for your plan. In all cases, jot down the main points of your answer; later, you can refine your plan and fit in subsidiary points in the most logical places.

Example

"Discrimination in the legal profession is a thing of the past" Discuss.

Introduction *— much discrimination on grounds of both race and sex in the past- refer to numbers of women / members of ethnic minorities qualifying as solicitors and barristers, also women not able to qualify as solicitors till well into the twentieth century — see Bebb v The Law Society.*

First section *Currently, still a lot of discrimination on grounds of sex — refer to small numbers of women partners in solicitors' firms, small numbers of female Q.C.s and small numbers of female judges. Also refer to research reports on women in the legal profession.*

Second section *Equally, still a lot of discrimination on grounds of race — refer to small numbers of solicitors, barristers and judges drawn from ethnic minority communities, also research reports on racial discrimination at the Bar and in the solicitors' profession.*

Conclusion *Although it appears there is still a lot of discrimination on grounds of race and sex in the legal profession, it is arguable that the situation is improving — use statistics to show increased participation in the legal profession by women and by members of ethnic minority groups.*

Your plan is there to help you; you do not have to stick with your original structure too rigidly. If you can see a better way of organising your argument once you have done a bit of reading, then adjust the plan. The plan in the example above is just a first draft. It provides a basic framework, but it does not contain enough ideas at this stage. In order to add more ideas, the student needs to go and do some more research and reading before amending the plan in the light of the additional information. However, this is a good start.

● **Reflect and evaluate**

When you have gathered the basic information, it is time to review your plan in the light of what you have discovered. Read through your notes, bearing in mind all the time the question you have been asked. Have you changed your mind about any of the points you want to make? Have you discovered additional information that you want to include in your answer? Where does it fit in to your argument? Now you will be able to make a new plan, indicating not only the main points you are going to make, but also any arguments or pieces of information drawn from your research that you wish to include.

● **Write a first draft**

Once you are satisfied with your revised plan, you can embark on the first draft of your essay. Before you start, read through the plan and make sure that all your points are relevant. To do this, look at the question again, and then look at your plan. Every argument you make should relate to the question you have been asked. This is what makes it relevant.

Here is an example of a first plan for an essay whose title is "Settlement of major litigation is a necessary evil." Discuss.

● Settlement definition.
● Settlement is necessary because a) saves court time b) saves expense c) saves litigants' time.
● But settlement is an "evil" because a) litigants are not equally experienced and do not have equal resources b) inexperienced litigants often go to lawyers who are not specialists in the relevant field & are not well advised c) inexperienced litigants can easily be put under pressure, e.g. by payment into court, delays (often manufactured by the other side), worries about cost, risk-aversion.
● Conclusion settlement is a necessary evil, but currently is so evil it is immoral and unacceptable.

Every point that is made relates directly to the quotation that is under discussion. This is an initial plan. After some research, you would be able to expand some points, and to insert the names of books or articles that you could use to justify the points being made. But you would still ensure that everything related to the quotation that you had been asked to discuss.

● **Remember the audience you are writing for**

When you write an academic essay in law, you can assume that you are writing for a reasonably intelligent reader who knows almost nothing about your subject. That means you have to explain clearly every step of your argument. At first, many students are ignorant of this convention. They know their essay is going to be marked by an expert, so they do not bother to include all the information about a topic, only to be told by their tutor "I cannot give you credit for anything, unless it is down in your essay. It's no use keeping things in your head".

● **Acknowledge your sources**

During the course of your writing, you will often put forward arguments and ideas that you have discovered in books or articles. If you do this, you must acknowledge that the idea is not an original one. You can do this expressly in the text by saying something like "As Bradney argues in 'How to Study Law'. Or you can use a footnote to indicate the source of the idea. What you must not do is to pass off someone else's idea as if it were something you had thought of for yourself. That is stealing their idea, and it is a practice known as plagiarism. In academic life, where people's ideas are of the utmost importance, plagiarism is regarded as a form of cheating. Ideally, you will use other people's ideas as a base from which to develop thoughts of your own, acknowledging their idea, and then going on to say something original about them. This is the kind of critical thinking which you are trying to develop.

● **Do not make assertions**

In academic writing, you must <u>always</u> be able to justify what you say. You cannot make assertions (an assertion is when someone says "X is the case", but provides no justification that proves that X is the case). You must always be able to provide reasons for your statements; in an essay, this is done by providing a reference or footnote. In a problem question, all the points of law you make need to be substantiated by a reference to some legal authority—usually the ration of a case, or a section of a statute.

Example

If someone writes "Small claims are proceedings involving £5,000 or less" that is an assertion. There is no evidence that the statement is true, the author is just expecting us to take their word for it. After a little research, it is possible to rewrite the sentence so as to include the evidence which proves the statement: "Under Part 26.6 of the Civil Procedure Rules, small claims are proceedings involving £5,000 or less." Alternatively, you could include the justification in a footnote. Then the statement would look like this:
Small claims are proceedings involving £5,000 or less.[1]

[1] Civil Procedure Rules 26.6.

● **Consider the style of your writing**

An academic essay is a formal piece of writing, so the style in which you write should not be too colloquial. Shortened forms of phrases, such as isn't and mustn't, are inappropriate. However, pomposity is equally inappropriate. Phrases such as "I submit that . . . " are out of place. Advocates make submissions in court, but you do not make submissions in an academic essay, even in law!

Aim for a clear, direct style, which conveys your arguments in a way which can be readily understood. Use paragraphs to indicate a change of subject, and keep sentences reasonably short. In general, academic writing is written in an impersonal style, so writers do not use phrases such as "I think that . . . ". They use alternative, less personal, phrases, such as "This indicates that . . . "

● **Be prepared to write several drafts**

Before you arrive at the final version of your essay, you should have produced several drafts. You should read each draft carefully, making additions and alterations that you then incorporate into the next draft. Although it is important to correct the spelling and the grammar in each draft, the primary reason for having several drafts is to give yourself the opportunity to examine your argument and make sure that it is as clear and convincing as possible. Think about what you are saying. Have you justified all the points you have made? Does the argument flow logically from one point to another? Is the material relevant?

● **Do not describe too much**

In general, the object of writing academic essays is to engage in critical analysis, i.e. thought and argument. Your tutors are not looking for detailed descriptions of subjects that they could, after all, read in any competent textbook. A certain amount of description is necessary, to explain what you are talking about, but the main emphasis in any academic piece of work will be on analysing. You are interpreting for the reader the significance of what you have described, and it is this process that is most important.

● **A few points about problem answers**

It is often said that it is easier to answer a problem than to write an essay, but this is largely a matter of personal preference. Problem answers are certainly easier in one sense, because they provide a framework for your answer by posing certain issues that you must cover. The research and planning process described above will help you when you are answering a problem question, just as much as an essay.

Problem answers do not need lengthy introductions. The convention is that you need to introduce a problem answer by identifying the main issue in the problem, but you do not need a lengthy introduction. Whenever you make a statement about the law, you must give the relevant legal authority; for example, "When X wrote to Y saying that if he did not hear from Y, he would assume that Y agreed to the contract, this has no legal effect, because silence does not imply consent (Felthouse v Bindley (1862) 11 C.B. 869)."

Remember that socio-legal information is not relevant in a problem answer. Strictly speaking, problem questions are just asking you to identify the relevant legal rules relating to the issues raised. There may be very interesting research studies on a topic, but these are not relevant to a problem answer.

EXAMS AND ASSESSMENT

9.10 ▶ It is likely that you will experience a number of different forms of assessment, including continuous assessment, based on written work submitted during the course of the academic year, and the traditional three-hour unseen examination. The strategies discussed above will help you to cope with the various forms of continuous assessment which you are likely to meet. This section will therefore concentrate on strategies designed to help you cope with the traditional unseen examination.

● **Make a revision timetable in good time**

It is important to make a realistic revision timetable well in advance of the examinations, allocating a certain amount of time for each subject you have to prepare. Most people find it best to study all their subjects concurrently, doing a bit of each one in turn, rather than finishing one before going on to the next one, which brings the danger that you might never get round to the last subject.

● **Reduce your notes to a manageable size**

At the beginning of the revision period, you are likely to find that you have a large amount of notes. It is a good idea to reduce the size of these, by taking even briefer notes from your original notes, so that you end up with a manageable quantity of material to work with. As the examinations approach, most people reduce their notes again, perhaps several times, so that a whole topic can be covered comprehensively, but speedily.

● **Question-spotting is a risky strategy**

It is sensible to consider what sort of subjects might come up in the examination. Consulting old examination papers is a useful way of finding out what is expected of you in the exam. However, it is unwise to "question spot" too precisely. It is unlikely that you will be able to revise the whole course; indeed, this would often be a waste of effort, but you need to cover several subjects in addition to the three or four which you hope will come up, so that you have plenty of choice when it comes to deciding which questions you will answer in the examination. Being familiar with a range of subjects is a sensible strategy because:

(a) Your favourite topics might not come up at all.
(b) Some topics might come up, but in a way which is unfamiliar to you.
(c) Your favourite topic might be mixed up with another topic which you have not revised.

● **Consider practising timed answers**

If you find it difficult to write answers quickly, it is a good idea to practice writing some answers in the same time that you will have in the examination. Use questions from old examination papers.

● **Make sure you get enough rest**

Studying hard for examinations is a very tiring experience. Try to ensure that you get sufficient sleep and exercise, so that you remain as fresh as possible. Burning the midnight oil is not necessarily a sensible strategy.

● **Feel as comfortable as possible during the exam**

Before you enter the examination room, make sure you have all the pens, pencils and so on that you need. Wear something comfortable, preferably several layers of clothing so you can discard some if the room is hot, or add additional layers if you are cold. Check whether you are allowed to take drinks or food into the examination room. If you are allowed to do so, it is a matter of personal choice whether you take advantage of this facility or not; some people find it helps to have a can of drink, others find it a distraction. Check that you know where you have to sit, and whether there are any attendance slips or other forms that you have to fill in. Ensure that you know whether or not you will be told when you can start the examination; you do not want to sit there, waiting for an instruction that never comes.

● **Read the instructions on the exam paper very carefully**
Make sure that you read the instructions at the top of the examination paper very carefully. The paper may be divided into different sections and frequently candidates must answer a certain number of questions from each section. Sometimes you will be asked to write certain questions in certain answer books. Always make sure that you comply with any instructions of this kind; the examiner may not give you any marks for material you have written in contravention of such instructions.

● **Develop good examination technique**
In the examination, plan your time carefully. Provided that all the questions carry an equal number of marks, you should allow an equal amount of time for answering each question. Sub-divide your time into reading the question, planning the answer, writing the answer and checking it. Planning is a very important part of good examination technique. If you spend a few minutes setting out a good plan, it will allow you to write a much fuller answer than if you are thinking out your answer as you go along, because all the basic thinking will be done at the planning stage, and you will be able to concentrate on writing a relevant answer. Do not spend more than the time that you have allocated for each question. If you run out of time, leave that question and go on to the next one, returning to the unfinished question if you have some spare time later.

● **Answer the question**
Read the question carefully. To gain the maximum number of marks, your answer must be relevant to the question you have been asked. If you are familiar with a topic on which a question is set, it is tempting to write down a version of your notes, which includes all you know about that topic, in the hope that you will get a reasonable number of marks. However, if you merely write all you happen to know about a topic, it is unlikely that you will be answering the question. You need to slant your information to the question, showing how the things you know relate to the precise question that you have been asked.

● **Answer the correct number of questions**
Under pressure of time, some people fail to answer the whole examination paper by missing out a question. Examiners can only award marks for what is written on the examination paper. By not answering a question, you have forfeited all the marks allocated to that question. However, it is often said that the easiest marks to gain are the ones awarded for the beginning of an answer, so if you do run out of time, it is much better to use those final minutes to start the final question, rather than perfecting answers you have already finished.

- **Remember that examiners are human, too**
  When you are writing an examination paper, you often feel as if the examiner is the enemy "out there", determined to catch you out. In fact, examiners do not want candidates to fail. They generally expect students who have done a reasonable amount of work to pass examinations.

INTERNATIONAL STUDENTS

The study skills discussed in this chapter are required by all law students. However, if English ▶ 9.11 is not your first language you may feel that you would like some extra assistance with studying in the United Kingdom. Most institutions which welcome students from around the world have a support service which offers different classes covering a range of English Language and study skills, and you should try and find out about these at an early stage in your course. Even if your English is very good, you might be able to pick up some useful tips about studying in the U.K. from such classes. The support service will also be able to help you familiarise yourself with the particular types of teaching and learning situations which you will find in British educational institutions, what might be termed the "hidden culture" of learning, such as particular ways of writing essays or behaving in seminars, which might be different to those with which you are familiar at home. This sort of information can be very useful, as it is impossible to discover beforehand, however good your English is. Many institutions also offer self-access materials, which you can go and use at a time that is convenient for you.

Further reading

If you would like to find out more about any of the topics covered in this chapter, you will find that there are many books on study skills available. The following books both cover a wide range of study skills.

R. Barrass, *Study! A guide to effective learning, revision and examination techniques* 2nd edn London: Routledge, (2002).

S. Cottrell, *The Study Skills Handbook*, 3rd edn London: Palgrave Macmillan, (2008).

Exercise 6

STUDY SKILLS

9.12 ▶ The exercises below concentrate on some of the most important study skills which you will need at college or university. They may help you decide if these are areas you need to improve in order to get the most out of your course.

Note-Taking

You will find that you have to take a lot of notes, in lectures, and when you are researching for essays and other assignments. Being able to take very good notes as quickly as possible is a very useful skill.

1. For this exercise, you are going to take notes of the first three pages of the article entitled "Women Solicitors as a Barometer for problems within the Legal Profession—Time to Put Values before Profits?" by Lisa Webley and Liz Duff, which you will find in Exercise 5 of this book. Before you start, re-read the suggestions about taking notes in Chapter 9 of the book, in the sections headed "Take Notes to Aid Concentration" and "Take Notes Which Will Be Useful in the Future".

   Once you have finished taking notes, compare them with the two pages of the article you were working on, and assess your notes according to the following criteria:

   - *Presentation* Can you read what you have written? Have you used underlining or highlighting effectively? Could you have used diagrams or lists?
   - *Clarity* Can you remember what your abbreviations mean? Are there words or phrases which occur frequently that you definitely need to invent an abbreviation for? Have you remembered to write down the full reference of the article you are working on?
   - *Content* Have you included all the main points? Do you have a full reference to any useful articles or other documents which were mentioned in the footnotes? Have you written down too much, so that your notes are not really notes, but involve copying out nearly the whole extract?

2. Find some notes that you took in one of your lectures. Now carry out the same exercise with them. Use the criteria above to assess how useful your notes will be to you if you need to refer to them in the future. Do they make sense to you now? Will you be able to refer to them when you are writing assessments or revising for exams? Have you noted down the references to any cases or statutes that were mentioned? How could you improve your notes.

Essay Writing Skills 1—using footnotes and references

One of the new skills you will have to master at this level is the ability to use footnotes or references in essays to justify what you are saying. Everything you write in an essay must be justified, and in order to do this, you need to include a reference to an appropriate document in your essay. You can do this by including footnotes or Harvard-style references. These two styles of reference are explained below. The explanation is followed by an exercise to help you practice the skill of referencing. You should find out from your tutor which style of referencing they want you to use, and then learn to use it as early on as possible in your course, so that when you have to submit an assignment, you know how to reference appropriately.

Using Footnotes

It is likely that your tutors will require you to use footnotes when you submit an essay for assessment. If you use footnotes, your essay will look like this:

> Historically, women were debarred from entering university law schools.[1] Today, women are to be found in larger numbers than men in university law schools.[2]

Note that the footnote number is inserted *after* the punctuation. The footnotes themselves are located at the foot of the page; look at them now. They contain the full reference to the work referred to, *including the page number*; it is very important to include a page number, so that the reader of your work can look up your reference and check that the material upon which you are relying really does back up what you have written.

You must adopt a consistent order for the information included in your footnotes: author; date; title; place of publication; publisher; page number.

Computers make it very easy to insert footnotes; in Microsoft Word, you will find a drop-down menu called 'Edit' or 'References'; you can then click on 'insert reference' and a footnote number will appear in the text. Practice inserting footnotes in a piece of text, so that you know how to do it *before* you have to submit your first essay.

Harvard-Style References

References can be included in the text (these are known as a 'Harvard-style' references), so that your essay would look like this:

> Historically, women were debarred from entering university law schools (Sachs & Hoff Wilson, 1978, 27–28). Today, women are to be found in larger numbers than men in university law schools (Law Society, 2006, 34).

Note that the reference in the text includes the page number at which you can find the material which is being relied upon.

If you use Harvard-style references, you <u>must</u> include a list of the *full* references to all the materials you have included in your essay. So at the end of this essay, the references would look like this:

[1] A. Sachs & J. Hoff Wilson (1978) *Sexism and the Law* London, Martin Robertson, pp.27–28, 31–33 & 170–174.
[2] Law Society (2006) *Annual Statistical Report 2005* London, The Law Society, p.34.

Law Society (2006) *Annual Statistical Report 2005* London, The Law Society.
Sachs, A. & Hoff Wilson, J. (1978) *Sexism and the Law* Oxford, Martin Robertson.

Note that the order of the information provided is: author(s); date of publication; title; place of publication; publisher. This order remains the same every time you write a reference.
Cownie et al, *English Legal System in Context* 4th edn, (OUP) p.209.

Reference Exercise 1

Here is a piece of writing about private security firms. Read it through. Imagine this is part of your essay. The footnote numbers have been inserted for you, but there is no content in the footnotes. On a piece of paper, write down the TYPE of material you would use to justify what you have said. The first footnote is completed for you as an example, to show you what to do.

Private Security
(adapted from Cownie et al, *English Legal System in Context*, 4th edn, p.209)

An increasingly important form of social control which has hitherto been largely ignored by those writing about the English legal system is the world of private security. Private security personnel are those persons engaged in the protection of information, persons or property. They are privately employed, have different legal powers to the public police, and are accountable for the exercise of those powers to a private individual or institution, rather than to the public.[1]

The term 'private security' is used, rather than 'private policing', partly to avoid confusion with the public police, but also because that term conveys more accurately the wide range of activities carried out by private security personnel in contemporary society, activities which go far beyond the policing activities carried out by the public police. The range of activities undertaken by the private security sector is very wide. It involves the provision of manned services - guarding, patrolling, transporting cash etc, as well as providing bodyguards, private investigators and involvement in the management of prisons and escort services. Private security entities are also involved in the provision of physical or mechanical devices, such as locks, safes and cash bags, supplying electrical and electronic devices, such as alarms, video motion detection devices etc. and 'security hardware' i.e the manufacture, distribution and servicing of a wide variety of security equipment.

It is impossible to obtain accurate figures relating to the number of persons involved in private security in Britain today. Estimates vary greatly, partly depending on the definition of private security which is used. Figures reported by the Home Affairs Select Committee in its 1995 report on the industry ranged between 126,900 and 300,000. The 1999 White Paper *The Government's Proposals for the Regulation of the Private Security Industry in England and Wales* estimated that there were then a total of 240,000 individuals employed in some 8,000 companies. All commentators are unanimous, however, in agreeing that the number of persons

---

[1] Reference to book or article about private security, which discusses what private security personnel do, and how their employment status, powers etc differ from the public police.

employed in the sector is growing rapidly and many have noted that it is probable that the number of persons employed in the private security industry is larger than the number of persons working in the police service. Thus in terms of quantity alone, we are dealing with a significant factor in the criminal justice system.

The answers to this exercise can be found at the back of the book.

Essay Writing Skills 2—Avoiding Assertions

A common mistake made by law students is that in answering essay questions, they fail to *justify* what they have written. Writing a statement without providing justification for it is called making an "assertion". Assertions are completely unacceptable in academic law essays.

Virtually every statement you write in an essay should be justified by reference to something which proves that it is a true statement. This might be, among other things, a reference to a case report, section of a statute, a particular page of an academic book (monograph), or a page of an academic journal article. In the exercise above the footnotes were inserted at appropriate places for you. In this exercise, you have to decide where to put the footnotes, as well as indicating what should go in them.

Read the following extract and identify the assertions that it makes. Do this by deciding where footnotes need to be inserted to support the author's arguments. Then, for each footnote, indicate the *type* of material which could provide the evidence which is needed (e.g. a section of a statute, a journal article, a Government document etc). The first footnote is completed for you as an example.

Reference Exercise 2
Uncovering Crime
(adapted from Cownie et al, *English Legal System in Context*, 4th edn, pp.224–225.
It is generally accepted that the number of crimes dealt with by the criminal justice system is less than the actual number of crimes taking place. This is because a large number of offences are not reported to the police, so they do not feature in statistics which record the number of crimes taking place. It is surprising to find that the police play a relatively small role in uncovering crime. Research for the Royal Commission on Criminal Procedure (the Phillips Commission) showed that most offences were reported to the police, either by the victim, or someone acting on the victim's behalf; many crimes were also reported by witnesses. When all these instances were taken into account, the researchers concluded that 75-80% of crimes are reported to the police, rather than the police discovering the crimes for themselves. This data is confirmed by other research studies, including research carried put for the Royal Commission on criminal Justice (the Runciman Commission) which found that the initial source of information linking the suspect to the offence came from the police in only 37% of cases.
Write down your answers like this:

Footnotes needed as follows:

Location	Content
After 'place' in line 3.	Reference to precise page of book or article discussing the fact that there is a large amount of unreported crime.

APPENDIX I

ABBREVIATIONS

The short list below contains some of the standard abbreviations that you are most likely to be referred to early in your course. It is not exhaustive. It will help you whilst you are beginning your study of law. The most complete and up-to-date list of abbreviations is to be found at *http://www.legalabbrevs.cardiff.ac.uk/*. This can be searched both by abbreviation, to find out what journal or law report is being referred to, and by journal or law report, to find out what the accepted abbreviation or the journal or law report is.

▶ A1.1

A.C.	Appeal Cases (Law Reports).
All E.R.	All England Law Reports.
C.L.J.	Cambridge Law Journal.
Ch.D.	Chancery Division (Law Reports).
C.M.L.R.	Common Market Law Reports.
Conv.(n.s.)	Conveyancer and Property Lawyer (New Series).
Crim.L.R.	Criminal Law Review.
E.L.R.	European Law Reports.
E.L.Rev.	European Law Review.
E.R.	English Reports.
Fam.	Family Division (Law Reports).
Fam.Law	Family Law
H. of C. or H.C.	House of Commons.
H. of L. or H.L.	House of Lords.
I.L.J.	Industrial Law Journal.
K.B.	King's Bench (Law Reports).
L.Q.R.	Law Quarterly Review.
L.S.Gaz.	Law Society Gazette.
M.L.R.	Modern Law Review.
N.I.L.Q.	Northern Ireland Legal Quarterly.
N.L.J.	New Law Journal.
P.L.	Public Law.
O.J.	Official Journal of the European Communities.
Q.B.D.	Queen's Bench Division.
S.I.	Statutory Instrument.
S.J. or Sol.Jo.	Solicitors' Journal.
W.L.R.	Weekly Law Reports.

APPENDIX II

FURTHER READING

A2.1 ▶ The number of books about law and legal rules increases each day. They range from simple guides, written for the GCSE student, to thousand-page, closely argued texts, written for the academic. Some are encyclopaedias; others are exhaustive surveys of a very small area of law. This short list of further reading is intended to be of use to those readers who want to take further specific themes raised in this book. The list is not a guide to legal literature as a whole. Readers who have specific interests should consult their library catalogues for books in their area.

Introductory books

P. Atiyah *Law and Modern Society,* 2nd edn (Oxford: Oxford University Press 1995).

J. Adams and R. Brownsword, *Understanding Law 4th edn,* (London: Sweet & Maxwell, 4th edn, 2006).

J. Waldron, *The Law* Routledge 1990.

Books on the English legal system

F. Cownie, A. Bradney and M. Burton, *English Legal System in Context,* 5th edn (Oxford: Oxford University Press, 2010).

K. Malleson, *The Legal System, 3rd edn* (Oxford: Oxford University Press, 2007).

S. Bailey, M. Gunn, N. taylor and D. Ormerod, *Smith, Bailey and Gunn on the Modern English Legal System, 5th edn* (London: Sweet & Maxwell 2007).

C. Stychin and L. Mulcahy, *Legal Methods and Systems: Text and Materials,* 3rd edn (London: Sweet & Maxwell, 2007).

R. Ward and A. Akhtar, *Walker and Walker's English Legal System*, 10th edn, (Oxford: Oxford University Press, 2008).

APPENDIX III

EXERCISE ANSWERS

Exercise 1

1. a) An offence under s.1(1) of keeping animals solely or primarily for slaughter for the value of their fur or for breeding so that their progeny are slaughtered for their fur.

   b) An offence under s.1(2) of knowingly causing or permitting another person to keep or breed animals for their fur.

   c) An offence under s.4(5) of intentionally obstructing an authorised person entering property to inspect under s.4(1) or to carry out a forfeiture order under s.4(2).

2. England and Wales, s.7(4).

3. Yes. S.5 came into force two months after Royal Assent, s.7(4). Sections 1–4 required a commencement order and could only be implemented after January 1, 2003, s.7(2).

4. You can find an Explanatory Note on the Statute at
   http://www.opsi.gov.uk/acts/acts2000/en/ukpgaen_20000033_en_1
   These notes are prepared by civil servants when legislation is being considered by Parliament. They explain the aims of legislation but are written before it comes into force.

5. No. It provides for the 'appropriate authority' to make a compensation scheme, s.5(4).

6. a) Mr McGregor is in breach of s.1(1). Since he no longer has a contract for rabbit meat he is only breeding the rabbits for their fur. He is presumably also breeding rabbits so that they can be killed for their fur.

   b) Potter Land Holdings Plc rents the land to Mr McGregor. The lease may specifically allow him to run a rabbit farm but even if it does, the company may not have sufficient knowledge of the business to realise that he is only keeping and breeding the rabbits for their fur. It would therefore not be 'knowingly' permitting this within s.1(2).

   c) It would be more difficult for Potter Land Holdings to avoid criminal liability if there were a mink farm because the only reason for keeping mink would be for their fur.

▶ A3.1

7. a) Mr Fisher appears to have acted lawfully. Under s.2 the court can make a forfeiture order without imposing any other penalty providing that there has been a conviction, s.2(1), (2). A forfeiture order allows the destruction of animals to which the order applies. As the order states "rabbits at. . ." it would appear to include Thumper. Mr McGregor's daughter could have protected Thumper by applying to be heard under s.2(5) and persuading the court to draft the order more clearly to exclude Thumper.

   b) It does not seem to matter that Thumper was only acquired afterwards because the forfeiture order is valid until the animals are destroyed, s.2(6). However, if Thumper was only bought after the other rabbits had been destroyed he would be safe, from forfeiture at least!

You can find the answers to the questions in Section B by using the *Current Law Statute Citator* or an electronic database such as *Westlaw* or *Lawtel*. If you do not have access to these resources, try to find the answers to questions 10b, 11 and 12 using the website of the Office of Public Sector Information (*http://www.opsi.gov.uk/*). You will need to include the purpose of the regulations in your search.

Exercise 2

1. The long title of the Act states that it is "an Act to make provision about hunting wild mammals with dogs; to prohibit hare coursing; and for connected purposes."

2. The Act came into force 3 months after Royal Assent which was November 18, 2004, s.15.

3. Exemptions to the ban are set out in Schedule 1 to the Act, s.2. In addition a person who "reasonably believes that the hunting was exempt has a defences, s.4".

4. a) "Hare Coursing" is not defined in the Act but a "hare coursing event" is, s.5(3).
   b) It appears that a hare coursing event could amount to hunting because hares are wild animals and dogs are set loose to catch them. However, it appears from the creation of a separate offence that the drafters of the Hunting Act considered that it was easier to create a separate offence than leave this issue to the courts. In addition the offence in s.5(1) is wider because those who "participate" or "attend" also commit offences, s.5(1)(a) and (b) these activities would not appear to come within the offence in s.3.

5. a) If Charles wants to continue stag hunting he must make sure his actions do not come within the ban in s.1 or are within the exemption in Schedule 1. If he hunts Stags without dogs his hunting is not caught by s.1. Alternatively, if he uses dogs to flush out the stags providing he satisfies all the conditions in Sched.1, para.1.
   b) using the meat to feed dogs would satisfy the first condition (Sched.1 para.1(b)) but he will need to satisfy the other conditions, for example hunt only on his

own land or with permission, (para.1(4); use no more than 2 dogs (para.1(5)); and ensure that the stags are competently shot, (para.1(7). The fourth condition (para.1(6)) does not seem relevant to stag hunting.

6. The powers of stop and search are set out in ss.8(2)and (3).

7. a) There is no power to enter Mr Jones' house, s.8(5)(b).
   b) The barn can be entered and the car removed so long as PC Smith reasonably suspects that Mr Jones has committed an offence under Part 1 of the Act (s.8(1)) and the car will be evidence in Mr Jones' trial (s.8(4)(a)) or could be subject to a forfeiture order under s.9 (s.8(4)(b)).

8. a) Allowing land to be used for hunting is an offence under s.3; permitting land to be used for hare coursing is an offence under s.5(1)(d). Neither of these offences are arrestable under s.7.
   b) s.5(2) makes no specific mention of ownership. It appears that the person must either enter the dog for the event, permit the dog to be entered or control the dog to commit an offence in s.5(2).

9. It appears that this activity would not fall within the exemptions in Schedule 1. These animals have not been released or escaped (Sched.1, para.7). They are possibly diseased but have not been injured (Sched.1, para.8). Although dogs can be used to flush animals out (Sched.1, para.1) it does not appear that the first condition would be satisfied—in an urban area rabies is a risk to man not to livestock.

10 a) i *Jackson v AG* [2005] UKHL 56
       ii *R. (on the application of Countryside Alliance and others and others (Appellants)) v Her Majesty's Attorney General and another (Respondents)* [2007] UKHL 52. The Court of Appeal decision in this case is reported at [2006] EWCA Civ 817; [2007] Q.B. 305; [2006] 3 W.L.R. 1017; [2006] HRLR 33; [2006] UKHRR 927; [2006] NPC 73; *The Times*, June 30, 2006
       iii *Friend v Lord Advocate* [2007] UKHL 53
       iv *DPP v Exeter Crown Court and others* [2008] EWHC 2399 (Admin)
       v *Director of Public Prosecutions (Appellant) v Wright (Respondent) : R.(on the application of Scott, Heard and Summersgill) (Claimants) v Taunton Deane Magistrates' Court (Respondents) (2009)* [2009] EWHC 105 (Admin), also reported at [2009] 3 All E.R. 726 and *The Times*, February 17, 2009. These cases were "conjoined appeals" that is they were heard together because they raised the same points.
10 b) He has to provide evidence that what he was doing came within an exemption in Schedule 1 of the Act. The *DPP v Wright* (above) held that the burden of proving the exemption was on the defendant.
   c) Not by the time this book was completed.

Exercise 3

1. Mr. Donachie. See paragraph 1 of the decision.

2. See the formulation by Lord Justice Auld. in paragraph 9 of the decision.

3. (a) 1. The Manchester County Court, before His Honour Judge Tetlow.
        See paragraph 1 of the decision.
     2. The reported decision is in relation to a hearing before the Court of Appeal
        (Civil Division).
        See the information set out at the head of the report.
   (b) Civil proceedings.
   (c) 1. In the Manchester County Court, the judge dismissed the claims for negli-
        gence and breach of statutory duty. (ie. Mr. Donachie lost)
        See paragraph 1 of the decision.
     2. The Court of Appeal (Civil Division) allowed the appeal unanimously. (ie.
        Mr. Donachie won)
        See paragraph 46 of the decision, setting out the conclusion of Lord
        Justice Auld, together with the following agreements by Lord Justice
        Latham (at paragraph 47) and Lord Justice Arden (at paragraph 48).
   (d) Yes.

4. See the grounds set out in paragraph 8 of the decision.

5. See what is set out at paragraph 8 of the decision.

6. See the formulation by Lord Justice Auld at paragraph 9 of the decision.

Exercise 4

1. (a) 1. High Court (Manchester District Registry)
        See at page 1124j in the report

     2. Court of Appeal (Civil Division)
        See at page 1122b in the report
        [See also the "running header" of the published law report]

     3. House of Lords
        See at page 1122c in the report

     4. Note also that the case had come before the Appeal Committee of
        the House of Lords on 23 July 2002 in respect of an application by the
        Defendant for leave to appeal. See at page 1139j in the report. At the
        same page it emerges that the case had also come before the Appeal

Committee of the House of Lords on 9 October 2002 when leave was granted to the Claimant to bring a cross-appeal.

(b) 1. Claim dismissed (ie. The claimant lost)
2. Appeal allowed by 2-1 majority (ie. The claimant won)
3. Appeal allowed by 5-0 majority (ie. The claimant lost)

Note that the outcome in the Court of Appeal is set out at p. 1139g-h, while the final outcome in the House of Lords is set out at p. 1166j.

2. 1. As regards the report of the Court of Appeal decision, compare the judgment of Longmore L.J. at page 1139f-g with the judgment of Ward L.J. at page 1137e and the judgment of Sedley L.J. at page 1138c.
2. In relation to the report of the House of Lords opinions, there is no dissert.

3. See those of Mr Bill Braithwaite QC, at page 1128d-f
Compare them with the arguments of Mr Raymond Machell QC, at page 1128f-g.
Then see page 1128h-j for the responses made by Mr Braithwaite QC.

4. See page 1137g–h.

Exercise 5

1. The article is concerned with the fact that women seem to leave the solicitors' profession at a greater rate than men and at an earlier age than men. The article is concerned with trying to understand why this is the case. It also looks at whether or not one of the suggested strategies for addressing this problem, the business case for equality of opportunity in the solicitors' profession, is, in fact, helpful.

2. The research is based on qualitative analysis. The two authors conducted interviews with 6 focus groups in London, Leeds and Manchester. However the study is based on quantitative analysis of the statistics for solicitors failing to renew their practising certificates.

3. There has been comparatively little research done on lawyers either in this country or elsewhere. If the authors just referred to research done on English lawyers they would have relatively little on which to base their arguments. American research provides them with a greater variety of ideas to think about. However they note that their concern is with the culture of the solicitors' profession. Cultures vary from country to country. American lawyers are trained differently to lawyers in England and Wales. Their working practices are different. Thus there is a question about how relevant arguments about American lawyers are to an analysis of solicitors in England and Wales. Here the question to be considered is does the benefits of the extra arguments that are made available by looking at research in America outweigh the disadvantage of the fact that we may not be looking at comparable forms of work.

4. The authors do not explicitly define what they mean by "masculinist cultures". However it seems to involve things like assertiveness, competitiveness, being in

authority, risk-taking and working long hours. The use of the term "masculinist" rather than "male" reminds us both that some men may not have or value these traits and that conversely some women may.

5. The numbers involved in the study were relatively small; they were self-selecting and were not chosen to be representative of women in the solicitors' profession taken as a whole. They also, of course, were taken from just one gender. This is not to say that their views are either incorrect or unrepresentative of women in the solicitors' profession or, indeed, both men and women in the solicitors' profession. Noting limitations in evidence is not the same things as saying that the evidence is worthless. Perfect evidence is rarely if ever presented. However we always need to be aware of its potential flaws.

ANSWERS TO *Reference Exercise 1*

2. Reference to the precise page of a book or article that discusses the wide range of activities carried out by private security personnel.
3. Reference to the precise page of a book or article that discusses the role of private security in relation to the supply of physical/mechanical/electronic devices and 'security hardware'.
4. Full reference to the 1995 Home Affairs Select Committee Report mentioned in the text.
5. Full reference to the 1999 White Paper mentioned in the text.
6. Reference to the precise page of a book or article which discusses the growth in private security personnel and concludes that the number of persons employed in private security is larger than the number employed in the police service.

ANSWERS TO *Reference Exercise 2*

It is generally accepted that the number of crimes dealt with by the criminal justice system is less than the actual number of crimes taking place. This is because a large number of offences are not reported to the police, so they do not feature in statistics which record the number of crimes taking place. It is surprising to find that the police play a relatively small role in uncovering crime. Research for the Royal Commission on Criminal Procedure (the Phillips Commission) showed that most offences were reported to the police, either by the victim, or someone acting on the victim's behalf; many crimes were also reported by witnesses. When all these instances were taken into account, the researchers concluded that 75-80% of crimes are reported to the police, rather than the police discovering the crimes for themselves. This data is confirmed by other research studies, including research carried put for the Royal Commission on Criminal Justice (the Runciman Commission) which found that the initial source of information linking the suspect to the offence came from the police in only 37% of cases.

Footnotes needed as follows:

Location	Content
After 'place' in line 3.	Reference to precise page of book or article discussing the fact that there is a large amount of unreported crime.
After 'witnesses' in line 7.	Reference to the precise place in the report of the research carried out for the Royal Commission on Criminal Procedure which discusses the fact that offences are generally reported to the police.
After 'themselves' in line 9.	Another reference to the report of the research carried out for the Royal Commission on Criminal Procedure, to the precise page where the researchers' conclusions are set out.
After 'cases' in the final line.	Reference to the report of the research carried out for the Royal Commission on Criminal Justice setting out the statistics referred to in the text.

Index

(all references are to paragraph number)